Noel Loos

White Christ
Black Cross

The emergence of a black church

Aboriginal
Studies
Press

First published in 2007
by Aboriginal Studies Press

Aboriginal Studies Press
is the publishing arm of the
Australian Institute of Aboriginal
and Torres Strait Islander Studies.
GPO Box 553, Canberra, ACT 2601
Phone: (61 2) 6246 1183
Fax: (61 2) 6261 4288
Email: asp@aiatsis.gov.au
Web: www.aiatsis.gov.
au/aboriginal_studies_press

National Library of Australia
Cataloguing-In-Publication data:

   Loos, Noel.
   White Christ black cross: the
   emergence of a black church.

   Includes index.
   ISBN 9780855755539 (pbk.).

   1. Christianity and culture — Australia
   — History. 2. Aboriginal Australians
   — Missions — Australia. 3. Aboriginal
   Australians — Religion. I. Title.

270.0899915

Printed in Australia by Ligare Pty Ltd

Cover image: Clay composition of Fourth
Station of the Cross (Jesus meets his
mother on the way) by Laurie Thomas.
Based on the *Fourth Sation of the Cross:
Yetjinmadilit Kana Kinyi Jesus Kala (Jesus
meets his mother on the way)* by Miriam-
Rose Ungunmerr-Baumann.

Aboriginal and Torres Strait Islander
people are respectfully advised that this
publication contains names and images
of deceased persons, and culturally
sensitive material. AIATSIS apologises for
any distress this may cause.

For Anthony Loos

Contents

Abbreviations

ABM	Australian Board of Missions. Now Anglican Board of Missions – Australia
AIATSIS	Australian Institute of Aboriginal and Torres Strait Islander Studies
AIM	Aboriginal Inland Mission
APNR	Association for the Protection of Native Races
CC	*Cooktown Courier*
CMS	Church Missionary Society
DAIA	Department of Aboriginal and Islander Advancement
FCAATSI	Federal Council for the Advancement of Aboriginal and Torres Strait Islanders
MM	*Mackay Mercury*
NAAC	National Aboriginal Anglican Council
NATSIAC	National Aboriginal and Torres Strait Islander Anglican Council
PDT	*Port Denison Times*
Pol. Com.	Commissioner of Police
QPP	Queensland Parliamentary Papers
QSA	Queensland State Archives
UAM	United Aborigines Mission
V & P	Votes and Proceedings of the Queensland Legislative Assembly

Sites of cultural interaction

A Story in Three Parts

This is a story in three parts that are progressively separate, together and apart.

There are the Aboriginal clans who suddenly found a group of white men and women occupying their land, informing them that there was only one belief system, Christianity, which replaced their old religion, their old languages, their old customs and values, and their old way of living.

There were the missionaries searching for their own significance in an alien culture they were determined to shape in a way they could accept.

Then there were the people who sat in the pews in the churches, and their priests and bishops who formed committees, subcommittees and a board of directors in cities sanitised from the reality of the lives of Aboriginal people and the reality of the missions. Here missionaries and the clans they controlled were bound together and yet apart, a small minority of blacks and whites living in separate strata in Christian compounds created to show the glory of the God revealed in Hebrew history and English practice.

The missionaries were fringe dwellers of the Aboriginal culture they chose to live among, and fringe dwellers of their own faith and culture which found it easy not to see the Lazarus in need in the land they occupied from which they derived all that was comfortable and sustaining in their own lives.

I have tried to hear the voices of these three groups of people and to let them speak for themselves. Questions keep recurring. What did the city-based Christians, through their mission agencies and their committees, expect the missionaries to achieve? What did they ultimately think would be the destiny of the Aboriginal people whose lives they were shaping with the support of the local legislatures and the nominal approval of the white Christian majority? From the hindsight of today, how have Aboriginal people responded to the faith brought to them in possibly the worst way imaginable?

I have tried to communicate what has been happening in the 150 years since the dominant Christian denomination in the Australian colonies, the Anglicans, formally committed themselves as a church to convert the Aboriginal people to what they said was the saving grace essential to the salvation of Aboriginal people and what they sometimes confessed was their only justification for their occupation of Aboriginal land.

Inescapably, this is my understanding of this complex history. It is a story, then, told in four voices.

1.

The Triumph of the Mynah Bird

You know, we had Jesus before you white fellows came.

What is the Bishop of North Queensland up to now?

Arthur Malcolm, a stocky Aboriginal in the maroon Fairmont, was in tears as the cavalcade of late model cars drove along the road towards the Yarrabah Aboriginal community. Two columns of painted dancers, almost naked in the afternoon sun, snaked forward singing a Gunganjdji welcome. They moved in front of and beside the cars, leading them along the road into Yarrabah. About one hundred metres from the turn near St Alban's Church, the Aboriginal police stopped the cars and asked everyone to get out. Ahead, the road in was lined with Yarrabah people and visitors clapping and cheering their new bishop, the first Aboriginal bishop in the Anglican Church. It was 13 October 1985.

At intervals, out of the shouting throng, an old man or an old woman came forward to greet Bishop Malcolm, people who were related to him or had known him all of their lives. Although his father was Koko-bera from south of Kowanyama in western Cape York Peninsula and his mother Olkolo from the Alice River north of Kowanyama, the Bishop was born at Yarrabah and grew up there. As a young man, he left to train as an evangelist in the Anglican Church Army. His parents had been sent to Yarrabah under the Queensland system of removals.

Torres Strait Islanders in traditional dress joined the Aboriginal dancers who continued rhythmically clapping boomerangs and brandishing spears to escort the Bishop and the rest of the official party to the church on Gribble Street, named after the founding father of the mission. An Aboriginal elder ritually presented Bishop Malcolm with a woomera as a symbol of his authority among them and of his spiritual power. Aboriginal priests, deacons, and Eucharistic assistants from Yarrabah in colourful High Church Anglican vestments processed with the rest of the official party of Bishops, including Indigenous bishops from New Zealand, Papua New Guinea, Polynesia and Melanesia. The crowd of different races and colours overflowed the large church on to the surrounding lawns beside Mission Bay with the rusting hulk of a shipwreck stark in the sea just off the beach. To the left was Gribble Point, and in the distance out of sight, False Cape and Cape Grafton, enclosing the broad expanse of Mission Bay. Cook's Anchorage, from which he landed at Yarrabah, is at the mouth of the bay half way between the two dramatic capes that he had named, directly in front of Karpa Creek.

Reeves Creek, named after Ernest Gribble's trusted assistant and brother-in-law, runs into Karpa Creek. To the south are the small settlements of Buddabadoo, Jajini and Oombunghi that date from early mission days.

The modern map of Yarrabah is just such a seamless garment, woven of sites and names from ancient times and the last hundred years of mission and government rule.[1] The sacred healing pool of Medicine Water is at the northern end of King Beach facing the Coral Sea and Fitzroy Island; to the south are Gunumburra and Gurrmba near the old Fighting Ground which is now only a site on the map. The old and the new live alongside of each other in the landscape and, often unknowingly, in the lives of the Yarrabah people.

Yarrabah itself was Ernest Gribble's Anglicisation of the Gunganjdji name, Ngiyaaba or Eyerreba, a meeting place. The ancestor of the Barlow family, John Barlow, had been Menmunny before he had accepted Christianity, surrendered two of his three wives, and been given the surname of the second bishop of North Queensland. Pompo Katchewan disappears from mission records, replaced by Patterson, the name he passed on to his descendants.

The past lives on in the present in so many ways that have yet to be revealed and the present projects itself back into the past. In 1977, seventeen years after mission control had been transferred to the Queensland Government, the Bishop of North Queensland, John Lewis, anointed Lorna Schreiber 'Queen of the Gunganjdji' because the people wanted it. Ernest Gribble had anointed her grandfather, Menmunny, King John Barlow to show his acceptance of mission authority and his willingness to work with the new regime. With its joyous memories and its bitter ones, mission life is inextricably part of the lives and history of Yarrabah as it is of so many Aborigines throughout Australia. For some Aboriginal people, it is not an aberration in their historical experience; it is as central as the Dreamtime.[2]

The extensive official party processed into St Alban's Church. They filed into an Anglican church past a back wall covered with photographs of mission days and mission personalities: the Gribbles, father and son, and mother Mary; James Noble, Aboriginal missionary at four Anglican missions, Ernest Gribble's lifelong support and, in 1925, the first Aboriginal to be ordained deacon in the Anglican Church; past Menmunny and other early Aboriginal visitors to the mission; past snapshots of mission life and visiting clerical dignitaries whose importance now was lost in time. The party proceeded down the aisle to the altar where the Eucharist would be celebrated. The procession passed the Stations of the Cross, magnificently drawn by Aboriginal artists, the two columns parting before the cross from which an Aboriginal Christ looked down upon the throng.

Throughout the service the constant background noise of little children voicing their own concerns and interests rose and fell. Elegant English accents blended with white Australian and Aboriginal English cadences in the readings from the Bible and in Arthur Malcolm's sermon.

Serious faced and still moved by the occasion, the Bishop read only the first page of his prepared sermon. 'Today I want to talk to you about Jesus...' he had said at the beginning before removing his glasses and talking directly to the people of Yarrabah and Palm Island, the two Aboriginal communities in which he had served since his return to North Queensland in 1973. Aunty Teresa and the small group of Yarrabah churchgoers had asked for Arthur and his wife, Colleen, to replace their frail old chaplain, Cyril Brown.

Although the Aboriginal people might think 'he had made the grade so to say', Arthur pointed out that it was the people of Yarrabah and Palm Island who had 'seen something in faith in his ministry'. He paid tribute to some of the white missionaries he had known as a young man such as Bert Moxham, the mission bookkeeper, and Father Cyril Brown. He also mentioned the two Aboriginal Christians from Yarrabah who had most influenced him.

Sister Muriel Stanley had volunteered for the Church Army College while Arthur was a child, graduated as an evangelist and as a nursing sister from South Sydney Hospital, the first Aboriginal to become a qualified nurse. She had returned to Yarrabah to become a legend as matron of the hospital and community health officer. James Noble was Arthur's uncle. Although Arthur had never met him, everyone at Yarrabah knew of his exploits as a missionary. The secular Yarrabah Council had named its new sports centre after the Reverend James Noble. The group of Aboriginal priests and deacons then emerging as black missionaries from Yarrabah formed themselves into the James Noble Guild.

Malcolm's talk was peppered with colloquialisms, words like 'blokes', and the grammatical structure of Aboriginal community English. He referred obliquely to, but did not name, his first job at Yarrabah, working on the goona cart, the 'shit' cart, a job many of the Aboriginal men had worked at. They understood. 'I hope and pray I will be the same Arthur Malcolm as before I was made Bishop'. How should he be addressed? 'Just call me Bishop Arthur'. To some whites present this seemed an awkward self-glorification and a distancing himself from his people. After all that's what generally happened with white bishops. Aboriginal Christians would delight in calling him Bishop and referring to him as 'the Bishop' when he was not present. They were delighted 'he had made it'.

The mynah bird had triumphed.

On the previous day, in St James' Cathedral in Townsville, the Reverend Arthur Malcolm and the Reverend George Tung Yep had been consecrated Assistant Bishops in the Diocese of North Queensland. The Australian media had not thought the consecration of the first Aboriginal Bishop and the first Chinese–Australian Bishop in Australia's history at all newsworthy, yet over 1000 people packed the cathedral to overflowing. In this throng it was the large Aboriginal and Torres Strait Islander attendance that caught the eye.

The consecration ceremony, dating back to medieval England was very dignified and grandly impressive to those churchgoers who loved the studied, formal Anglican ritual. It had lasted for two hours and even the introduction of the Yarrabah and Palm Island choirs and the swooping, soaring hymn singing of the Torres Strait Islanders could not disguise the fact that it was a very long service indeed. The actual consecration was moving not only for those immediately involved but also for the black and white members of the congregation. The feeling of being present at a unique historical event was almost tangible and the celebration of the Eucharist or Mass had made everyone present actual participants. Yet these two central events, the consecration and the distribution of the bread and the wine, had somehow become almost submerged in the ceremonial, the Anglican pomp and circumstance.

At the end of the ceremony, a number of local dignitaries, perhaps too many, came forth to congratulate and welcome the new bishops. Then Bishop Lewis invited Michael Connolly, an Aboriginal Christian from Yarrabah to speak. He had actually asked the bishop if he could bring greetings from the people of Yarrabah. As he stressed how important and how gratifying it was for Aboriginal people to at last have their own bishop, Michael Connolly's speech gradually became more compelling.

He paused and gazed intently at the congregation. Then he told them the story of the mynah bird.

Recently at Yarrabah a man had stayed in the church praying after a Sunday service and noticed a mynah bird with a foot caught in a crack in the ceiling. Other mynah birds were flying around their trapped companion, darting in to pick at him viciously with their beaks. He was horrified, aghast, to see the bird's blood running down the wall of their church. What could it mean? Why had God done something so horrible to them in their church just before this wonderful event?

Then Michael Connolly told of the prophecy he had received. The trapped mynah bird being picked to death by his companions was John Lewis, the Bishop of North Queensland, who had fought long and hard to create the Aboriginal bishopric. The birds that inflicted such pain and suffering were those in the church who had opposed this move. They were, said Connolly, like the Pharisees and hypocrites and vipers in the Bible. They were living in the past whereas Bishop Arthur and Bishop George were babes in the spirit willing to learn their new roles. He asked the Yarrabah and Palm Island choirs to sing one verse of a hymn they had sung earlier in the service. During the singing, Connolly suddenly moved across to the thin, pale, ramrod straight Lewis and, in tears, embraced him. Some people in the congregation thought there may have been tears in John Lewis's eyes as well.

Michael Connolly had electrified the congregation. Although some were unaware of the controversy and others offended, there was a burst of enthusiastic applause when he returned to his seat. To some he had validated the consecration of the Aboriginal bishop with his directness and charismatic spirituality. He had also presented an Aboriginal perspective of the white church politics that had developed as a result of Bishop Lewis's proposal that an Aboriginal bishop be appointed with an Australia-wide responsibility for Aboriginal Anglicans and a Torres Strait Islander Bishop for Torres Strait Islander Anglicans. In New Zealand the Anglican Church had already consecrated Hiu Vercoe, Bishop of Aotearoa, in December 1982, with an Episcopal responsibility for Maoris throughout New Zealand which coexisted with the territorial responsibility of the diocesan bishops. The opposition to replicating this situation in Australia was surprising in its extent and its intensity. Some considered it wrong to consecrate someone bishop because he was Aboriginal, ignoring the fact that everywhere the Christian church had always found Indigenous people to assume leadership at all levels as soon as that was possible. Roman, Greek and North African bishops had emerged in the first three hundred years of Christian evangelisation and had continued as a natural consequence as Christianity spread throughout Europe, the Middle East, and North Africa. Some thought the monarchical bishop an inappropriate model for Aboriginal people and recommended a shared ministry.[3] Some thought it wrong, discrimination in reverse, to create bishoprics for Aboriginal and Torres Strait Islander people and not for other ethnic minorities, in effect denying the significance of the invasion and colonisation of Aboriginal and Torres Strait Islander Australia. It was really a well-intentioned desire for everyone to forget the past. Nothing could be done to change it; contemporary Australia was a reality and Aborigines and Torres Strait Islanders were part of it and should be treated like everyone else, their argument ran. Some wanted Aborigines and Islanders to be part of their congregations and really couldn't understand why they weren't there already. In Christ there was neither Jew nor Greek, why then should black Australians need or want separate identities? A strange response from people who identified as Church of England or Anglican.

Within the institutional structure of the church there were some strong objections on 'practical' lines. Bishops had responsibility and authority within certain carefully defined geographic areas. The idea of another bishop with overlapping responsibility was difficult to contemplate, for some impossible. Episcopal land rights apparently could not be challenged.

Some North Queensland churchmen were opposed in principle to the creation of assistant bishops on the grounds that the ordained ministry was there to assist the bishop. Throughout the whole drawn out controversy, there was nothing intentionally racist or even malicious, yet it was clear that some Aboriginal Christians had interpreted this as yet another attempt by whites to keep Aborigines down, to deny them equality. To the whites, ignorant of the scars of history the Aborigines bore, it was just church politics.

It was, however, the Torres Strait Islanders and the Aboriginal people who first put forward the idea of cultural bishops. In 1976, Anglican Torres Strait Islanders in Townsville had talked about the possibility of a bishop for their people, and not long afterwards the Yarrabah congregation made a similar request. The Bishop of North Queensland had then taken up the proposal.[4] Subsequently, in May 1984 after intense debate, the North Queensland Synod had passed a motion recommending the establishment of such bishoprics in the National Church in 1988 to coincide with Australia's bicentenary. This proposal was to be presented to the next meeting of the General Synod of the Anglican Church of Australia to be held in August 1985.

It became clear that the proposal would be rejected, partly because most church leaders who would vote at General Synod had no understanding of the issues involved. Few had any contact with Aboriginal or Torres Strait Islander people and fewer still any sympathy with the North Queensland proposal. Bishop Lewis, then one of the longest serving bishops of the Australian church, was often a controversial figure known for his outspokenness and direct, even radical, solutions to the problems confronting him or his diocese. On my visits to the Anglican Board of Missions' Archive in Sydney I was regularly asked: 'What is the Bishop of North Queensland up to now?' There's little doubt that some of the opposition to the consecration of Indigenous Australian bishops was stimulated by a suspicion that John Lewis was 'up to something' or that it was another one of his outlandish innovations. There was little appreciation that Aboriginal and Torres Strait Islander Christians would see such opposition as a rejection of their worth on grounds of race.

The Australian Primate, Archbishop John Grindrod, referred a position paper by the Rev. Dr Allen Brent of James Cook University to the Doctrine Commission of the Anglican Church where it received an unsympathetic response partly because members of the Commission could not comprehend the need for 'cultural' bishops.[5] If Bishop Lewis wanted Aboriginal or Torres Strait Islander bishops, he could consecrate them as assistant bishops within his diocese.

Archbishop Grindrod visited North Queensland to consult with the Aboriginal Anglicans at Palm Island and Yarrabah and with Torres Strait Islander Anglicans in Cairns and Townsville.[6]

Five supporting submissions were made from Torres Strait Islander Anglicans in Townsville while Torres Strait Islanders in Cairns also indicated support; the Palm Island Anglicans supported the proposal; and, at Yarrabah, seventeen submissions and a petition signed by 342 Aborigines out of a total population of approximately 1300 were presented to the Archbishop.[7] He was convinced of their seriousness of purpose and proposed the compromise which was accepted by the North Queensland Synod and General Synod: that an Aboriginal be consecrated assistant bishop in the Diocese of North Queensland on the understanding that he could visit other dioceses, when invited, to minister to his people; and a Torres Strait Islander be consecrated assistant bishop in the Diocese of Carpentaria, based at Thursday Island in the Torres Strait, but able to visit other relevant dioceses as required.[8] The historic Anglican compromise had once again struck! Episcopal territoriality had been maintained and the concept of cultural bishops able to cross diocesan boundaries had been accepted, even if only at the level of assistant bishop.

Bishop Arthur Malcolm meeting Pope John Paul II at Alice Springs, 1986. Courtesy Catholic Parish of Our Lady of the Sacred Heart, Alice Springs.

Subsequently, Bishop Arthur Malcolm and the Torres Strait Islander bishop, Kwami Dai, both functioned as bishops to their people outside of their dioceses. They met Pope John Paul II as representatives of their people when he visited Alice Springs. Bishop Malcolm represented Aboriginal people at such occasions as the bicentennial celebrations in Canberra, and at an act of reconciliation in Sydney with the Anglican Primate for the 200 years of conflict and injustice, and at the World Council of Churches meeting in Canberra in January 1991.[9] He had previously represented the Anglican Primate in October 1985 at the handover of Uluru, Ayers Rock, to the Aboriginal owners in the Northern Territory.[10] The acceptance of Bishop Malcolm as a religious leader had stretched across the denominational boundaries without in any way threatening to destroy them. However, because Anglican Australia's cultural bishops have been fitted into the existing structure, an assistant bishop of an existing diocese, there was a danger that there would be no further growth beyond the existing subordinate status, or that the concept would wither on the vine. The compromise was seen as an interim measure by the Diocese of North Queensland.[11] When John Lewis informed his 1985 synod that in New Zealand Maori bishops remained assistants for nearly fifty years, he clearly hoped that there would be no such delay in Australia.[12] He is still waiting.

The desire of many Aboriginal Anglicans in North Queensland to have their own bishop, the emotion generated by the attempts to frustrate their proposal, the enthusiasm and large attendance at the consecration, and the moving reception at Yarrabah were signs of the importance of Christianity in their lives. To this can be added the importance attached to the event by Aboriginal Christians of other denominations. Even many non-Christian Aborigines were pleased that one of their race had been made a bishop in a mainstream church. In an increasingly secular Australian society in which the Christian churches had long been marginalised, it may seem surprising that so many Aboriginal people were witnessing to the Christian faith, or at least saw it as important.

To the Greeks, or in this case secular Australians, it may have seemed foolishness; or at least that simple minded, poorly educated Aborigines were dupes of the missionaries. Yet the Aboriginal Christian leaders of the 1980s were only too aware of the meaning of mission control as they had grown up under it. At Yarrabah, a paternalistic mission regime had existed until 1960 and on the other Anglican missions dealt with here, till 1967 or 1968. There had been open conflict with Yarrabah superintendents during the 1950s, a strike, and a mass walk off of residents. On all the Anglican missions, probably on all missions, Aboriginal Christians of the last decades of the twentieth century were aware of the poor living standards they had endured, the primitive housing, the minimal supply of clothing, often hand-me-downs from comfortable white congregations, and the inadequate monotonous food rations. They were aware of the limited schooling and health care provided which had depended on the ability of the missionary agency to attract suitably qualified Christian volunteers. The Aboriginal Christians still living in the secular Aboriginal communities that had been missions, and those who had left them to live elsewhere, remembered with greater bitterness a few who had been harsh and unjust. Some they remembered with the greatest affection. Some, like Ernest Gribble of Yarrabah and Forrest River, JW 'Chappie' Chapman of Mitchell River and Edward River, and John Warby of Lockhart, many regarded as legendary heroes of these new creations, the missions that had become their homes. Most, however, were just remembered as whites who had worked and lived with them on their missions, who had been part of the only life they had known. And regardless of their personalities, these white emissaries from the colonising culture had brought them not only the new faith, they also introduced them to the new way of life more deliberately and more systematically than any other group of colonists. They were well-intentioned despite their limited understanding of the

Aborigines they were living with and their arrogant scorn of Aboriginal languages and culture.

For despite the limitations of the missionaries and the changes they caused in the Aboriginal way of life, by being there and establishing their control in the communities they were creating, they did less harm than any other group of colonists coming into contact with Aboriginal people.[13] Indeed, most of the Aboriginal communities that now exist in North Australia were once missions.[14] Until governments began developing communities on reserves, there were no other colonists working with Aboriginal people, either wisely or misguidedly, 'for their own good'.[15] The other colonists were content to allow Aboriginal people to be shot down and poisoned on the frontier, and to be exploited sexually and for their labour behind the frontier. They allowed them to live and die in disease ridden, unhygienic fringe camps and allowed the children to be casually appropriated as cheap labour or domestic pets without effective protest, or most often without any protest at all. Well into the twentieth century, settlers could take the law into their own hands to intimidate or 'punish' Aborigines and the police take extra-legal action to maintain their control and prevent Aborigines interfering with settler interests. And if some whites working on the missions abused their authority, or lost their temper and struck Aboriginal people or systematically used corporal punishment or occasionally became sexually involved with Aboriginal women, in the secular society beyond the missions where Aborigines interacted with colonists such abuses and worse were infinitely more frequent. Missionaries attracted contemporary criticism not only for not practising what they preached, that is, they were regarded as hypocrites, but also because they exposed colonial society for its inhumanity towards the people they had dispossessed.

Modern writers often savage missionaries for being cultural imperialists attacking and destroying much of Aboriginal culture to impose their own values and beliefs upon a vulnerable, defenceless people. They have little or no sympathy with the Christian imperative at least as interpreted by these zealous advocates.[16] There is a good deal of substance in such criticism as a Christian writer on mission history, John Harris, has pointed out.[17] Like their contemporaries, missionaries were also prisoners of their own culture.

Aboriginal people throughout Australia were not going to be left alone undisturbed. It was a matter of which particular colonial interest would impose itself upon them. From the hindsight of history many Aboriginal communities may be grateful that they first came into contact with missionaries and not pastoralists, miners, or even government bureaucracies.

In the communities that are the subject of this study, missionary control lasted from twenty-nine years at Edward River to sixty-eight years at Yarrabah. On each community the Anglican Church is still accepted but individual allegiances vary greatly. On visits I have made to these communities there seemed to be no bitter resentment of the missionary past, except at Yarrabah where the Aboriginal Christian presence is most obvious. Here a minority were prepared to wear black armbands at the centennial celebrations to be held in June 1992. Yet John Harris found that 'memories of regimentation and oppression run as a common thread through the majority of [Aboriginal Christians'] stories'.[18] It would be surprising if it were otherwise.

Some older residents of these missions saw missionary times as almost a golden age when community life was more stable and disciplined. 'At least families were families then', I was told and this sentiment was repeated on a number of occasions. This also is not surprising given the enormous challenges the people face with regard to economic and community development, unemployment, education, health and housing, and the tensions on such communities today between the different clan or tribal groups, the friction and violence associated with the consumption of alcohol, and the generation gap that has widened because of the accelerating changes of the last thirty years.

It was my doctoral study, part of which was published as *Invasion and Resistance*, that first made me interested in this extraordinary group of people, the missionaries to the Aborigines. Yet there is truth in the Christian cliché that most of them were very ordinary people trying to do extraordinary things. Confronted with the horrifying nature of the colonisation of Australia, I became fascinated by this splinter group of western colonial expansion that was trying to civilise the process as best they could and to offer the colonised the greatest gift they personally believed they could offer, Christian salvation. It was clear that the missionary agency of their church and most of the missionaries thought this a matter of great importance for Aboriginal people and for themselves. They eagerly confronted Aboriginal societies they saw as satiated with Satanism, as barbaric and immoral, and were repelled, initially at least, by almost everything they saw. I was astonished and often horrified at their attitudes towards the Aboriginal people they were determined to convert and yet equally as astonished at the dedication, self sacrifice and achievements of so many of them in creating villages, Christian communities in their eyes, in environments as alien to their places of origin as it is possible to imagine.[19]

In 1989 a modern missionary, Philip Freier, later Bishop of the Northern Territory and Archbishop of Melbourne, took me to the site of the first Mitchell River Mission at Trubanaman. It had been abandoned in 1917 when the fresh water creek which supplied the mission became salt. I looked at what seemed undisturbed Australian bush. The wilderness had reclaimed the mission site. Then our old Kunjen and Koko-bera companions pointed to the cement floor where the bakery had been. Over there were fragments of a huge shattered clam shell that had been a baptismal font, and here was where houses and buildings had been erected. Out there were the horse and cattle paddocks and the gardens and farms. I picked up a Bovril™ bottle whose contents had probably nourished patients in the bush hospital.

'How on earth could a couple of white missionaries ever imagine they could build a township on their own out of this!'

'They weren't on their own', Freier pointed out, having to state the obvious, 'they had the Aborigines to do most of the work for them'.

That raised another problem. Why did the Aboriginal people at Kowanyama and the other missions surrender their independence and that of their children to these strange whites? The country was teeming with game and fish and plant food. They could have given the mission a wide birth for another generation if they had wanted to. How then did these missionaries establish their control, a group of people who were in many ways fringe dwellers of their own society? Some were even found uncomfortably zealous or naïve by many in their supporting churches except when they were on their distant mission fields.

I was also intrigued by the way some Aboriginal Christians obviously retained aspects of their traditional religious life. Before I began my research, an old friend, Mrs Gladys Thompson, told me about the healing properties of a sacred pool at Yarrabah. The right words had to be said and a ritual propriety observed for it to be efficacious. Yet she would not miss a Sunday service at St Peter's Anglican Church in Townsville. She was Anglican to her bootstraps. Much later at Kowanyama, I interviewed Mrs Alma Wason, a Eucharistic assistant in the Anglican Church and one of the most influential Christians in the community. We spoke for hours. She told me of a conversion experience she had had a few years previously which led her to involve herself more actively in the faith of her childhood. Near the end of the interview I asked her if there were any changes she would like to see at Kowanyama.

'Yes', she said after thinking about it for a while, 'I think the Old Men should tell more of their stories'. By this she meant the local Aboriginal creation myths.

'Do you think they believe those stories?' I asked. Kowanyama had been Christian for over eighty years.

'Of course!' she said, with just a hint in her voice that she was talking to a simpleton.

I paused and then asked as casually as I could: 'And do you believe in them?'

'Of course,' she said, 'the Old Men tell them'.

Here was a mystery for me to unravel I thought. How could a profoundly Christian Aboriginal believe as profoundly in her Aboriginal belief system? I encountered other examples of this phenomenon. It fascinated me and I thought it would be a great challenge to explain it. In effect, I discovered there was really no mystery. Aboriginal people took the new into their old intellectual universe. They were not empty wine skins waiting to be filled, but wine skins holding good old wine. The new wine blended with the old and produced a wine that is newer to Christianity in many ways than that which the white missionaries took in with them. Especially in the first generation of converts, the old wine produced a flavour that often seemed strange to western observers.[20] 'Syncretism', some would declare from the heights of their western experiences, forgetting that their society had been involved in this process, especially in the first five hundred years of the Christian era.

In later generations some Aboriginal Christians came to see their old belief system as a forerunner to Christianity. It assumed a similar relationship to western Christianity as the Old Testament had to the New Testament. Christianity was seen as completing or fulfilling their old belief system not destroying it. In the process many came to modify the old in the light of the new whether white Christians liked it or not or even knew about it, as Christians had done with the old law in the Old Testament. The missionaries had tried to force a complete replacement. Increasingly, I discovered they had failed and many Aboriginal people retained those aspects of their old religion which they still found relevant and acceptable to their new understanding.[21]

I sat in on a workshop designed by Pastor George Rosendale, an Aboriginal Lutheran Pastor from Hopevale in North Queensland, while a group of Aboriginal Christians from Townsville and Palm Island pored over some Aboriginal creation myths searching for Christian values.[22] They obviously found it a totally absorbing experience.

At times I could not understand the connections some Aborigines were making and tended to dismiss them as indicating a partial understanding.

'You know, we had Jesus before you whitefellows came', one Townsville Christian, Roman Catholic Deacon Monty Prior, told me in casual conversation. Initially I thought that this simply indicated a misunderstanding of historical developments and did not pursue the matter. I did not wish to embarrass him. Afterwards, when I encountered other expressions of this concept, I realised it was I who did not understand. My friend, in his own way, was enunciating a theological concept that western Christians have termed 'the cosmic Christ', one that the early church had accepted and declared in the prologue to John's gospel, 'In the beginning was the Word...'. If God had created all things through Christ who was part of the Godhead, then this 'Word of God' must have spoken to Aboriginal people and been present in their culture even if not identified initially as the Jesus of history.[23]

I concluded then that it was not for me to try to explain how Aboriginal people had come to understand Christianity and were continuing to do so. The fact that this had happened under the worst circumstances imaginable began to interest me more. But, of course, as a white academic I later found myself exploring this mystery, but always aware how tentative any conclusions were.

I decided to study the work of one mission agency, its relationship to Aboriginal people, to the white Christians supporting it, and the evolution of these Aboriginal communities this had created. The Australian Board of Missions (ABM) had directed most of its Aboriginal mission work to North Queensland — my own backyard, Don Aitken termed it when interviewing me for a research grant. ABM was the officially constituted missionary agency of the Anglican Church of Australia which claimed the adherence of by far the largest number of white Australians throughout the nineteenth century and much of the twentieth. Its name has been changed to Anglican Board of Mission — Australia but I will refer to it throughout as ABM which is how most Anglicans still refer to it. Such a study would reveal how white Christians throughout Australia in a mainline church responded to the process of the colonial dispossession of Aboriginal people which resulted in their pauperisation and misery. At the same time they were developing the capacity and structures deemed necessary for the white colonists whose way of life derived from exploitation of Aboriginal land. One might think that in such circumstances the missionary agency would distance itself from the culture creating the Aboriginal people's suffering. Such was far from the case, for mission agencies and churches were inextricably part of the culture that benefited from the dispossession of Aborigines.

Yet the surprising situation has been revealed by John Harris, in his study of Aboriginal mission history, that a higher percentage of Aboriginal people are Christians than is the case in the rest of the population. He goes further and suggests that this situation has existed since the 1930s.[24] Consequently a study of mission history is in fact the study of how a major change in Aboriginal culture was effected. As such I hope it will be a useful resource for Aboriginal people to understand more fully historical developments that have affected them. Many of my Aboriginal students at James Cook University were part of the history described in this study and were eager to know as much about it as possible.

In the Diocese of North Queensland, the missionary organisation developed by Aboriginal Christians, the James Noble Guild, had adopted a coat of arms in which two boomerangs embrace a cross. On the crest of the shield was a Crown of Thorns with a mynah bird with bleeding chest emerging triumphantly from it.

Anyone who had been to the consecration of Bishop Arthur Malcolm could be forgiven for thinking that it was an extraordinary compliment to Bishop Lewis. However, at the welcome at Yarrabah, and later in his diocesan newsletter, Bishop Lewis had deliberately enlarged Michael Connolly's interpretation to include all of those who struggled and suffered for a cause, in this case the creation of the Aboriginal bishopric. In the official description of the coat of arms, the mynah bird with bleeding chest rising above the Crown of Thorns was seen as symbolic of the Resurrection. Aboriginal Christians had experienced the crucifixion of colonisation and contempt. Now it seemed that as a people they would experience the triumph over suffering of the resurrection. The banner below the shield proclaimed their confident faith even in the midst of a dominant white society: Jesus is Lord. For many Aboriginal Christians, it seems, white domination, past or present, is not the ultimate reality. As well, the modern Pharisees and hypocrites and vipers Michael Connolly had referred to had been diplomatically distanced from the scene.[25]

During the consecration and in reports of it, Bishop Lewis singled out the Anglican Church Army for its role 'in encouraging and nurturing vocations amongst Aboriginal people'. Bishop Ken Mason, the Chairman of the ABM which had been directly associated with Yarrabah since its foundation in 1892 until 1960 when its administration had been handed over to the Queensland Government, was described as 'also present' and the Rev. Richard Tutin, ABM's Queensland representative, was given a special mention as a guest. Both ABM officials seemed to be just that, mere guests at the feast. In part this reflected the shallow memory of the Anglican Church of Australia of its own history. In part it reflected the determined independence of the Diocese of North Queensland. In part it reflected how changed the role of the missionary body had become and how remote it was in the 1980s from grassroots developments in its old Aboriginal mission communities.

It was certainly not always thus.

2.

Agents of the Aboriginal Holocaust

One of the troubles of a colonising nation is the decent disposal
of the native inhabitants of the country, of which the
latter have been dispossessed.

Scenes from the Frontier

James Morrill was an Essex seaman who was shipwrecked on the Great
Barrier Reef in 1846. After forty-two days adrift on a raft, seven survivors
were washed ashore at Cape Cleveland near the present city of Townsville.
Three died after landing. The remaining four were befriended and nursed
back to health by Aborigines, who regarded them as deceased relatives
returned as whites to their previous state of existence, a factor which
often seems to have determined whether whites were received kindly or
regarded as dangerous intruders. The Europeans moved south to the Port
Denison district, hoping for rescue, and lived there for about two years.
After the other three died from natural causes, Morrill moved back to the
local group at Mount Elliott who had accepted him when he first landed.
He lived with them for the next twelve or thirteen years as an Aboriginal.
When news reached him of European settlement to the south, he made
his way back to the mouth of the Burdekin River.[1]

On 25 January 1863, Morrill made contact with the advancing white
settlers at Inkerman Station. At Bowen, Rockhampton, and Brisbane he
was soon able to describe the nature of first contact between the white
pastoralists and the Aboriginal people he was living with. Rarely has the
impact of the European invasion of Aboriginal land been chronicled by
an Englishman from an Aboriginal perspective. Although Morrill retained
a sense of responsibility for the relatives and friends he had lived with for
seventeen years, he elected to return to British colonial society. He even

participated in the establishment of a new port at Cardwell. His role was to attempt to communicate with the local Aborigines. He told them 'they must clear out and tell others to do so as we wished to occupy the land, and would shoot any who approached'. Asked many times to tell of his adventures he eventually dictated his reminiscences, which were published by the Queensland Government Printer in 1863.

He was able to shine an intimate, revealing light on the process of dispossession associated with the pastoral expansion that led to the rapid colonisation of eastern Australia.

A pattern of contact had developed in New South Wales and was perpetuated in Queensland which was referred to by the euphemism, 'keeping the blacks out'. This was done to protect the lives of the settlers and their capital in cattle, sheep, horses and property. This could result in conflict that lasted for several months or intermittent conflict that could persist for decades, largely depending on the terrain and the population density of the colonists. The next stage of this colonising process was referred to as 'letting the blacks in'. Their resistance had been broken and they could be controlled by the settlers themselves with the assistance of the local police and police magistrates.

From 1849 in New South Wales, pastoralists had the Native Police, a paramilitary force, to assist them to occupy new country. When Queensland separated from New South Wales in 1859, it inherited this force and expanded it and used it systematically for the remainder of the nineteenth century. It was the new colony's only instrument of frontier policy as Aboriginal people were being dispossessed.[2]

Morrill told of misunderstanding, fear and malice even before the actual colonisation of North Queensland began in 1861. In 1860, a ship, which Morrill believed to be the *Spitfire*, engaged in Dalrymple's Burdekin exploration, hove to at Cape Cleveland. The Aborigines tried to make the Europeans understand that there was a white man living with them in accordance with Morrill's request. The Europeans grew alarmed and fired upon the apparently menacing 'savages', killing one of Morrill's friends and wounding another.

The next encounter Morrill heard of occurred about three years later. Some Aborigines were lamenting the death of an old man when an unnoticed settler fired upon them killing the old man's son. Presumably, this was the opening gambit of 'keeping the blacks out'. Later the Aborigines induced this settler to dismount and killed him. Thinking the horse was also rational and malevolent, they tried to kill it too.

Reports of the encroaching whites increased, each one bringing fresh evidence of their ruthlessness. A party of Native Police with squatter volunteers shot down the Aborigines Morrill had lived with at Port Denison. Next, fifteen members of the tribe Morrill was then living with were shot while on a fishing expedition. By 1863, 'keeping the blacks out' meant that the Aborigines could not safely win their livelihood from their own country.

They also realised that their tribal lands were being changed by the mere presence of the white man. Some had watched while a herd of cattle drank a waterhole dry, exposing the fish, which they were afraid to come forward to take. Morrill had commented on the great variety of edible plant life used by the Aborigines, much of which would have been consumed or destroyed by the vast numbers of voracious, hard-hoofed cattle pouring into the region. At a simple economic level, the food and water resources, which were just sufficient to support the tribes in a dry season were being limited and free access to them denied. Eventually, Morrill persuaded the Aborigines to let him go as an emissary to attempt to come to terms with the invaders.

Morrill made it clear to the Aborigines that the Europeans would dispossess them of their land, a prospect that caused great distress. They requested Morrill to ask the Europeans to let them keep some of their tribal lands, even if only the coastal swamps which were valueless to the invaders. Morrill probably helped formulate the proposal and gave it much emphasis in his pamphlet published in 1863. The Queensland Government, however, made no response and a unique opportunity in Aboriginal–European relations in Queensland was lost.[3]

It was not because Morrill was held in low esteem. Governor Bowen conversed with him on several occasions and, 'finding him to be a very respectable and intelligent man', obtained a job for him at Bowen.

In this infant frontier town, Morrill married an emigrant girl 'and was universally liked and respected'; the chief journals of the Australian colonies were much interested in his experiences, as was the Secretary of State, the Duke of Newcastle.[4]

Morrill's eagerness to act as mediator was deemed a failure before the close of 1863. It was rumoured that the squatters were dangerously hostile to him because they believed him in league with the Aborigines to destroy their flocks while, it was said, the Aborigines had come to mistrust him because of his association with the settlers. In his obituary in the *Port Denison Times*, mention was made of the government's fear that he would rejoin the Aborigines and 'cause mischief'.[5] Apparently being sympathetic to Aborigines on the frontier was considered racial treachery.

It was unlikely that a squatter-dominated government would legislate to give land rights to a race it regarded as nomadic savages. Even the sympathetic Governor Bowen had claimed the Aborigines only 'wandered' over the country. Europeans would only accept the land rights of nomadic hunters and food gatherers if they were forced to do so. Morrill did not understand the basic conflict of cultures which required more than goodwill to provide a solution.[6]

As early as 1863, Morrill was able to describe the depopulation in the Burdekin district resulting from frontier conflict which was still continuing: 'the work of extinction is gradually but surely going on among the Aboriginals. The tribe I was living with is far less numerous now than when I went among them'. Morrill indicted the settlers and the Native Police but also blamed 'the wars, fights…and the natural deterioration of the people themselves'. Yet Morrill had previously said that traditional Aboriginal 'wars' caused little loss of life.[7] Similarly Morrill spoke of the 'natural deterioration of the people', presumably implying their decline in health and in number. Morrill was probably indicating the increased inter-tribal warfare and an unnatural deterioration in the physical and, possibly, mental health of the people consequent upon the chaos into which Aboriginal life was thrown by the European invasion. The very basis of the Aborigines' economic, social, and religious life was disrupted, natural resources restricted, land trespassed upon, dietary habits changed, and the security of their sacred life shattered.

My research into Australia-wide frontier conflict over many years indicates that the havoc Morrill witnessed on the Burdekin in the early years of colonisation was not unusual. In the Queensland Police Commissioner's report to Parliament for 1868, he commented of the Aborigines from Mackay south to St Lawrence: 'The blacks in this district are very bad…complaints and requests for assistance are every day received'. Of the Aborigines north of Mackay, he reported:

> The coast country all along from Townsville is inhabited by blacks of the most hostile character. On some of the stations north of Bowen, such as Woodstock, Salisbury Plains, and some others, it is almost impossible to keep any cattle on the runs; and south of Bowen some stations are or were about to be abandoned, in consequence of the destruction of property by the blacks.[8]

DT Seymour, who was Police Commissioner from 1864 to 1895, was not one to exaggerate Aboriginal hostility. It was more typical of him to blame the settlers for not taking adequate precautions to protect their own lives and property or to accuse the local newspapers of exaggeration.

Even though the number of Native Police at Seymour's disposal was reduced greatly as a result of economic measures associated with the 1866–70 commercial depression and the use of the Native Police as gold escort, he went to extraordinary measures to pacify the Townsville to Mackay coast. At a time when he was giving each detachment a larger area to patrol, he was unable to reduce the Native Police on the Townsville to Mackay coast and had to establish two 'flying detachments'. These had no settled camps but patrolled constantly, one between Townsville and Bowen and the other between Bowen and Mackay.[9]

The Commander-in-Chief of the Native Police was describing guerilla warfare resistance in terms of destruction of property and capital.

When I was doing doctoral research in the early 1970s, I came upon one of the few detailed accounts of what could happen on a Native Police patrol. The attack was referred to at the time as a 'dispersal', another frontier euphemism. Extracts from the Burketown correspondent to the *Brisbane Courier*, 9 June 1868, make clear what happened:

> I much regret to state that the blacks have become very troublesome about here lately. Within ten miles of this place they speared and cut steaks from the rumps of several horses. As soon as it was known, the Native Police, under sub-Inspector Uhr, went out, and I am informed, succeeded in shooting upwards of thirty blacks. No sooner was this done than a report came in that Mr Cameron had been murdered at Liddle and Hetzer's station, near the Norman. Mr. Uhr went off immediately in that direction, and his success I hear was complete. One mob of fourteen he rounded up; another mob of nine, and a last mob of eight, he succeeded with his troopers in shooting. In the latter lot there was one black who would not die after receiving eighteen or twenty bullets, but a trooper speedily put an end to his existence by smashing his skull.

The complacent tone of this report and the absence of any hostile reaction or an inquiry demonstrate the official attitude towards Aboriginal resistance even more strikingly than the ferocity of the deeds themselves. They suggest that this was, perhaps, only the most successful act of revenge and bloodshed in the Burke district. The Burketown correspondent concluded: 'Everybody in the district is delighted with the wholesale slaughter dealt out by the native police, and thank Mr Uhr for his energy in ridding the district of *fifty-nine* (59) myalls'.[10]

Presumably some wounded Aborigines escaped the slaughter. This report was copied in the *Queenslander*, 13 June 1868, and in the *Port Denison Times*, 4 July 1868. It was clearly regarded as a good news story that would interest the colonists.

In their determination to break Aboriginal resistance, the settlers often provoked it. Thus they deliberately destroyed or appropriated such important Aboriginal equipment as spears, fish nets, wallaby nets, rugs, and tomahawks which the Aborigines had been forced to abandon. More provocative, of course, was the indiscriminate slaughter of unoffending Aborigines which was inherent in the policy of 'keeping the blacks out' and the associated Native Police policy of 'dispersal', as a brief report of what was probably a routine Native Police reprisal indicates.[11] In retaliation for heavy stock losses, Inspector Isley and six troopers swept south from Bowen 'dispersing' two 'mobs' of Aborigines on the Don River, through the Proserpine District to the Mackay District where Isley attacked at least five more 'mobs' several of which were termed 'very large'. In the area he had passed through, the Aborigines had re-commenced killing cattle so, on his return north, he attacked them, driving them over the ranges. One can only guess at how many Aborigines were killed in these dispersals. Even frontiersmen well-disposed towards the Aborigines believed this was unavoidable, justifying it on the grounds of tribal, and often, it seems racial responsibility for particular offences against the settlers. Thus one commented: 'each tribe is fully aware that it is responsible not only to the whites but to other tribes of black fellows for the acts of its members'.[12] Aboriginal social and political organisation rendered this expectation unreal and Aborigines must have often concluded that the invaders were inexplicably and irrationally murderous.

Another common source of great provocation during this period of frontier conflict was the kidnapping of Aboriginal women and children. This practice was common throughout the whole North Queensland frontier and indeed throughout Australia. It was also a feature of life in the pacified areas.

However, even while frontier conflict raged, squatters and other settlers took Aboriginal women from their tribes to provide concubines for themselves, for white employees, and for the Aboriginal employees they brought from the south. These women soon became useful sources of labour. In the predominantly male society of the frontier, it was widely known and accepted that some squatters and their white employees turned to Aboriginal women to satisfy their sexual needs either on a casual basis or through some more permanent relationship. Writing at the time, Charles Eden gave an example of two squatters who 'took a fancy to a certain gin'.[13] Children, too, were commonly taken from their parents or kin to work on the stations during this period of frontier conflict. Eden, a Police Magistrate at Cardwell, recorded in his reminiscences his kidnapping of a twelve-year-old boy because he thought the boy would be useful; while Richard Anning described how his father, who had taken up Reedy Springs on the Upper Flinders in May 1862, had captured a young lad to work on the station — 'catchem young' he recorded.[14] Even in the

Burketown District before hostilities developed, settlers were insensitively exploiting the Aborigines for their labour and their women. Sometimes, in this chaotic new situation, the Aboriginal women and children either accepted their fate or came to prefer it to their tribal life. Thus, in the Burketown District before the outbreak of hostilities, an Aboriginal parent reclaimed his son only to have the boy run away to return to the station.[15] Some old Aborigines have also told me of their reluctance to return to tribal life after being taken into stations as children.[16] However, the removal of Aboriginal women and children from their kin was as destructive of traditional Aboriginal life as the killing of the men and often no more humane.

I have chosen examples of frontier conflict that I have personally researched but there is no shortage of examples of violent dispossession of Aboriginal people from other parts of Australia. In his study of the applicability of the term, 'genocide', to Australia's history, Reynolds has underlined the obvious contradictions implicit in the British Government's expressed platitudinous concern for Aboriginal people in the first fifty years of Australian colonisation and the realities of what was happening as Aboriginal land was occupied. The settlers were allowed to take the law into their own hands and, if they thought it necessary, the colonial administrations supported the settlers with whatever force was necessary: the declaration of martial law, the use of British troops, the creation of a Mounted Police force, then of Border Police, and finally the acceptance of the use of the Native Police as a paramilitary force to support the settlers.[17] The decision to grant the colonies in eastern Australia self-government reflected the lack of real concern for the fate of Aboriginal Australians. The Colonial Office had frequently accused the colonists who would control the colonial legislatures of trying to exterminate the Aboriginal people they were dispossessing.[18]

Reynolds examines what he terms 'genocidal moments in colonial Australia', occasions when settlers set out to exterminate a group of local Aborigines as retribution for Aboriginal resistance that had resulted in the killing of white settlers and the destruction of their capital in animals and property. He chose five well-researched 'massacres'. The first two are the Hornet Bank massacre of 27 October 1857 in which eleven Europeans were killed and the Cullin-la-ringoe massacre of October 1861 in which nineteen Europeans were killed. Both of these 'massacres' have come down to us in history because it was the whites that were massacred. After Hornet Bank it is estimated that settlers and Native Police killed between 150 and 300 Jiman people in planned punitive expeditions that lasted for weeks. After Cullin-la-ringoe, Queensland's Governor Bowen estimated that seventy Aborigines were killed by settlers and the Native Police, people now identified as of the Wadja tribe or language group. Both of these massacres of Aboriginal people occurred in the Dawson River district of southern Queensland without due process of law and without subsequent inquiry.[19]

In the Channel Country of south-west Queensland, the settlers and police were engaged in conflict with the Karuwali, Mitaka, Marrula and Karanguru people over twenty years, with possibly six major massacres in which it was intended to exterminate particular groups. In Central Australia, within a four hundred kilometre radius of Alice Springs, between the 1860s and 1890s, it has been estimated that between 650 and 850 Aboriginal people were killed by punitive expeditions.[20] These were from the Aranda, Antakininga, Matun, Tara, Anmatjea, Kaititja and Iliaura tribes.

In 1894–95 in the west Kimberley, after a period of conflict which culminated in the killing of a police constable and two stockmen, and of course an unrecorded number of Aborigines, the local sub-inspector of police was given permission to take whatever action he considered necessary. Settlers were sworn in as special constables to accompany the police and Aboriginal trackers on a series of punitive expeditions. The inspector in charge recorded killing forty-nine Aborigines. As with the other examples Reynolds used in this chapter to suggest genocidal intentions and actions, no due process of law was followed, no attempt was made to arrest and put suspects on trial. Official correspondence to the Premier, John Forrest, indicates that there were many other occasions when Aboriginal people in the Kimberley were being killed in 'a war of extermination'.[21] In Chapter 6, we will explore an incident very similar to the one described above that occurred as late as 1926.

Reynolds has used these examples of 'sudden and terrible retribution' because intent is expressed and they therefore can be accepted as examples of genocide as defined in 1946 by the United Nations. There are others where the intent of the perpetrators and government of the day was not expressed, or expressed in terms that would not stand up in a court of law to substantiate the charge of genocide. However, the norm Australia-wide was generally small scale, indiscriminate and sporadic, what, in 1878, the editor of the *Cooktown Courier* described as 'our present fitful scheme of haphazard little massacres'.[22] For the Aborigines, they were still 'sudden and terrible', whether one was killed or one hundred.

In *Australian Race Relations*, Andrew Markus has a chapter, 'Dispossession', which examines the process Australia-wide from 1788 to the close of the nineteenth century. His analysis, in this necessarily brief chapter, is insightful and balanced. In his introduction, he begins by stating the obvious: that in the eighteenth and nineteenth centuries, 'Europeans dispossessed indigenes to the extent that they were able to and needed to...Brutality was the norm, not the exception. There were no high standards to be emulated when the British first occupied Australia. The age was characterized not by cultural relativism but by the certainties that Christianity was the one true religion and that European civilization was the pinnacle of human progress'.[23]

The Australian colonists were not uniquely evil. Most of them would no doubt have liked to dispossess the Aborigines as easily and painlessly as possible but, if Aboriginal people resisted and threatened their occupancy of Aboriginal land, they took whatever action they thought necessary to break this resistance so they could wrest the economic potential of the land from the Aborigines and enrich themselves, their families and their descendants. In the process 'the first affluent Australians' became paupers.

To the Aboriginal people occupying their land as they had 'from time immemorial', their loss of authority occurred with dramatic suddenness reinforced, where the settlers thought it necessary or desirable, by a ruthlessness of tragic proportions. The clans were progressively dispossessed as European settlement spread. They were forced to accept the status of an inferior caste in the multicultural society that was being created in the pacified areas, although the concept, 'multicultural society', was not then recognised as the Aboriginal people were not seen as part of it. This process began in 1788 and continued as the frontier spread rapidly and violently across Aboriginal lands. The last known official, punitive expedition occurred in 1928 although one was planned as late as 1933 but abandoned after public protest.[24]

By the end of the nineteenth century, the dispossession of Aborigines had progressed so far that the only uncolonised areas were remote and apparently useless for European economic exploitation. Some parts were set aside as reserves although it was not envisaged at that time that this would prevent future colonisation of Aboriginal and Torres Strait Islander land. Within the settled areas, colonial governments, and later the Federal Government and states, were confronted with what they saw as the problem of how to dispose of and control the Aborigines and Torres Strait Islanders who had survived the frontier violence, the introduction of exotic diseases that caused catastrophic depopulation, the debilitating food supplies, and the unhygienic living conditions, and had found no useful place in the colonies; that is, useful to the white settlers in those developing, whites-only democracies.[25] As the *North Queensland Register* noted on 11 October 1893:

> One of the troubles of a colonizing nation is the decent disposal of the native inhabitants of the country, of which the latter have been dispossessed.

The colonising governments of Australia proved equal to the task of 'disposal'. Between 1869 and 1911, throughout Australia, those governments responsible for significant concentrations of Aboriginal and Torres Strait Islander people made them wards of the state and segregated them on Christian missions and government reserves when they were not economically useful to white society or were ill, diseased, addicted to alcohol or opium, or guilty of what whites considered crimes. From this period until after the Second World War, the history of Aboriginal and Torres Strait Islander administration is one of increasing attempts to control the wards the bureaucracy was administering. The control was never as thorough as the white administrators would have liked, because they were provided with very limited funding, but it was sufficient to make the Aborigines and Islanders conform to white expectations, although not without determined resistance. It was certainly more thorough than the Aborigines and Islanders would have wished. It is important to note that, while the twentieth century saw the gradual extension of the benefits of liberal democracy to white Australians, it saw an ever-increasing denial of liberty to black Australians. In Queensland, this paternalism was still very evident in the Aborigines Act 1971–1979 and the Torres Strait Islander Act 1971–1979.[26] Indeed, it was not until Aboriginal land tenure was partly acknowledged in 1984 in the Deeds of Grant in Trust land legislation that this state began to encourage Aboriginal local government on Aboriginal communities.[27]

The overall result was that an inferior caste status was imposed upon Aboriginal and Torres Strait Islander people.[28] Its scope and significance in the economic, legal, social, political, educational and religious spheres is clear.

Throughout most of the twentieth century, most Aboriginal and Torres Strait Islander people have been legally wards of the state or, as many of them would say, second class citizens. Their struggle for justice, for voting rights, for the right to move freely in towns and cities, to attend schools, to have their medical needs treated effectively, to retain their own culture and identity and to control and manage their own affairs on land that is recognised as irrevocably theirs, is an heroic story that all Australians can be proud of. It is an attempt to create a just society in which all of us can live.

From the time frontier conflict ceased and Aboriginal and Torres Strait Islander people were allowed to participate in the developing Australian society as an inferior caste, they have been discriminated against socially. In areas where the whites had settled, they were not allowed to make many major decisions affecting their own lives or to move wherever they wished. They were also regarded with extreme contempt by white Australians. In Australia, white racism probably reached its high water mark, not in the nineteenth century but in the 1920s and 1930s. It was part of the racist flood manifested so clearly throughout the British Empire, and even more clearly in Nazi Germany where Hitler took the concept of the master race to its logical conclusion and attempted a final solution. In Australia, determined attempts were made to prevent further miscegenation, which was believed to be a degradation of the race. In Queensland, Western Australia and the Northern Territory, for example, light coloured Aborigines of mixed descent were taken from their families and consigned to institutions so they could grow up and 'better themselves' in white society. The darker Aborigines were left isolated from the dominant culture, but in the main, under supervision on missions, reserves or pastoral properties. This final solution of 'the half caste problem' included attempts to prevent intermarrying or having sexual relations with whites.[29]

The Policies of Colonisation

Throughout Australia's history governments applied a number of policies to the Indigenous people. These varied somewhat from state to state as did the time spans during which they operated.

The first policy was, of course, *dispossession*. This was based on the legal fiction that Australia was wasteland, a colony of settlement not a colony of conquest: *terra nullius*, as the concept, colony of settlement, was in Australia, later designated. The land was said to be unoccupied, or at least unoccupied by people that the British colonists recognised as civilised. They became in theory British citizens when the land became the property of the British Crown. When they resisted the white invaders, they became outlaws.[30]

In the first three decades after 1788, it was assumed that Aboriginal people would acknowledge the alleged superiority of British civilisation, model themselves on the invaders and be assimilated into the colonial working class. This did not happen. Because of rapid depopulation, for the rest of the nineteenth century and the first two decades of the twentieth century, Aborigines were considered a doomed race, doomed to extinction.

The policy of *protection and segregation* on reserves and missions was in part a response to the doomed race theory and in part to colonial racism. It began in Victoria in the 1860s. Policies and practices varied greatly in the different colonies (states and the Northern Territory in the twentieth century) within the broader framework of European colonisation.

However, even in Queensland where controls were most pervasive and segregation on reserves and missions most energetically pursued, in the 1940s, about 60 per cent of the Aboriginal population still lived in fringe camps, on cattle stations, and in remote communities where they had limited contact with white settlers. Local police officers were appointed protectors of Aborigines in their districts and they, with other settlers, ensured Aborigines did not interfere with the developing white society. They were 'kept in their place'.[31]

This policy was maintained until the outbreak of the Second World War, which interrupted progress towards the new policy of *assimilation*. The eras of protection and assimilation were both accompanied by increasingly stringent controls over Aboriginal lives as they were forced to accommodate to the needs and aspirations of the white colonists.

The policy of *assimilation* was adopted as a national policy in 1951 but its implementation varied from state to state. There was an attempt in the 1960s to make it less offensive to Aboriginal and Islander people and their supporters and the policy was briefly termed *integration*. In effect, the policy of assimilation was maintained until the 1970s.

In 1972, the Federal Labor Government enunciated its policy as *self-determination* for Indigenous Australians. The Liberal–National Party Government modified this to *self-management* in 1975. With both parties, the rhetoric was not matched by surrendering ultimate power and authority to Aboriginal and Islander people to make and implement decisions affecting their own lives, even though Aboriginal land rights was legislated for in the Northern Territory.

In 1990, the Commonwealth Government created the Aboriginal and Torres Strait Islander Commission (ATSIC), bringing together the Department of Aboriginal Affairs and the Aboriginal Development Corporation. It was an attempt by the then Labor Government to involve Aboriginal and Islander people in meeting their own needs. ATSIC was the third such attempt by the Commonwealth Government to create a nationwide body to speak for Aboriginal and Torres Strait Islander Australians. Now it too has been terminated and an advisory council established.

The prominent activist, and first Aboriginal Secretary of the Federal Department of Aboriginal Affairs, Charles Perkins, in 1989 pointed optimistically to the dawning of a new age:

> There are no experts in indigenous affairs. Similarly, there are no magic solutions. Nevertheless, the developments in the past decade have been remarkable...Poverty, dispossession, prejudice and unhappiness still abound but not to the same extent...The time for crying in our beer is over.[32]

Aboriginal people have had much to cry over and the transgenerational consequences of their history can be seen still in the twenty-first century.

* * * *

Nearly all missions established in the nineteenth century or the first half of the twentieth century actively participated in the separation of children from their parents. The cruel reality of contemporary practice, the effect on those separated and on subsequent generations is graphically told in *Bringing Them Home: The Report of the National Inquiry into the Separation of Aboriginal and Torres Strait Islander Children from their Families.*[33] It caused the then Leader of the Opposition, Kim Beazley, to weep in Parliament.

The removal of children from their parents and relatives was always aimed at the destruction of their Aboriginal identity and the creation of a new institutionalised identity that would make them tractable participants in the institutional community of the mission or in the broader white dominated society in which they could only become the hewers of wood and drawers of water.[34] The missions, supported by the ABM, followed the policy and practices of the day. They split up even resident families by separating children from their parents, Aboriginal authority, and Aboriginal culture. At Yarrabah, Mitchell River Mission (now Kowanyama), Lockhart River Mission, and Forrest River Mission young children were placed in dormitories, one for the boys and one for the girls and unmarried women, and allowed very limited contact with their parents living in the mission village. The girls remained in the dormitories until they were married to husbands approved and often selected by the white missionaries.

Some missions, like Forrest River Mission and Yarrabah, and 'half-caste homes' like St Mary's in Alice Springs, were used as repositories for children deemed by state governments to be neglected children, often because they were in desperate need, but more often simply because they were Aboriginal children of mixed descent. Yarrabah, especially, was used by the Queensland Government for such children. Forrest River Mission in Western Australia was also used for this purpose. The Anglican Church missionaries were thus willing accomplices to the government's policy of removing families to their missions and then separating children from their parents or other family support.[35]

The story of Yarrabah, for example, tells of local Aborigines of the Gunganjdji and Yidinjdji tribes over time coming to the mission established in their land and accepting the reality of missionary control because there was no real alternative. They had lost their authority to live as they might determine and increasingly the ability to maintain or support their old way of life. With increasing contact with the colonists, Aborigines were developing new needs for the exotic 'material' culture, such as its food, tobacco, alcohol, opium, tea, sugar, metal containers, glass, axes, knives, wire, and sheets of iron. The mission was an alternative way of life to that which would have encroached on their land, and was already beginning to do so when it was founded in 1892.

Very soon after Queensland's 1897 Aboriginal Protection Act was passed, children and young women of mixed descent were identified by the police in their role as Protectors of Aborigines, hunted down, removed from their families or situations considered unsuitable, and sent to Yarrabah. They came from the far north of Cape York Peninsula, Coen, Lockhart River, Maytown, Laura, and Cooktown in central Cape York Peninsula, from the Daintree and Cairns, in the south of the Cape, from the Atherton Tableland, from Cloncurry, and over the years from anywhere in North Queensland where a Protector found a child of mixed descent or other Aboriginal child he deemed in need of *protection*, or, from the 1960s, *assimilation*.

The most extensive single removal occurred in 1904 when about one hundred Aborigines, adults and children of mixed descent, were brought from Fraser Island in southern Queensland. Fraser Island had been set up in 1897 as a government reserve for Aborigines. The Anglican Church was asked to take it over in 1901. Ernest Gribble, the founder of Yarrabah, soon concluded Fraser Island was unsuitable for a mission and, with government support, transferred a very disgruntled group, to far North Queensland. Most of them had lived in the Maryborough area.[36] This was all done legally with efficiency, economy and, of course, as far as the missionaries were concerned, with the best of intentions. They were cooperating with their government's policy.

Rosalind Kidd has recently shown how far from the truth were the good intentions the government stated whenever they had to report on their policies and practices in the administration of Aboriginal affairs. If Aboriginal children and adults were being removed to government communities or missions, one would expect to find that they were being provided for humanely and that their new living conditions were satisfactory. This was as far from the truth as it is possible to imagine. Until the 1970s Aboriginal people under government or mission control were fed debilitating, disease producing diets, and housed in leaking hovels, with disgracefully unsafe and inadequate water and sanitary provisions. They were made to live in communities where easily preventable diseases and parasites were allowed to flourish. Aboriginal children and adults died unnecessarily in these conditions with the full knowledge of the Aboriginal administration and the governments of the day. Reports of these conditions were received from government medical officers and nothing was done.

The Queensland Government supported each Aboriginal on Queensland missions at rates that were approximately one-third to one-half of the pitifully inadequate rate they provided per capita on the government communities. Children sent to Aboriginal reserves or missions were only subsidised at 20 to 25 per cent of white orphanage rates. The supporting churches were never able to find enough resources to make up this difference, let alone to resource their missions adequately. And this persisted until the missions finally relinquished control to the government in the 1960s. Senior Aboriginal department administrators, government ministers, and politicians still alive were complicit in the obscenity of crucifying a people because they were black and powerless.

I have taught the history of black–white relations in Australia for over thirty years. I knew how cruelly oppressive were government policies in Queensland and other states. Yet Kidd's revelations shocked me. She was able to obtain access to the carefully guarded Aboriginal administration files and detail the cruel hypocrisy behind Queensland Government practices. She revealed the 'machinations' of senior officials and governments to administer the Aboriginal department as cheaply as possible, often with less care for the welfare of their wards than for farm animals, while proclaiming they were acting in the best interests of Aboriginal people.

The deliberateness with which some white Australians allowed Aborigines to starve and live in conditions that produced ill health, stunted physical development, psychological and social dysfunction and abundant deaths horrified me. It shouldn't have but it did. I had been teaching about something that was at times evil and called it less than that.

In Queensland and in other states, Aboriginal workers were paid at a fraction of the white rate and, on missions and government communities

31

they received only a fraction of that. The remainder went to support the institution in which they or their families lived. In Queensland, regular percentages of their wages were also diverted to the Aboriginal administration so that, increasingly throughout the twentieth century, Aboriginal earnings were used to fund the department and government that oppressed them for services that were part of government infrastructure. On top of all this, they paid income tax and other deductions on their earnings, like other citizens. As Commonwealth Government provisions such as the maternity allowance, child endowment, and unemployment relief were made available to them, these resources were diverted from the Aboriginal recipients to the institutions, and Queensland Government funding reduced by equivalent amounts.

Overarching all of this was the system of control that created a colonial situation where white administrators or missionaries attempted to govern every aspect of Aboriginal lives: the language they spoke, their housing, their labour, their wages, their education, their movements to or from their communities, their expression of sexuality, their religious practices, their marriages, and their children. Especially their children. This was the ideal, not always realised of course because of inadequate resources, but the consequences of these institutionalised controls reverberate down the generations of Aboriginal people.[37]

It is perhaps not too late for Australia to have its own Truth and Reconciliation Commission. Many of the victims of generations of suffering are still alive. So are many of the officials, missionaries, parliamentarians, and government ministers who created the suffering or allowed it to persist. After the truth is accepted, a real reconciliation based on terms mutually acceptable to Indigenous Australians and the state and federal governments might be possible.

I have focused on Queensland because four of the five missions supported by ABM were in Queensland: Yarrabah, Mitchell River Mission (now Kowanyama), Lockhart River Mission, and Edward River Mission (now Pormpuraaw). The other, Forrest River Mission, in the Kimberley in the far north of Western Australia was funded at a much lower level even than the Queensland missions, despite the fact that from 1921 to 1930, the Western Australian government sent to it most of the children of mixed descent removed from families in the east Kimberley. None of the state governments or the commonwealth provided anywhere near adequate funds for the administration of Aboriginal affairs as black lives were thought of as much less important even than those of poor, needy whites. Western Australia's funding was the poorest per capita of all of these administrations and it is no surprise to discover that the Western

Australian Aborigines Act of 1905 was based closely on Queensland's 1897 Aboriginal Protection Act.[38]

Throughout the twentieth century, the response of the missionaries and such missionary agencies as ABM was varied. They functioned within the racist mindset that regarded Aboriginal people as inferior human beings and inferior citizens of the emerging white democracy, a child race that needed to be controlled in whatever ways white interests dictated. They aided and abetted the governments they worked with in the disempowerment and pauperisation of Aboriginal people because they could see no alternative. Founding missionaries, such as Ernest Gribble, actively encouraged not only the removal of children but also the development of a community of adults who were the necessary cheap labour to build and maintain the mission's infrastructure, indeed to be the mission. Thus, as governments accepted missions as a cheap, *de facto* government social service, the existing missions shaped government policy and practice. When it seemed desirable or necessary to extend government control over Aborigines living in some remote area, governments could always request one of the churches to establish a mission. In this way Mitchell River, Lockhart River and even Forrest River missions came into being, as we will see, as well as others such as Mapoon, Weipa, Aurukun and Mornington Island. Although AO Neville, as Chief Protector, only 'tolerated' missions in Western Australia, he used them extensively in the far north.[39] When government policies in the 1930s changed, under the influence of eugenics, to the biological absorption of Aborigines of mixed descent, churches supported this policy, as they did in the 1950s when the policy changed to the assimilation of all Aboriginal people into the broader community. Indeed, missionaries, mission agencies, and such influential Christian academics as anthropologists, AP Elkin and Arthur Capell of Sydney University, were advocates of assimilation long before governments enunciated it, admittedly of a more sophisticated kind than that implemented by governments. Elkin and Capell were both ordained Anglican ministers who were consulted by mission agencies and governments.[40]

But the marriage of government and missionaries was not without its problems and sometimes degenerated into a tense marriage of convenience, held together by their dependents, the Aboriginal people, who were in reality the reason for the existence of both the missionaries and the Aboriginal Affairs administrations.

The Western Australian and Queensland governments strongly supported the use of Aborigines as cheap labour and wanted them available for employment from early adolescence. The missionaries often opposed this policy, especially in the early years while they were establishing the infrastructure of their missions. It was practised extensively on government communities such as Cherbourg, Woorabinda, and Palm Island in Queensland and Moore River and Moola Bulla in Western Australia. It was a way of removing Aborigines as a cost on government and provided government revenue in Queensland. It also supported white employers and ultimately the economy of each state. Throughout most of the twentieth century, ABM supported missions, as did other missionary agencies, aimed at creating self-perpetuating Christian village communities. The missions tried to retain as many adults as possible to build and maintain the infrastructure and to produce as much food as possible on the missions to reduce costs. The ideal of a self-supporting mission involved attempts to find one or more cash crops or other sources of income. At Lockhart River, for example, the missionaries tried employment in the pastoral industry, trochus shell, cotton, mining, and retail shopping.

The missionaries were often confronted with a dilemma. They realised how Aborigines were exploited and defrauded of their meagre wages when sent to remote pastoral properties to work. Moreover, the girls and women regularly returned pregnant. Consequently the missionaries' reluctance to supply wage earning, outside labour was often a source of friction with the government administration. Ideally, they would have liked to keep families together on the mission, despite their third world poverty, and often resisted the temptation to send Aboriginal men and women out to work to raise funds and lower their costs.[41] Repeatedly they requested increased funding from government and pointed out the crippling effects of government funding on the people the government committed to their trust. However, they were caught in a no-win situation. Despite reports from government medical officers their requests were routinely rejected.[42] Then, to survive and to provide work for their growing populations, some also sent Aboriginal mission residents to outside employment.

Most church requests and protests to government were buried in government files, but not always. In 1935, the Queensland Government found itself publicly criticised at the Science Congress in Melbourne and subsequently in the press for the way it denigrated Aboriginal culture and defrauded Aborigines of their wages and savings accumulated in government accounts. The Director of Native Affairs, J.W. Bleakley, turned for support to Reverend John Needham, Chairman of ABM and the Association for the Protection of Native Races (APNR). The APNR secretary, Rev. W. Morley, had pointed out that in Queensland there were '17,000 voiceless and voteless fellow-creatures…held in conditions of economic slavery'.[43] Needham was probably the most highly respected administrator of a mission agency in Australia at the time. After consultation with Bleakley, he publicly supported Queensland Government policy in ABM's Annual Report: 'the native is not an economic slave, but most truly a cared for ward of the State'. So successfully had Bleakley hoodwinked him, lied to him, that he added that the government 'did not receive one penny from native taxation'.[44]

The limited expectations of well-intentioned white Australians for Aboriginal people are probably nowhere better illustrated. Needham had been superintendent at Yarrabah and had first hand knowledge of what Aboriginal people had been experiencing for over thirty years. It would take the Second World War and the new international awareness of the plight and rights of colonised people in the third and fourth worlds before prominent administrators of missions realised that Aboriginal and Torres Strait Islander people were not responsible for their oppressed, impoverished lifestyle, but were the victims of imperialist conquest. In 1958, in response to Queensland Government allegations that mission stations had utterly failed to provide satisfactory conditions for the Aboriginal residents, the chairman of ABM, Archdeacon Frank Coaldrake, laid the blame for the failure firmly on the shoulders of the Queensland Government.[45]

In 1962, Bishop John Matthews, the Bishop of Carpentaria Diocese which then incorporated far North Queensland and the Northern Territory, appealed to the Freedom from Hunger Campaign in London for funds to support undernourished Aborigines on Anglican missions. He publicly blamed the parsimony of the state and federal governments for the poverty of the Aboriginal people that had been entrusted to them.

At this time, government reports revealed that Aboriginal stillbirths and premature baby deaths occurred at four times the white Australian rate, deaths under one year at more than six times, and for children under four more than thirteen times the white Australian rate. Malnutrition was the main cause of death of 50 per cent of children under three years old, and 85 per cent of children under four years. Indeed, malnutrition was the base cause of other illnesses and the diminished resistance to disease. Almost half of the deaths under sixteen years resulted from gastroenteritis or pneumonia, singly or in combination. Endemic hookworm and un-safe water supplies were also part of the destruction of the health of Aboriginal people on missions and government communities.[46] Although Bishop Matthews may not have intended it, this appeal to Freedom from Hunger shared the sentiment of those involved with the establishment of the Aboriginal Embassy on the lawns of Parliament House in Canberra. Aborigines were foreigners in their own land. The church had to seek support for them from an overseas charity.

In the early 1970s I wanted to live on Palm Island to record oral histories. My request was politely turned down by the Manager because, he said, he could not offer me accommodation. Through contacts in the Queensland Education Department, I was able to get a teacher's flat during the summer school vacation and spent one week there introduced to members of the community by Fred Clay, the Chairman of the Council, and his wife Iris. When I applied to return for a second visit to the nice modern teacher's flat, the Manager had to again politely reject my request because there was a widespread outbreak of gastroenteritis that had already resulted in a number of deaths. This was a regular feature of Palm Island life in summer. The Manager told me that it would be irresponsible of him to allow me to visit while this epidemic was raging. I appreciated his concern for my wellbeing. Of course the Aboriginal people were still there suffering from fifty years' accumulated neglect, malnutrition, and unsanitary living conditions. It required funding and community health education to attempt to bring Palm Island up to the white Australian norm. The Manager was respected by the people, a good man trying to do an impossible job, but he certainly did not want a white academic dying of gastroenteritis on his watch. And, of course, he knew that an historian was *persona non grata* to Paddy Killoran, the legendary head of Aboriginal Affairs.

While missionary agencies such as ABM wished to maintain control of the mission communities, they were ultimately under the authority of the state government. They could demand more resources and protest to the department responsible for Aboriginal affairs or directly to government ministers. On occasions, if they were determined enough, they could raise issues in public, but finally the government called the shots, even to insisting that Ivens, Gribble's successor at Yarrabah, be sacked, because he refused to accept any more removals. In this Ivens had been supported by ABM.

In 1914 Bleakley had drafted plans to take over administrative control of the ten missions which contained many more Aborigines than the government communities. The Queensland Government rejected his proposal because the ten missions would have required four to five times as much funding if they were administered by the government. As the various mission agencies came nowhere near to making up the shortfall which would bring the missions up to the deplorable conditions on the government communities, the even more deplorable conditions on the missions persisted into the 1960s.[47]

In *One Blood*, John Harris, the son of CMS missionaries and a committed Christian, noted:

One very obvious trend throughout the history of Christian missions in Aboriginal Australia is that, as missionaries gained increasing control over the lives of Aborigines, they either became more authoritarian, domineering people or the missions tended to attract this kind of person…Somehow, having power over people's lives changed them.[48]

He contrasts those who had such authority with those missionaries who visited Aborigines in fringe camps or rural reserves or were attached to government reserves but not part of the controlling administration. These, he claimed, were more often remembered with affection than those who had authority over them because they had to win the interest and commitment of the people they came to serve. Clearly, he is saying more than 'power corrupts' but that is part of it. The other factor that fostered such authoritarianism, regimentation and control was the contempt with which most missionaries regarded Aboriginal culture and the racism of white Australian society which persisted through much of the twentieth century.[49] The missionaries did not regard the Aborigines as equals before God or Man.

Yet, given their totally inadequate resources and their personnel, the missions often achieved surprisingly positive results. In Queensland in 1922, ninety-three Aborigines on government communities died out of a population of 1634, while fourteen died on the ten missions which had a much greater population.[50] As noted, the missionaries often also tried to protect young Aboriginal men and women from exploitation, and the women from virtual prostitution, by limiting outside employment when such a policy alienated the government and those seeking cheap labour. It was also a great financial sacrifice to keep the young on the missions.[51]

Each mission was unique with its own history, its own changing constellations of personalities, black and white, and its own relationship with the outside world. For example, in 1913, Chief Protector Bleakley asked Mitchell River Mission to provide wives for the Aboriginal men at Abingdon Downs Station. This request was refused because the missionaries wanted the women to marry and have families at Mitchell River. In 1936 Bleakley requested Mitchell River Mission to supply mixed-race Aboriginal wives for Mapoon which Bleakley had designated the mission for Cape York Peninsula 'half-castes'. This request was strongly supported by Bishop Stephen Davies and five women were sent from Lockhart River to Mapoon. Other missions also cooperated. The mission superintendent at Mitchell River at the time, 'Chappie' Chapman, refused the request. May Smiler best expressed his philosophy: 'Oh, leave them with their families, they're happy here'. At Kowanyama, I met May Smiler, one of the women to be transferred. She had previously been saved by Chapman from another unwanted marriage with a suitor of mixed descent from Urandangie. Bleakley's attempt to control marriage based on 'caste' with the support of the bishop was quietly but firmly avoided by Chapman who did not regard the people he was responsible for as commodities to be moved around without consideration of their own wishes.[52] Missionaries such as Chapman are remembered with respect for their humanity.

The contradictions inherent in the British Government's policy for Aborigines in the first fifty years of the colonisation of Australia are starkly obvious. Solicitous concern was expressed while officials supported dispossession by allowing the settlers to treat them as enemies of the state and supporting them with as much force as was necessary. These contradictions seem minor compared with those confronting colonists for whom their faith in Christ was central to their understanding of themselves as human beings. Their relationship with Christ implied, in theory the potential of a Christ-like relationship with all other human beings, a relationship that also implied a respect for all members of what Christians refer to as 'the body of Christ'. The challenging end-times idealism dramatically enacted in the Gospels became institutionalised and ritualised in the ongoing lives of the generations that followed, and then an integral part of European culture. History then modified and shaped the expression of the faith within the kaleidoscope of political structures and regional cultures that have emerged since Christianity became the official religion of the Roman Empire. Christianity became one of a number of integrating ideologies of the various European polities. Most often Christianity was made to serve what was assumed to be the greater good of the nation state, alliance, or empire.

In my doctoral research, I studied the first generation of Christian missionaries to work among the Aboriginal people in North Queensland, most working on the frontier itself. I became quite fascinated by this group of people. Some like John Gribble, Ernest Gribble, 'Chappie' Chapman, Nicholas Hey of Mapoon, and Pastor Schwarz of Hope Valley, devoted their lives to offering their culture, their faith and religious practices to Aboriginal people in the remotest parts of Australia living in the most primitive conditions. Yet they were always agents of the invaders, allowed to offer their ministry by grace and favour of those who were intent on destroying Aboriginal culture wherever necessary. I once commented to Archbishop John Grindrod, then Primate of the Australian Anglican Church, that I could not imagine Christianity being offered in worse conditions than it had been to Aboriginal people from the earliest years throughout most of Australia's history. Regrettably, he did not reply.

What I found equally as fascinating is the fact that there are still many Aboriginal people committed to the faith that was taken to their ancestors only one or a few generations ago. If it is true that the percentage of practising Aboriginal Christians is greater than that of white Australians, given the history to which I have briefly alluded, it must be worthy of inclusion in whatever canon exists of modern miracles.

I decided to focus on the official missionary outreach of the Anglican Church to Aboriginal people through ABM, known for most of its existence as the Australian Board of Missions, now more humbly as the Anglican Board of Mission–Australia. It represented the single largest Christian denomination for much of Australia's history. Anglicans occupied influential positions in all aspects of society throughout Australia's history, including the legislatures and the public service. ABM supported institutional missions in remote areas as well as chaplaincies on government reserves. Inevitably as the place of Aborigines in Australian society changed in the twentieth century the Anglican Church has found itself challenged to respond to broader issues. Those associated with ABM were the ones most likely to be aware of these changes and to communicate them to other Anglicans, and ultimately to those who sat in the pews.

The response of Aboriginal people historically linked to the Anglican Church, possibly the most formal or staid of mainstream churches, is also fascinating. Mine has been a privileged position as a participant observer of developments of the last few decades as most of ABM's outreach to Aborigines has been in North Queensland, my 'backyard', as Don Aitken had said. Here, as we have seen, an Aboriginal Assistant Bishopric has been created which not only has an administrative function within the Diocese, but also by invitation to Aborigines in the rest of Australia.

* * * *

For most of my life I have lived among Aborigines, first as a teacher in western Queensland, and later as an academic. As a child in North Queensland in the 1940s and 1950s, I had known there were 'Blacks' Camps' on the fringes of Townsville at Stuart and on the Common and, of course, I knew of Palm Island. On one occasion at least, I saw a group of Aborigines in a wired-off enclosure boarding a boat to return to Palm Island. I also saw Palm Islanders giving spear throwing demonstrations before the start of Rugby League matches. I did not meet an Aboriginal, however, until I was in my final years of secondary school. Ernie Hoolihan, now an old friend but then a feared opponent, played tennis, cricket and rugby league for Townsville Grammar and I for the Townsville State High.

The next Aboriginal I met on equal terms was a very good cricketer, whose name I have forgotten, who worked for a stock and station agency in Longreach. He had such a natural dignity that as a twenty-year-old school teacher I felt quite inadequate in his company. These two were clearly such exceptions that it was not until 1955 when I was sent unwillingly to a one-teacher school, Quamby, in north-west Queensland that I got to know a wide range of Aboriginal men working in the pastoral industry or as fettlers in the railway. They were not under the control of the Aboriginal Affairs Department, not 'under the Act'. Nor were their families. I met their wives at the school where I taught their children. I occasionally ate with Aboriginal men and often drank in the pub with them. About half of my pupils were of Aboriginal descent. Between whites and blacks there was clearly a social distance that did not preclude a wide range of human interaction.

And then there were the Aboriginal pastoral workers from missions and Palm Island who were 'under the Act' and generally regarded by whites as inferior others. They did not eat in the hotel dining room; they did not drink at the bar although there was always someone who would provide them with alcohol when they sat in small groups in the backyard of the hotel during the local Quamby race meetings. And, finally, there was Freddie, the six foot 'black boy' who worked at the hotel or at the publican's nearby pastoral property. The publican, his wife and family were fine people, highly respected throughout the district and by me. They had bought the pub so they could live there and send their kids to school. Freddie ate with the publican's children in the kitchen while the adults ate in the dining room. He slept on a swag in the laundry. I had a room to myself, the white cook had a room to herself, and most nights there were rooms vacant. At the time, I accepted this situation with as much equanimity as everyone else. On the odd occasion that someone purchased alcohol for him, Freddy occasionally dropped in on me in my room. On one such visit, he made it clear he hated being 'under the Act'. He wanted me to help him 'get out from under the Act'. 'Let's talk about it in the morning, Freddy,' I said, an offer of support that was pretty hollow, as I think I probably realised even then. In the morning, he would be sober.

I began to read about Aborigines; one of the first books being *The Australian Aborigines: How to Understand Them*. Professor Elkin apparently did not envisage Aboriginal people ever reading what was then the standard anthropological text. I then applied to be an assistant teacher at Palm Island, stating in my application that the Aborigines had suffered greatly and I wanted to help them in whatever way I could. Not many, if any, Queensland state school teachers applied to teach at Palm Island in the early 1950s. Needless to say I did not get the job. People with such warped attitudes were presumably not wanted at Palm. (For the record, I received a promotion instead.)

In 1969, when I decided to undertake post-graduate research, the history of Aboriginal–European relations was the obvious choice even though no one at James Cook University at the time was familiar with the area.

* * * * *

I use the term 'holocaust' because the Aboriginal experience in Australia since colonisation has been just that, 'a holocaust'. From the Aboriginal perspective, it is important to explore the complexity of historical factors that contributed to this situation, to examine the process, to reveal it as truthfully as possible. It is important for all Australians. But for me, and I suspect for many Aboriginal people, the one word that crystallises the two hundred years of colonisation is 'holocaust'. I have studied the Holocaust inflicted upon the Jews by the National Socialist regime and their allies. I am not attempting to do a 'compare and contrast'. This is not the Holocaust of the Jews. This is the Aboriginal holocaust. Their experience is worthy of the name.

Early population estimates for the whole of Australia before European colonisation was about 300,000. More recent estimates suggest at least 750,000 and probably one million. The Australian Bureau of Statistics estimated it to have plummeted to 31,000 by 1911, the lowest level suggested. These figures suggest a depopulation of perhaps 90 per cent, or even 97 per cent. If the population estimates were accepted conservatively as reducing from 750,000 to 100,000, a depopulation of 87 per cent would be indicated. More detailed studies support such human devastation. One estimate is that the population decline in Tasmania in thirty years was 96 per cent; in Victoria, at least 90 per cent in thirty-five years; on Victoria River Downs approximately 90 per cent in sixty years; and perhaps 97 per cent in the Alligator River district.[53] At what level would the term, Aboriginal holocaust, be unacceptable: 80 per cent, 70, 60...?

Frontier conflict contributed to the immediate depopulation, as the British eyewitness James Morrill reported, but, more importantly, it created the situation where devastating exotic diseases were introduced to Aboriginal communities without any attempt to control the circumstances or to lessen the impact such contact would have in each new frontier area. The effect of smallpox was known by 1789, one year after the First Fleet arrived, and the impact of other diseases such as measles, venereal disease, tuberculosis, leprosy, hookworm, dysentery and gastroenteritis were reported regularly throughout the nineteenth and well into the twentieth century and accepted by government administrators and politicians with apparent nonchalance. If such carnage had occurred among the white colonists, their response would have been deafening. Governments would have used all known measures to reduce the death toll, and there were simple ones always available, like isolation, providing nourishing food, sanitation, shelter, hospitalisation, contemporary medication and nursing. During this time, governments intervened energetically when diseases, such as leprosy or venereal disease, threatened white populations.[54] By the end of the nineteenth century, missions had shown that much could be done with very limited expenditure and inadequately qualified staff, if only the white settlers and their governments cared what was happening to Aborigines.

The catastrophic consequence of deliberate aggression, benign indifference, and calculated neglect was the Aboriginal holocaust.

3.

In the Beginning

The Australian Board of Missions, the Anglican Church and the Aborigines 1850–1900

I have always felt that the Aboriginal was the Lazarus of Australia.

> The more religious and thoughtful people in Australia have long felt that we owed aborigines a very considerable debt for our past treatment of them…I have always felt that the aboriginal was the Lazarus of Australia. Poor, ragged, and sick with sores which are the result of the contact with the diseases of the white man…It is largely due to the real if tardy efforts of the Church that the nation is slowly awakening to its duties and responsibilities in this matter.[1]

A slow awakening indeed.

The Australian Board of Missions (ABM), now renamed the Anglican Board of Mission – Australia, is the missionary organisation of the General Synod, the national legislative and administrative body of the Anglican Church of Australia. It attempts to coordinate missionary outreach within Australia and overseas on a nationwide scale and to educate Anglicans about what ABM and the General Synod see as their missionary responsibilities. ABM describes its function as facilitating the sharing of the resources of knowledge, personnel, and finance with other Christian communities and emphasises its 'special responsibility to support Aboriginal and Torres Strait Islander ministries within Australia'.

In the last two decades of the twentieth century, from one-quarter to almost one-third of the Mission Grants were directed to Aboriginal and Islander ministries. The Diocese of Carpentaria whose cathedral was at Thursday Island in the Torres Strait received almost two-thirds of the Aboriginal and Islander Mission Grant. In 1996, Carpentaria was incorporated into the Diocese of North Queensland. An analysis of the ABM budgets would lead to the conclusion that ABM, and through it, the Anglican Church in Australia is at present fulfilling its responsibility 'to support Aboriginal and Torres Strait Islander ministries within Australia' as far as its meagre income will allow.[2] In the first half century of its existence this was far from the case.

There are a number of other Anglican missionary organisations represented in Australia: the Church Missionary Society (CMS), the Bush Church Aid Society, the National Home Mission Fund, the Church Army, the South American Missionary Society, and the Society for Promoting Christian Knowledge in Australia. Of these CMS is now by far the largest, much larger than ABM, and since 1908 has had a continuous, direct involvement with Aboriginal missions in the Northern Territory.[3] The Bush Church Aid Society, the National Home Mission Fund, and the Church Army also provide some direct or indirect ministry to Aboriginal people. Until the 1960s all Anglican ministry among Aboriginal people was regarded as 'missionary work' rather than a Home Mission responsibility. As the CMS limited its involvement to Aboriginal missions to the Northern Territory, 'missionary work' among Aborigines elsewhere was seen as requiring the support of ABM.

Throughout its history, the Christian religion has often found itself associated with the expansionist energies of powerful European states. Indeed, the colonising propensity of human beings has generally been accompanied by the spread of the expanding power's dominant religious belief. From its inception in 1850, the ABM was confronted with the fact that Christianity in general, and the Anglican Church in particular, were challenged to work among the Aboriginal people of Australia. Like other colonising Christians, the Board of Missions realised that the devastation their society had inflicted and was continuing to inflict upon those it had conquered and dispossessed had placed upon them the responsibility for offering assistance, and, in their eyes, salvation to the colonised survivors.

On the expanding frontier, as we have seen, British colonists asserted their authority over Aborigines, a process which often led to bloodshed and the fierce hatred that is a consequence of wars of conquest. After pacification, this authority was maintained by the social gap between the races and the use of legal and extralegal intimidation. This assertion of authority disrupted traditional Aboriginal society and, combined with exotic diseases, malnutrition, and the unhygienic living conditions associated with acculturation, had a disastrous effect. The Aborigines were then accepted as cowed and inferior sojourners in the developing society dominated by the European colonists. Although generally regarded as parasitic nuisances, they provided a pool of menial and cheap casual labour. As long as they didn't offend the colonists, they were largely ignored except for the appropriation or abduction of their women and children to meet the sexual and employment needs of pioneer society.[4]

It was the Christian missionaries, however, who aimed to assert the most complete and pervasive authority. The Christian ideology contained within it, in the example and teaching of Jesus of Nazareth, a clear acknowledgement of human equality and a concern for the physical, psychological, and spiritual wellbeing of men, women, and children. However, Jesus claimed to have, and was believed by Christians to possess, a unique relationship with the one true God revealed in Hebrew history such that he alone offered salvation to all people. All his followers in theory, but few in practice, accepted this imperative of converting non-Christians to their faith. For nineteenth century Christians, this involved an acceptance of the superiority of the Christian religion over all others. As Christianity's strongest power base was then in Europe, it inevitably gained European accretions, which its followers accepted as essential to Christian belief, although they dropped others that the first Hebrew Christians regarded as essential to their veneration of God in the light of Christ's teaching, for example, circumcision. Christian missionaries in the nineteenth century, therefore, were determined to change not only the religious beliefs of Aborigines but also other aspects of their culture that the missionaries found unacceptable to their own cultural value system.[5]

During the period of European colonial expansion, a large number of missionary societies, groups, and organisations had come into being. Three Anglican societies, the Society for the Promotion of Christian Knowledge, the Society for the Propagation of the Gospel, and the Church Missionary Society, played an important role in establishing the Australian and New Zealand dioceses in existence in the 1850s.[6] Yet, despite this, the six bishops of Australia and New Zealand who met in Sydney in 1850 and committed the Church of England to missionary enterprise in the South Pacific, deliberately turned their backs on the use of missionary societies and committed the responsibility to the whole church by setting up a board of bishops for this purpose. At first it was called the Australasian Board of Missions, but after 1872, the Australian Board of Missions or, more commonly, ABM.

The driving force behind the creation of the ABM was Bishop George Selwyn of New Zealand. The meeting of the six bishops of Australia and New Zealand, held in Sydney during October 1850, was the first such meeting. Its main purpose was to discuss colonial church government but one night was set aside to hold a public meeting to promote missions in the south-west Pacific and to create a Board of Missions on which the six dioceses would be represented. Selwyn's immediate goal was to marshal support for his missionary outreach to Melanesia. In this he was remarkably successful. The 1300 people who attended donated almost £1000, enough to purchase a schooner to sail among the islands.[7]

Selwyn, a High Churchman, was also determined to involve the whole church through diocesan committees, which would correspond with and be coordinated by a Board of Missions made up of the bishops of Australia and New Zealand. He also wished to avoid using voluntary missionary societies, especially the evangelical or low church CMS with which he had very strained relations in New Zealand. After the formation of the board, Selwyn invited the CMS missionary in Auckland to be a member of his diocesan missionary board, an offer CMS in London firmly rejected, partly because it was by then suspicious that Selwyn wished to weaken CMS, and partly because it was strongly opposed to Selwyn's plan to educate Indigenous evangelists in English at a college remote from their home areas. CMS believed 'that the truths of religion can be taught only in the vernacular language of the country'.[8] The rift between Selwyn and CMS had widened considerably.

This concept, that missions were the responsibility of the whole church through the bishops, had already been implemented by the Anglican Church in the United States, the Episcopalians. Thus, from its inception ABM had attempted to occupy the high ground, which was in reality High Church ground. The founding bishops had also given ABM the prophetic role of challenging all Anglicans to participate in the mission Christ had entrusted to his apostles in his Great Commission: 'Go therefore and make disciples of all nations' (Matthew 28:19). The missionary societies aimed specifically at the dedicated few who would support their missions and their churchmanship. This idealism, with its inherent problem of rousing an apathetic, inward looking, poorly organised Australia-wide church to meet the challenge, was to haunt ABM throughout its whole existence. It still does today.[9]

The establishment of a 'Board of Missions for the evangelisation of the indigenous peoples of this continent [the Aborigines] and the inhabitants of the islands contiguous with the same [the Melanesians]'[10] did not do away with the existence of missionary societies in the South Pacific nor prevent them from operating there. The CMS founded in England in 1799 was to complement ABM in its missionary outreach within Australia and overseas and to compete with it for human and financial resources.[11] By not turning to any of the established societies, the bishops had ensured that, for a good deal of its history, ABM would become actively involved in establishing and managing missions. However, although the bishops had turned their backs on CMS, CMS had not turned its back on mission. And, as Keith Cole has put it: 'The CMS of Australia, as in England, is a *church* society in the Evangelical tradition, founded on "the church principle, but not on the High Church principle"'. CMS could thus count on Evangelical support if ABM proceeded further along the High Church road.[12]

The dating of the birth of ABM from the meeting of the bishops in 1850 proved to be largely of symbolic significance, for the Board of Missions made no attempt to evangelise within Australia or overseas for another generation. No administrative structure existed until 1872 when the first General Synod of the Church of England in Australia approved a constitution for the ABM. Board members were the bishops of the church in Australia. New Zealand had, by this time, been excised from the Province of Australia. As the bishops could only meet at irregular and infrequent intervals, an executive council was created to carry out the decisions of the board. The structure looked impressive and encompassing but nothing of any substance was achieved for yet another twenty years. In these forty years, the Aboriginal holocaust went on unabated as the Aborigines were dispossessed throughout most of Australia. In each colonised area, depopulation was so obvious that Aborigines were considered a 'doomed race'. And in their sanitised cathedral cities, the ABM members and committees thought about the problems. As Canon John Needham, Chairman of ABM from 1922 until 1942, remarked with apparent bemusement: 'There is no evidence forthcoming to show that anything in the shape of missionary work was attempted'.[13]

At the second General Synod in 1876 it was decided to undertake work among the Aborigines on the Queensland Government reserve at Mackay but nothing was to eventuate as the small amount of finance required was considered beyond the board's resources. Subsequently, the reserve was closed as part of governmental economy measures.[14] In 1879, the board cautiously began life as a missionary agency by engaging a Chinese catechist to work among the Chinese in Sydney. In the same year, the board agreed to provide £50 to the Warangesda Aboriginal Mission, which John Brown Gribble had started on his own initiative with some support from the Bishop of Goulburn. The Diocesan Corresponding Committee of ABM acted as the controlling body until August 1885, when the mission was handed over to the Aborigines Protection Association.[15]

Missions were extensively discussed at the 1886 General Synod. The British annexation of New Guinea in 1884 provided a new challenge that stimulated yet more enthusiastic committee work. The constitution was amended to specifically include New Guinea as a missionary target and immediate action to found a mission there was called for.[16] For the next five years, New Guinea dominated the attention of the executive council as it tried to obtain the funds and personnel to open the mission the church had demanded but was loath to support. It was not until July 1891 that Albert McLaren and Copland King sailed to establish ABM's first extra-diocesan venture. The cost of the New Guinea Mission was estimated at £1500 per annum, a commitment that was a challenge to the pitifully meagre resources of ABM.

Before McLaren and Copland King had departed, ABM was embarrassed by a request from the zealous John Gribble for support in establishing an Aboriginal mission in North Queensland. Initially, ABM did nothing except to express sympathy and recommend that it receive 'practical support' from church people.[17] Gribble had to inspect, at his own expense, sites recommended to him by the Victorian Government botanist, von Mueller. The Queensland Government granted him a reserve of eighty square miles (204.8 square kilometres) south of Cairns. Six months elapsed before ABM recognised it as a mission. Even then Gribble was held responsible for raising all the establishment costs.[18] The executive council undertook to rouse active interest in the mission, known at first as Bellenden Ker Mission and subsequently as Yarrabah, and to supply funds 'as far as possible'; yet it clearly expected that the North Queensland Diocese would contribute significantly and supervise the mission, and that the Queensland Government would contribute an initial £500 and a boat, as had been promised to Gribble, plus £240 per annum, a pound-for-pound subsidy, and the use of Gribble in his area of influence to provide governmental assistance to the Aborigines. Gribble was so buoyed by his discussion with the Colonial Secretary, Horace Tozer, that he requested three separate sites, salary for teachers, £300 for school buildings, and a mission cutter.[19]

Gribble's dream of a missionary empire vanished instantly when he returned to Queensland in 1892. Tozer informed Gribble that papers had been forwarded from Western Australia 'relating to the great agitation on the treatment of the blacks of that colony during my [Gribble's] sojourn as a Missionary therein'.[20]

Because of Gribble's exposure of atrocities against the Aborigines in Western Australia, Tozer withdrew all offers of financial assistance although every other Queensland mission founded after 1885 had been assisted. Two weeks later, Bishop Barlow of North Queensland informed Gribble he could expect no financial support from his diocese. Barlow had been as alarmed as Tozer by the reports from Western Australia and had warned Gribble 'against saying anything about the doings of the whites to the blacks' and even threatened to close the mission if Gribble exposed North Queensland atrocities. The North Queensland Diocese was still in its pioneering stages and the bishop of this impoverished diocese did not wish to alienate his white congregation. 'My opinion of my Diocesan is not an exalted one', Gribble confided to his journal.[21]

Worse was to follow. Although the founder had not set eyes on any of the fifty or so Aborigines living on the Yarrabah reserve, after he had been there a few months, he was invalided back to New South Wales where he died in June 1893.[22] His young son, Ernest, initially determined not to work as a missionary among Aborigines, had been persuaded by his father to take charge of Yarrabah.[23] By the end of 1892, ABM had accepted financial responsibility for the mission.[24] It was at last forced to confront the consequences of Aboriginal dispossession.

In 1900, when ABM celebrated its jubilee, it needed emancipation from fifty years of the Anglican Church's apathy and tokenism. Unlike the Jews, whose jubilee year, the 'year of the Lord', they symbolically commemorated, they had not reached the promised land envisaged by the bishops in 1850 and, for this, bishops were largely to blame. The constituted missionary body of the Australian church was responsible for two small extra-diocesan missions, one in New Guinea and one for Aboriginal Australia, Yarrabah, which ministered directly or indirectly to at most three hundred Aborigines.

The Rev. AE David, writing in 1908, pointed out how far the Australian dioceses were from achieving the hope Bishop Broughton of Sydney had expressed in the bishops' meeting of 1850: 'That one uniform system might be established throughout all Colonial Churches (uniform, that is, as to all vital and essential observances), so that they might be bound together in one great system of unity'. The church instead had split itself into 'congeries of dioceses, each one constituting an autonomous and self-contained whole'.[25] It proceeded along the path to 'diocesanism' from which it has never recovered.

It would have been strange had the first General Synod in 1872 not set up some sort of missionary body, but, given the inability of Australia's General Synod until 1962, to bind the dioceses to accord with a determination of General Synod, it was probably inevitable that it too would become a victim of diocesanism. The Australian church had to have a missionary body. With ABM, it had one. However, until the end of the nineteenth century the dioceses still saw themselves as the recipients of mission, rather than contributors to mission.[26] They had churches to build and staff in the settled areas and the challenge of the outback still to overcome. As new dioceses were created, they had cathedrals to build and administrations to create.[27] But the problem went further than dependency on the church in England, diocesan insularity, and parochialism.

By 1872 the churchmanship divisions of the Anglican Church in Australia were well established. In that year, four of the ten dioceses were Evangelical. Included in this number were the two wealthiest dioceses, Sydney and Melbourne. By 1915, only four out of twenty-four were predominantly Evangelical, but this numerical disproportion is misleading, as once again it was mainly the least viable dioceses that were High Church or Anglo-Catholic.[28] From its inception ABM was thus dominated by High Church bishops, some enthusiastic Anglo Catholics who favoured Episcopal missions such as Melanesia, New Guinea, and later Carpentaria.[29] Proudly protestant Low Church Evangelicals believed the High Church party's renewed focus on its pre-reformation, heritage — which stressed ancient liturgies, sacraments, and priesthood — was a regression towards Rome. Consequently, whatever Evangelical support there was for mission was overwhelmingly directed towards CMS. However, as Wetherell has pointed out, there was little enthusiasm at all for missions. Not only was the church's energy sapped by the drawn out churchmanship controversy, there was also a suspicion that energies devoted to converting the heathen were misplaced if not harmful.[30] At a joint meeting of the ABM board and its executive council in October 1896, Archdeacon Whitington, who had been general secretary of the board from 1891 to 1893, 'drew attention to "the main difficulty" viz. that there was no enthusiasm for a board', while in its jubilee handbook, ABM confessed mournfully: 'Many in every age have scoffed at Missions. A still larger number have been lukewarm'.[31] The Great Commission was apparently not even an embarrassment to Australian Anglicans.

A study of the minutes of the board and its executive council since their legal institution in 1872 clearly illustrates 'the main difficulty'. It had been a struggle to have Diocesan Corresponding Committees set up in the dioceses and harder still to have them function effectively, if at all.[32] Those bishops who were not opposed to ABM because of its High Church domination and direction were not interested in diverting their resources to a board that was, in reality, a subcommittee of General Synod. Looking back on this period, the then Chairman, Canon John Needham, demonstrated the depths of the existing apathy with sure and acknowledged measuring sticks: 'It is hard to realise a missionary body without a full time Secretary and a monthly magazine'.[33] The plight of Aboriginal people was presumably of even more remote concern. Indeed, the reluctance of the Australian church to commit itself to missionary outreach was nowhere more in evidence than in its work among Aboriginal people. Samuel Marsden had soon diverted his missionary zeal from the Aborigines to the Maoris although the CMS had conducted the Aboriginal mission in Wellington Valley from 1832 to 1842.[34] Archdeacon Matthew Hale had established a mission, Poonindie, at Port Lincoln in South Australia in 1850. In 1862, the Church of England in Victoria commenced work at Lake Condah near Warrnambool. The Aborigines almost died out so the survivors were moved to Lake Tyers which was eventually taken over by the Victorian Government. The Anglican Church maintained a chaplaincy there. The London based Society for the Propagation of the Gospel had responded, in 1867, to a request by the Governor of Queensland, Sir George Bowen, to establish a mission to the Aborigines and Torres Strait Islanders at Somerset at the tip of Cape York Peninsula. This had closed after eighteen months.[35] In 1880 the Rev. John Brown Gribble established the Warangesda Mission, after seeing the misery of the surviving Aborigines along the Murrumbidgee River. At first Gribble worked without outside support. He left to establish a mission on the Gascoyne River in Western Australia in 1885, an initiative which was aborted because of the hostility aroused by Gribble's previously mentioned exposure of settler brutality. The Anglican Church surrendered its control over Warangesda but maintained a chaplaincy through visits from the nearby Vicar of Whitton.[36] These few fleeting attempts were the only significant efforts by the Anglican Church to reach out to the Aborigines from the first settlement until J.B. Gribble committed his church and its national missionary agency, ABM, to a mission at Yarrabah. In his 1908 review of Anglican church expansion in Australia, David made an important, contemporary assessment for his church. He was scathing in his criticism of its neglect of the Aborigines:

> Notwithstanding these evidences of care for the aborigines, it must be confessed that the Church of England has been slow to realise her responsibilities in this respect. The scarcity of clergy, and the extreme difficulty of the work, account for a good deal, but do not excuse the supineness shown in neglecting opportunities.[37]

Supine indeed, for the plight of the Aborigines that followed white colonisation and the opportunities for converting uncontacted tribes were known from the earliest decades of European settlement in New South Wales, not only by Evangelicals like Marsden and the CMS missionaries at Wellington Valley but also by High Church clerics.[38] Three of the six bishops at the first meeting of ABM in 1850 specifically referred to the

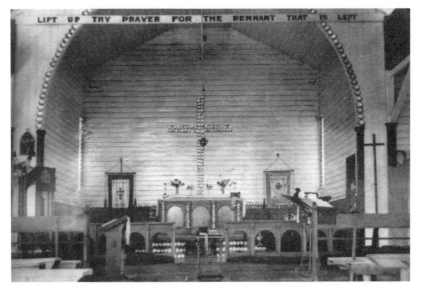

Interior of St George's Church, one of three churches on Palm Island. Courtesy Joy Cavill Collection, James Cook University.

devastation being wrought upon Aboriginal society and the responsibility of the church to convert the Aborigines to the saving grace of Christianity. Pride of first place was again given to them in the 1872 Determination and in each subsequent amendment to ABM's constitution. At public meetings sponsored by ABM in Sydney in 1879 and 1881 the claims of the Aborigines were vigorously advanced. The President of the Legislative Council and former Chief Justice of New South Wales, Sir Alfred Stephen, a prominent Anglican layman, had not been able to attend the 1879 meeting but had written a letter of support which was read out:

> It is impossible, I think not to recognise the duty which is proposed to be undertaken for taking possession of the land over which, until we came, the native inhabitant roamed at will. We are assuredly bound to do whatever may be possible to extend to him the blessings which, as Christians, we enjoy.[39]

At the same meeting, Archbishop Barker of Sydney reported how Aborigines 'were regarded as vermin and to be killed like kangaroos and snakes'. Mr Alexander Stuart, prominent in commerce, a devout and influential layman, and a future premier of New South Wales, pointed out that Aborigines 'were capable of being improved and it was an obligation upon the people of the colonies to improve them'. Other evidence was brought forward to demonstrate the educability of Aborigines. The success of the Moravian Brethren in establishing 'flourishing' missions in Victoria was referred to as an example. Bishop Stanton, who was in attendance before proceeding to the new Diocese of North Queensland, was urged to take up the missionary challenge in North Queensland and promised support from ABM.[40]

The 1881 meeting indicated an increased pessimism. A catalogue of current Anglican missionary endeavours was heralded as a sign of increased missionary zeal. By any measure, it was a short list. The Anglican Church was compared unfavourably with other denominations, such as the Wesleyans and Presbyterians. Indeed, the Dean of Melbourne urged Anglicans 'to wake to their responsibilities and become equal with other denominations in mission work'. As far as Aborigines were concerned, the school for Aborigines that had been started in association with the Mackay Reserve had closed after a few months when the Queensland Government had closed the reserve. Bishop Parry of Perth was the most optimistic and reported that Aborigines were attending two schools in his colony's settled districts. Some children had been sent out as servants. He mentioned the mission he was planning in the Gascoyne District. Warangesda, in New South Wales, where there were sixty-two Aborigines, was the church's greatest achievement. Bishop Stanton of North Queensland now spoke with admiration of the progress being made in Western Australia. Obviously the hopes for the Aborigines of North Queensland, expressed in 1879, had come to nothing. In another few years, the Bishop of Perth would have the same experience. The initiatives being attempted for Aborigines, a Chinese catechist, and religious instruction for indentured South Sea Islanders at Maryborough, however, led the Rev. W. Wilson to conclude that 'the church had taken a fresh start, and there seemed to exist a desire to carry on mission work…The time, however, had arrived when they must enter upon their work with greater zeal than ever'. Archbishop Barker of Sydney pointed out 'that a great responsibility rested upon those persons whom God had permitted to occupy this land'. These meetings clearly indicated that God's gift of colonial expansion had been accepted with much greater enthusiasm than his gift of missionary responsibility towards the colonised.[41]

When reflecting upon the first half century of the ABM, it would be easy to conclude that the Anglican response to the Lazarus at their gates had resulted largely in pious platitudes and hypocrisy. Those involved with the Board of Missions confronted a cruel apathy and a racial prejudice that Anglicans shared with the rest of the Australian community. At both meetings, the educability of the Aborigines had been repeatedly stressed because the colonists almost universally believed otherwise. It was the opinion of well-intentioned Anglicans at the meetings that the Aborigines were 'degraded', even more than the 'Negroes' in the Americas. This reflected a current Christian belief that those human groups whose standard of civilisation was believed not to be equal to European civilisation had regressed from that indicated in the Genesis story of creation. Some Christians were optimistic that this process could be reversed. Thus Bishop Parry of Perth stressed that the challenge was not hopeless:

> He had frequently heard it said that the Australian aborigines were too degraded for any good to be done with them; but his experience had taught him otherwise. In Australia we were brought into contact with a race which appeared to be representative of one of the oldest nations in the world; but, at the same time, one that had sunk into a degraded condition. It appeared that very little had been done to bring that race into a better condition — certainly that had been the case in Western Australia, where the natives had been employed in large numbers as shepherds and teamsters, but who had not been taught even the ordinary principles of morality.[42]

This speech to the 1881 meeting was probably the most positive and optimistic with regards to the future relationship between the church and Aborigines. Despite Parry's ethnocentric perspective he believed Aborigines were educable, at least to the level of the British working class. This represented the highest expectations of ABM and indeed other contemporary missionary organisations.[43] Such limited expectations would determine mission strategies and practices until after the Second World War.

Thus a domination determined in terms of race and colonialist expansion was designed to place missionary Aborigines into the lowest level of the Australian class structure. In 1952, seventy years later, the Chairman of ABM, Archdeacon CS Robertson, informed his board:

> we have simply provided him [the Aboriginal] with food and clothing. We have attended to his educational [and] physical needs, but we are still looking upon him as a 'hewer of wood and a drawer of water'.[44]

The idea that the food, clothing, education and physical provisions provided in the 1950s to Aboriginal people on missions was adequate reflected the low expectations of the needs of Aboriginal people held by someone as enlightened as Robertson. Yet, his admirable honesty revealed that the racial attitudes of the first half century of ABM cast a very long shadow. Paternalistic practices being developed at Yarrabah at the end of the nineteenth century were to be the pattern on all ABM missions until the 1950s.

The racial ideology of white Christians was of course an expression of the dominant white supremacist ideology inherent in their culture. At approximately the same time as ABM was commencing its work at Yarrabah in Queensland, the colonial government was formulating draconian legislation and a system of reserves to control Aborigines and make them wards of the state, a situation that remained virtually unchanged until the 1970s. Indeed these controls were still being removed in the 1980s after the Deeds of Grant in Trust land legislation had been passed.[45]

Australia's severe economic depression of 1893–94 threatened the existence of ABM's infant missions at Yarrabah and New Guinea. Bishop Montgomery of Tasmania sponsored a 'self-denial effort'; nine different leaflets were sent out, a million in all. The result was a paltry £3300, of which £868 came from New Zealand. This represented, on average, approximately a half-penny from each person identifying as Anglican in Australia. Missionary giving actually declined after this special appeal because of its drain upon the existing goodwill for missions. Although it was clear that not many Anglicans had denied themselves much at all, the desperate appeal had aroused sufficient interest for ABM to report on an optimistic, even triumphalist note:

> Progress — amid prevalent financial depression, notwithstanding conflicting claims and counter interests...Progress in those supremely important missions, which are directly under the Episcopal supervision of the Primate...Not many years ago few of us thought that in so short a time sympathy with missionary work would be so deep, development in various directions would be so substantial, and enthusiasm would be so roused as has been the case during the last few months. The Self-Denial Effort...has undoubtedly largely contributed to this result. The actual amount raised was not so large as many of our friends hoped.[46]

A determined search of ABM records has failed to uncover adequate grounds for this enthusiasm. In 1894, there were two priests, four European layworkers, and five South Sea Islanders on staff in New Guinea, and Ernest Gribble, his wife, and mother at Yarrabah, with two other European layworkers, a South Sea Islander, and an Aboriginal. These were the missions for which ABM was directly responsible. There were also Chinese catechists in the dioceses of Sydney, Riverina, Brisbane, and Tasmania.[47]

With the echoes of Christ's first recorded sermon in its title when he referred directly to the jubilee year of the Jews (when the poor were to be comforted, the oppressed, imprisoned, and enslaved liberated, the debts remitted (Luke 4.16–19)) ABM prepared to celebrate in 1900 the conclusion of its first fifty years. Like their Saviour, they expected a new age of mission and ministry to begin. Although this might seem an astonishing effrontery, given the poor harvest of the first fifty years, in hindsight, there were some grounds for such determined optimism.

As early as 1890, there had been a proposal to appoint a missionary bishop to take charge of the Northern Territory and North West Australia to supervise missionary outreach largely with Aborigines.[48] In 1898, the Reverend Montagu Stone Wigg was consecrated as first Anglican Bishop of New Guinea. ABM's jubilee celebrations held in Sydney in August 1900 raised £9660. This not only assisted the existing ABM missions at Yarrabah and in New Guinea but also contributed to the foundation of the Diocese of Carpentaria which then incorporated the Northern Territory and far North Queensland. Plans were made to divide Western Australia into three dioceses, one of which, in 1909, would be North West Australia.[49] The incorporation of the Northern Territory into a diocese, based in far North Queensland with its cathedral on Thursday Island, resulted from the efforts of Bishop Barlow of North Queensland to subdivide his diocese. North Queensland's non-Indigenous population had increased from 19,000 in 1878 to 130,000 in 1898. On a visit to England in 1897–98, Bishop Barlow had raised £5500 to endow the new diocese and, after a subsequent visit to England in 1898, managed to increase Carpentaria's foundation endowment to £10,000. Archdeacon Gilbert White of North Queensland was consecrated as the first Bishop of Carpentaria on 24 August 1900. With no large centres of population, the Diocese of Carpentaria was destined to remain a missionary diocese, dependent on the support of the rest of the Anglican Church in Australia, channelled to it largely through ABM. The sparsely populated diocese was soon faced with a severely declining population as mining declined, and Cooktown, Normanton, Croydon, Georgetown, and Burketown became mere hamlets. In 1900, Gilbert White accepted the missionary challenge of his diocese and immediately began preparing to establish a mission for Aborigines on the western side of Cape York Peninsula on the Mitchell River.[50] In time, three of the five Aboriginal missions associated with ABM would be in the Diocese of Carpentaria.[51]

The final manifestation of optimism for missionary outreach to Aborigines led in 1900 to the Brisbane Diocesan Board of Missions accepting responsibility for the Aborigines at the Queensland Government reserve on Fraser Island.[52]

By the end of 1900, ABM obviously felt it could take on no more commitment for Aboriginal missionary work. New Guinea was still absorbing most of its interest and resources; its expenditure on Aboriginal missions was increasing; and it was making a small contribution to the

Anglican Melanesian Mission situated in the New Hebrides, Santa Cruz and Solomon Islands. When the Lutheran Church and the Queensland Government requested that it take over the Bloomfield River Mission south of Cooktown, it reluctantly declined.[53] There were the prospects of future expansion in Carpentaria and New Guinea and at Fraser Island, the increasing cost of Yarrabah, and the still unproved commitment to mission through ABM of the Anglican Church.

Christ's commission, 'Go therefore and make disciples of all nations' (Matthew 28.19), was all but ignored as far as Aborigines were concerned. Australian Anglicans were also as aware as other colonists, almost all at least nominally Christian, of the suffering, powerlessness, and vulnerability of Aborigines in the wake of colonial expansion but, as Gilbert White pointed out, chose not to act, not to hear or see the Lazarus at their gate. The rare exceptions like JB Gribble and Matthew Hale counterpointed the dominant theme of casual, callous neglect.

4.

The Golden Age of Missions
1900–1950

The work at hand is to run an institution of a peculiar kind—
the building up of a community.

The Industrial Missions

If little was achieved in the first half century of ABM's existence, in
the period from 1900 to 1950, much was accomplished with always
inadequate resources. This suggested that ABM had fulfilled a good deal
of the expectation generated at the 1900 Jubilee. Indeed, looking forward
from 1900, or back from 2006, ABM's second half century seems one
of considerable achievement, especially as two world wars and the Great
Depression dominated the history and developments of this period.

The creation of the missionary dioceses of Carpentaria, based on
Thursday Island, in 1900 and the North West, now based on Geraldton,
in 1909, accorded with High Church Anglicanism's ideal of missionary
outreach. A diocese was defined as the geographical area over which a
bishop had authority with regard to all matters involving the church which
was then fully represented, actually or potentially, by the three orders of
bishop, priest, and deacon who then could teach and minister to the laity.
As the bishop could ordain or license priests and deacons for his diocese,
the church was self-perpetuating — complete for the area and people to
which it was relating. Where the Bishop is, there is the church.[1]

The replication of the English diocesan structure in unevangelised
or barely evangelised areas initially placed an extra load on the back of
such struggling missions. An administrative structure was needed for the
diocese, as well as to relate to the church beyond the diocese. A cathedral,

even a temporary one, was required, and an ordained, stipended ministry. The bishop then had to minister to his clergy and laity through regular visitations and was expected to bring those working in his diocese together on regular occasions to confer with him and to become an integral part of the diocesan family. Missionary societies such as the Church Missionary Society require less extensive structures in the area to be evangelised. They can expeditiously decide to withdraw from an area as the Society for the Propagation of the Gospel had from Somerset in 1868 after only eighteen months.[2] The creation of a diocese takes a tenacious grip on the future.

In 1900 Yarrabah was the only Anglican mission to the Aboriginal people. Ernest Gribble had established it in 1892 after his father, John Brown Gribble, withdrew through ill health. Gribble had established a mission village community with a school, a dormitory each for the boys and girls, and cottages for the married Christian couples. The centre of Christian life was the church where morning and evening prayer services were held each day. On Sunday there was also a communion service, and on feast (special) days the communion service replaced morning prayer. The Christian Aborigines or those who were undergoing instruction lived within the mission compound. Local Aborigines who wished to maintain a more independent lifestyle lived in a camp near the mission but were rigidly separated from it by Gribble who nevertheless still intervened to prevent activities of which he did not approve. The camp population fluctuated in size. The local Aborigines, the Gunganjdji and their neighbours, the Yidinjdji, used the mission as part of their subsistence economy or visited relatives, including children they had entrusted to the mission. The mission used their labour in return for food. Only those who worked were fed, except for the sick and aged.[3]

A daily timetable was soon established which was very much like that of a boarding school or a community established by a religious order: 6.00 a.m., ring bell; 6.30 a.m., matins (morning prayer service); 7.30 a.m., breakfast; 8.40 a.m., work bell; 12 noon, cease work; 12.30 p.m., dinner for the Aborigines; 1.45 p.m., school bell; 5.00 p.m., evening bell; 5.30 p.m., tea for the Aborigines; 6.35 p.m., evensong (evening prayer service); 9.30 p.m., the bugle for lights out. On Sunday there were church services at 7.00 a.m., 11.00 a.m., and 6.30 p.m., and religious classes at 3.00 p.m. During the week there were singing classes and drill classes on Tuesday at 8.00 p.m.; choir practice on Thursday at 4.00 p.m.; night school for adults on Wednesday at 8.00 p.m.; parade on Friday at 4.00 p.m. Sewing classes were held at 2.00 p.m. daily except Wednesday and Saturday afternoons which were free for the Aborigines to organise their own activities under the guidance of the mission staff. This timetable encompassed both adults and children.[4] The Aborigines were segregated according to age or sex, at work, church, school, and on outings such as Saturday picnics. Under Gribble, church attendance was compulsory for Aborigines in the mission compound. Mission life was dominated by bells.[5]

The aim of the Christian missions throughout Australia was to create a theocracy. The members of the Aboriginal community would lead good, useful lives where they would be 'made to live by rule'. Thus, at Yarrabah, the timetable included inspecting the cottages of the married couples each day at 11.00 a.m. — 'the floors having been swept and washed, and the blankets put to air immediately after breakfast' and cleanliness and sanitation insisted upon.[6] On all Aboriginal missions, to accomplish the aim of creating a new society, a pervasive system of education of children and adults was necessary not only to continue the process of religious indoctrination but also to produce the skills necessary for the first and subsequent missionary generations. There were adult education classes, classes for married women, and practical training in child care, homecraft, and simple industrial skills. As Nicholas Hey, foundation missionary of Mapoon Presbyterian Mission, pointed out, the Aborigines were given a way of life.[7] It was also goodbye to much of the old way of life.

By 1900, the Anglican Church and the Queensland Government had proclaimed Yarrabah a triumphant success: Daniel Craig has succinctly described the nature of this 'success':

> After only eight years [i.e. by 1900] the institutional structure of the community was well established with Gribble as its undisputed head... In order to live in the mission, Aborigines had to espouse Christianity and forsake their traditional life styles. Gribble and his fellow missionaries controlled every aspect of the settlement's life: they taught school, adjudicated disputes, dispensed medicine, limited travel, and set codes for everyone's conduct. All letters to and from Aborigines passed through the staff's hands 'for perusal'...Before residents could marry, the intending groom had to build a thatch hut for himself and his bride in the area designated for married couples...He had to promise never to remove his wife or family from the mission should he take a job off the reserve. The couple had to marry according to the rites of the Church of England, and Gribble set the date. Moreover, he reserved the right to postpone or cancel a wedding if one of the parties misbehaved or was deemed unfit for marriage...If a married man left the reserve for any reason, Gribble moved his wife back into the dormitory until he returned...The missionaries gave the wives rations to make their own bread and tea, but a central kitchen served everyone's meals.[8]

As early as 1896, ABM was reporting cautiously but confidently to the Anglican Church through its missionary journal, *Missionary Notes*, of the 'spiritual progress' among their charges:

> There are not wanting signs of real spiritual and moral improvement in the people, while the efforts made to enable them to clear and cultivate the soil must tend to their material welfare, showing them that Christianity is a religion which has the promise of the life which now is, as well as of that which is to come.[9]

A number of small satellite settlements were created for trusted married couples and their families, lessening the tensions Aborigines experienced in the larger village setting. Gribble also hoped that it would discourage the Queensland Government from cancelling any reserve land to make it available to colonists.

The Queensland Government was impressed with the work of the Lutheran, Presbyterian, and Anglican missionaries in North Queensland and realised that they could be used as a cheap control agency and dispenser of social services. In 1898, the Northern Protector of Aborigines, Dr Walter Roth, had reported most favourably. The missionaries cared for the sick as best they could, provided a sure if meagre supply of food, protected mission Aborigines as much as possible from opium and alcohol, and saved the women from sexual exploitation. The representatives of government seemed most impressed by the way the missionaries were producing village communities moulded on European–Christian values. Roth related with enthusiasm the skills of the Aborigines in carpentry, agriculture, basket-making and homecraft skills. He praised the choir and the playing of the piccolo, cornets, accordion and the organ. He was impressed with the mothers' meetings, prayer meetings, confirmation classes, and the church service. He thought the 'promotion' system by which girls and boys received in-service training in domestic service and farm work excellent. He thoroughly approved of the way the missionary arranged marriages so that a stable mission community was set up. He noted the excellent health of the community (although it was excellent only when compared with the deplorable health of Aborigines living in the fringe camps throughout the state) and that at Yarrabah there had only been six deaths in six years and fewer at Hope Valley. Of Yarrabah he concluded,

> To attempt to describe the noble self-denying work of these missionaries in sufficiently eulogistic terms would be futile: the organisation, management and discipline leaves nothing to be desired: the aims and objects of the mission are practically Christian.[10]

No pun was intended.

The factor that most impressed the authorities was the control that the missionaries could assert over the Aborigines. The Lutherans at Bloomfield River Mission were criticised by Roth because the Aborigines came and went as they pleased:' [T]he mission people have no control over them and herein lies the secret of what I would call their non-success'.[11]

Government approval of the missionaries and their desire to use them to implement government policy was very early made apparent. In 1899, Gribble was appointed superintendent of the reserve under the terms of the 1897 Aboriginals Protection and Restriction of the Sale of Opium Act.[12] In fact Roth and Home Secretary JF Foxton, were convinced that in North Queensland the Aborigines could be raised to 'a higher scale of social order' only 'by the influence and precepts of the missionaries'.[13] In 1903, Foxton stated publicly that he intended to divide Cape York Peninsula into Aboriginal reserves, apportioning to the interested Presbyterian and Anglican denominations geographical spheres of influence expanding as far 'as the enthusiasm of the Church members would carry it'. He made it clear that any denomination could have an Aboriginal reserve.[14]

Foxton believed that there were then 25,000 Aborigines in Cape York Peninsula and he was willing to deliver this number into the hands of the missionaries. As the new century opened, it seemed that a new age of a new faith was about to come to Aboriginal Queensland. After the early frustrating years, the efforts of such pioneers as Flierl and Schwarz of Hopevale, Hey of Mapoon, and Gribble showed promise of rewards that none could have imagined.

Although Gribble's authoritarian rule was at times harsh, he was held in great respect, even loved and revered by those who remained part of the mission community at Yarrabah, and later at Forrest River in Western Australia. The long periods of his life he was willing to dedicate to the creation of his mission community (seventeen years at Yarrabah and fifteen at Forrest River) allowed the Aborigines to adjust to his ways. His commitment to Aboriginal people and his encouragement of Indigenous leaders within the mission were factors that perhaps allowed them to forgive his flaring temper, his arrogance and his sometimes cruel punishments. The regime at Yarrabah was similar to that on other contemporary missions.[15] Indeed, Yarrabah became the model for Anglican missions to Aborigines, although the relationship between the Aboriginal 'inmates', as they were termed by the church and the government until after the Second World War, and mission staff depended greatly on the personality of each superintendent. For, as John Best, Chaplain-Superintendent at Forrest River Mission from 1942 to 1947, remarked: 'The Superintendent was

God'.[16] This system of white domination continued largely unchanged until the 1950s.

In 1895, the Queensland Government made its first attempt to develop a comprehensive Aboriginal policy when it appointed Archibald Meston as a special commissioner. His report and that of the police commissioner, WE Parry-Okeden, led to the formulation of the 1897 Aboriginal Protection and Restriction of the Sale of Opium Act. In 1897, the government, on Meston's advice, had sent some Aborigines living in southern Queensland to Fraser Island to isolate them from alcohol, opium, and sexual exploitation. Here they were expected to recover their health, dignity, and self-respect if left to their own devices and allowed to hunt and fish. Most had grown up within the developing colonial society and found their forced return to an unfamiliar Aboriginal lifestyle most unwelcome. Many of the women had been brought up from childhood in white settlers' houses. Home Secretary Foxton, concluded that this was not the future for Queensland's Aborigines and appealed to the churches to take charge of Fraser Island Reserve. The government would provide a yearly grant and the salary for a school teacher. The Anglican Church grasped the opportunity and requested Gribble's advice. Within two weeks, Gribble was at Fraser Island and had assumed authority.[17] In 1904, the Fraser Island Reserve was closed and 117 Aborigines were transferred to Yarrabah.[18] The Brisbane Diocese, through its ABM committee, had been providing most of the funds for Fraser Island and could not sustain the financial strain, especially when the Queensland Government reduced its subsidy. Nationally in 1905, ABM was confronted with rapidly increasing expenses from the New Guinea Mission while support for the Chinese missions in Australia and the Melanesian Mission in the South Pacific had dropped considerably. Overriding all of this was the belief that Fraser Island was an unsuitable site for an industrial mission, that is, a mission where a primary industry could be developed to provide employment and training along western lines for the Aboriginal 'inmates'.[19]

By 1903, the Bishop of Carpentaria, Gilbert White, was ready to establish the first of three ABM supported missions in his diocese. He and Bishop Frodsham of North Queensland requested the support of 'the whole Church' through ABM in the establishment of a mission near the mouth of the Mitchell River on the western side of Cape York Peninsula. To prevent competition by the two dioceses for support for their Aboriginal missions, the bishops requested coordination of funding through ABM. As the North Queensland Diocese had a colonist population of only 80,000 and Carpentaria a mere 12,000, neither diocese could support an Aboriginal mission from its own resources. It never occurred to anyone that the Aborigines should be given a higher priority than the establishment of white churches in white parishes. Yet, the two bishops justified the creation of such missions, firstly, in surprisingly elevated terms of Aboriginal rights to land as 'the original owners and inhabitants of the country'; secondly, their consequent first claim upon the spiritual commitment of the colonists to atone for dispossession; and, thirdly, the diseased and demoralised state of Aborigines subsequent to colonisation:

Claims of Aboriginal Work

> It will scarcely be questioned that the Aborigines of the soil have a primary claim on the Missionary service of Australian Churchmen. Not even New Guinea demands our aid so imperatively as the original owners and inhabitants of the country in which we dwell, whose land we have taken and whose means of subsistence we are daily diminishing, while our vices and diseases have swept them away like a pestilence, except when they have been shielded and preserved by Missionary effort. Not only have the Aboriginal Missions a first claim on Churchmen, but they also appeal to many who are deaf to every other Missionary appeal. There is an element of justice, of reparation, of plain and obvious duty about this work which commends itself to the hardened man of the world who cannot enter into the enthusiasm of the Gospel.[20]

For 1903, this was an extraordinary statement. Although there was no suggestion that colonisation was wrong or unchristian, Aborigines were declared central to Australian history and first in their claim upon Christian conscience and commitment. Time would show that the bishops' values were not shared by Australians in general or the Christian churches in particular. Their optimism that the unique place of Aborigines in Australian society would be accepted even by 'the hardened man of the world' was also misplaced. For despite the emphasis given to Aboriginal people, they were still seen as dependent on missionary outreach which was equated with charity, not seen at the time as essential to the individual's expression of Christianity, nor to that of the parish church or diocese.

Gilbert White had visited Yarrabah in 1902 to study Gribble's methods and was impressed. At White's request, Gribble immediately set out overland, attaching himself to a police patrol for protection. He inspected the area White had previously visited. White and the Northern Protector of Aborigines, Walter Roth, had intended to meet Gribble's party at the proposed site of the mission. As Gribble's party was delayed, this did not eventuate but the subsequent reports from Roth, White, and Gribble to Queensland's Home Secretary, Foxton, led to the gazettal of five hundred square miles (approximately 130,000 hectares) between the Mitchell and Nassau rivers as an Aboriginal reserve. Gribble made another two inspections before selecting a lagoon the Aborigines called Trubanaman as the site for the mission. Between May and July 1905, White and Gribble laid the foundations for the Mitchell River Mission. A number of Aboriginal Christians from Yarrabah had accompanied Gribble's overland expeditions: James Noble and his wife Angelina, Peter Bendigo, John Grady, Ernest Bungie, and Dinaroo. John Grady and Bendigo, who came from the area, remained at Trubanaman with the white missionaries, Miller and Williams. Miller, the first superintendent, was soon succeeded by the Rev. Selwyn Chase.[21] Mitchell River was then gradually developed as an industrial mission like Yarrabah. Increasingly the cattle industry became its industrial base. Associated with it was the supply of pastoral workers to other northern cattle stations.

The next Aboriginal mission to be developed with ABM support was in 1913 at Forrest River in the far north of Western Australia. The desire to establish a mission in north-west Australia had a long history. JB Gribble's 1885 attempt to establish a mission on the Gascoyne River was aborted the following year by the Anglican Church in Western Australia as a result of the opposition of the colonists. Another decade passed before the next attempt to establish an Aboriginal mission was made.[22] Harold Hale, son of the first bishop of Perth, spent some time at Yarrabah studying Gribble's methods before, in 1896, attempting to re-establish the Gascoyne Mission. As he soon concluded that this area was unsuitable, the Western Australian Government offered an alternative site at Forrest River, north-west of Wyndham. Here two of the five missionaries were attacked by Aborigines so the mission was moved within a few months to be adjacent to Wyndham and then abandoned in 1897.[23] In April 1913, Bishop Trower of the North West attempted to establish a diocesan mission at Forrest River under Robins, the Anglican priest at Derby. Both Trower and Robins had missionary experience. Although there was no support and some outright opposition from the Kimberley pastoralists, the mission was established at Hale's old site. At the outset, Robins was confident and optimistic but left the mission in November 1913, thoroughly cowed by the Forrest River Aborigines.

At this time Ernest Gribble was rector of Christ Church, Gosford. He had been ordered to leave Yarrabah in 1909 in a state of physical and emotional collapse. In September 1913, Bishop Trower telegrammed for his temporary assistance in re-establishing Forrest River Mission. With a promptness that reflected his enthusiasm, Gribble arrived in Wyndham in December 1913. Although just as vulnerable to the hostility of the numerous Aborigines as the others who had attempted to move into the area, he established a working relationship with the local Yeidji, Wembra, Andjedja and Arnga people without much difficulty. James and Angelina Noble, Aboriginal Christians from Yarrabah, joined him in April 1914. Gribble stayed at Forrest River Mission until 1928, the Nobles until 1933, and together they established Forrest River as an industrial mission modelled on Yarrabah. Gribble and later superintendents struggled against an uncertain rainfall, limited agricultural and pastoral potential, remoteness, and extraordinarily difficult communications with the outside world to make Forrest River Mission economically viable, or at least a major contributor to its own economy. The paternalistic authoritarian domination by white missionaries persisted unquestioned by the Perth committee of ABM, who had immediate responsibility for the mission, or the ABM board and executive council until the 1950s. Any attempts by Aborigines in the mission compound or in the camps adjacent to the mission to challenge missionary authority were effectively quashed, if necessary with the assistance of the Wyndham police.[24] John Best, superintendent from 1942 to 1947, summed up the Forrest River Mission experience: 'The mission has never flourished and its whole history is the story of a never ceasing struggle against environment and circumstances to keep it in existence'.[25] As we shall see, this was the white missionary perspective of the Forrest River experience.

Forrest River Mission was a small part of the vast (1.6 million hectare) Marndoc Aboriginal Reserve, which the Western Australian Government had created in 1911 to provide hunting grounds for the preservation of the local Aboriginal people. They were able to live traditional satisfying lives which most of them considered much more attractive than living under the autocratic Gribble regime and those which followed. This entailed living within the compound and surrendering their children to the dormitories where they lost control of their children's culture and their future. If they wanted to work for whites, they could live in the camp outside the compound and move on. They also had stations like Nulla Nulla where their labour was needed for the pastoral and agricultural pursuits being developed there. The government had excised one-fifth of the Marndoc Reserve after the First World War as part of its War Service Land Settlement Scheme. Leopold Overheu and Frederick Hay occupied Nulla Nulla in 1922 and needed Aboriginal labour to harvest and weed their cotton and peanut crops.

In 1928, there were only 111 'inmates' at Forrest River Mission, more than half from beyond the Marndoc Reserve, most were under seventeen years of age, many sent there from distant places by the government to become part of the Stolen Generation. Thirty-seven were pensioners.[26]

Another decade was to pass before the next ABM Aboriginal mission was established, at Lockhart River on the east coast of Cape York Peninsula. In the meantime, however, in 1919, ABM's Aboriginal sub-committee made a creative attempt to rethink its Aboriginal missionary policy and practice. Bishop Gilbert White who was then pioneering another new diocese, Willochra, in South Australia chaired the sub-committee and was the author of its report. The language was still paternalistic. The Aborigines on missions were still referred to as 'inmates'. There was still the belief that Aborigines were a doomed race unless they were segregated from contact with 'white civilisation'.

White pointed out the tokenism of the missionary outreach in meeting this limited aim. All the denominations combined had only twelve missions to 'wild Aborigines' in the north of Australia, containing no more than 2400 Aboriginal residents and having contact with approximately twice that number of non-residential Aborigines, a combined total of 7000 Aborigines at most that the Christian churches had any contact with. White believed this to be about one-tenth the estimated Aboriginal population of Australia. The conclusion the sub-committee reached was that the churches were neglecting 90 per cent of the Aborigines in Australia and thus dooming most of them to oblivion while they concentrated on a cosseted minority. The most experienced missionary bishop in Australia commented:

> The Mission native is more or less of a hot-house product. Many of the natural factors of life are necessarily eliminated. He is cared for in all things, and the discipline of the struggle for existence is removed.[27]

While the sub-committee went on to stress a loving indulgence allowed to the Aborigines that mission Aborigines might have had difficulty recognising, it clearly depicted the dependence on the white missionary structure that mission practices inculcated. White suggested firstly that the missions should 'endeavour to save and influence the whole people even if Christian endeavour takes a less concentrated form', and secondly, that the missions should prepare Aborigines for assimilation into the wider Australian community. 'What we want', urged White, 'is to develop the Aborigines and half-castes in such a way that they may be fitted to hold their own in the future, and to make them of real service to the State, while increasing and developing their self-respect'.[28] The rejection of the policy of paternalistic segregation in favour of paternalistic assimilation did not become commonwealth and Western Australian policy, as we have seen, until 1951 and was not accepted by Queensland until 1957.

It was beyond the resources of the churches to implement a policy that reached out to all Aborigines in northern Australia. White suggested that the commonwealth, Queensland and Western Australian governments establish a further twelve stations for Aborigines and 'half-castes' not more than twenty-five miles (forty kilometres) from the coast, with outstations on the coast, plus another four inland stations. Together with the existing Aboriginal missions, this would have provided a network of stations not more than 240 kilometres apart across northern Australia in the two states and the Northern Territory which was administered by the Commonwealth Government. Health services and the administration of these reserves were to be the responsibility of the relevant governments. Each reserve would have one chaplain provided by the churches, the reserves being apportioned to interested churches in proportion to the numbers of each denomination in the national census, a condition that would have favoured the Anglicans. The school teacher was to be paid for by the government but appointed by the denomination concerned. White suggested that the cattle industry could be developed on each of these northern missions. Despite the fact that White had pointed out the unrealistic expectations the public had that missions should become economically self-sufficient, he believed that the infusion of sufficient capital by the governments and the development of community infrastructures would allow these reserves to become self-supporting, and even to repay the government its initial capital investment. White also suggested that the Aborigines could be used as 'a permanent corps of drilled but unarmed scouts' to patrol the almost empty north in peace and to serve as a coast watch and coast guard in war. It would 'save the State from real dangers and be one-tenth the cost of any system of coast guard'.[29]

Given the grey sameness of policy and practice in Anglican missions throughout this whole period after the foundation of each mission was accomplished, the 1919 proposal of ABM's Aboriginal sub-committee leaps out of the archival records at the unwary historian. More amazingly, the Board endorsed it.[30]

This scheme, which would have accelerated the change in government and mission policies by over thirty years, brought no known constructive response, although many of its suggestions would later eventuate for other reasons. It would have required the three governments and the various churches to take Aborigines seriously and to regard them as potentially equal citizens. It would have entailed a coordinated approach, a hefty investment of developmental capital, and the creation of costly community infrastructures and services. It would have also meant rejecting the concept that Aborigines were societal failures only in need of Christian charity. Although the proposal was a generation ahead of its time, there were certainly negative aspects. Thousands more Aborigines in the Northern Territory, Queensland, and Western Australia would have been brought under a paternalistic control that most would escape for a generation.

As early as 1921, there were negotiations between Bishop Newton of Carpentaria and the Queensland Government with a view to establishing a mission for Aborigines on the east coast of Cape York Peninsula. The first site suggested was the Pascoe River, about 64 kilometres north-east of the eventual site of the Lockhart River Mission. Although the Queensland Government offered a foundation subsidy of £200 and a further £200 per year thereafter, ABM was unable to provide its estimated share of funding of £300 foundation cost and £300 per year.[31]

In the previous year, Yarrabah had been apportioned an annual grant from ABM of £1900, Mitchell River Mission £1529, and Forrest River Mission £1500. Out of a total budget of £32,729, £6279 (19 per cent) was to be provided for the running costs of Aboriginal and Torres Strait Islander missions. The board believed it needed a further £3000 to maintain the existing Aboriginal missions adequately yet it had to pare its 1920 budget to £31,000. The board estimated that its 1921 budget had to be raised by another 20 per cent. This was not the time for a new mission.[32]

By April 1924, the board was able to respond favourably to the Queensland Government's request for the establishment of a mission in the area. The Lockhart River site was chosen to avoid interference from existing and future mining operations. The Queensland Government had raised its support at the request of the then Bishop of Carpentaria, Stephen Davies, to an establishment grant of £1000 with an additional £500 per year for running costs. ABM agreed to contribute £500 per year.[33] The Queensland Government was clearly indicating the value it continued to place on missions as cheap agencies of control and social welfare.

HR (Harry) Rowan was licensed as a lay missionary and appointed superintendent. As with the other missions, Rowan made optimistic attempts to set up a western industrial base centred on agriculture, trochus shell and bêche-de-mer fishing, and later mining. The Aborigines in the area had experienced contact with pearl-shell and bêche-de-mer fishermen and sandalwood gatherers since the 1870s, and later with miners. A few South Sea Islanders, Torres Strait Islanders, and white settlers had established permanent or semi-permanent bases. Japanese pearlers visited the area and they and the other intruders exploited the Aborigines for their labour and possibly used opium and certainly other trade goods to sexually exploit the women. The population had been greatly reduced on the north eastern coast of Cape York Peninsula because of this prolonged contact, through introduced diseases such as venereal disease and influenza. A modified form of English was widely used.[34] Chase stressed that, though the Lockhart River Aborigines had experienced extensive prolonged contact and their culture had considerably changed as a result, a cultural continuity predominated that was, even in the 1980s, distinctively Aboriginal.[35] In different ways, this is true of all the Aboriginal communities dealt with in this study.

The people who formed the Lockhart River Mission were composed of a number of Aboriginal groups originally living on a 200-kilometre stretch of land north and south of the mission site. A sandalwood gatherer and fisherman, Hugh Giblet, had exercised control over the Aboriginal community at Lloyd Bay. After Giblet's death, this community became the nucleus for the Lockhart River Mission.[36]

Throughout its existence as a mission, Lockhart River was inadequately staffed; insufficient capital was invested to provide an acceptable level of community facilities for either European staff or Aboriginal residents or to produce a viable industrial base. Even in 1961, a report by the then superintendent, JT Currie, of the health, housing, buildings, and working

St James' Church at the old site of the Lockhart River Mission, 1950s. Photograph by John Warby, Noel Loos Collection.

conditions was of an isolated, colonial slum, despite the improvements John Warby had implemented throughout the 1950s. White Australia was willing to tolerate such living conditions for Aborigines and missionaries in such places as Lockhart River and Forrest River, while the pittance given for their support provided a comfortable Christian consolation to the people in the pews and the church hierarchy.[37] The conscience of the church towards Aborigines was easily ignored. Parishes had to become viable and staff educated and paid for, churches and cathedrals had to be built.

The establishment of the Edward River Mission was a long drawn out process. The Queensland Government gazetted the land on the west coast of Cape York Peninsula between the Mitchell River in the south and the Edward River in the north as an Aboriginal reserve on 14 January 1922; however, until November 1938, Edward River was merely an outstation of Mitchell River Mission.[38]

The Thaiore and Munkan Aborigines at Edward River had relatively little contact with white settlers and were considered warlike, fierce, and treacherous by the missionaries. In reality, this meant that whites intruded into the area at their own considerable risk. The legendary superintendent of the Mitchell River Mission, 'Chappie' Chapman, made brief visits between 1923 and 1938, and on at least two occasions unsuccessful attempts were made to establish a mission community. Although there was an abundant natural food supply, some Aborigines were willing to work for tobacco on the farms Chapman began establishing. In 1932, Chapman was surprised to find Aborigines visited Edward River from as far north as the Holroyd (sixty-four kilometres away) and as far east as Coen (190 kilometres away). Those visiting the mission site from the more distant areas suffered more from disease than the local Aborigines; and it may be that those from areas of greater contact were refugees from the settlers. Old Edward River Aborigines today have vivid memories of 'wars' between hostile Aboriginal groups, some of which may have resulted, at least in part from such displacement. Chapman had been powerless to prevent the more determined conflicts.

In 1928, the chairman of ABM, John Needham, expressed his fear that the Queensland Government would eventually give in to pressure from pastoralists, sandalwood-gatherers, pearl shell and bêche-de-mer fishermen, and other colonists to occupy the reserve unless the Anglicans showed 'that we care enough about the natives to make some effort on their behalf'.[39] In 1939, Bishop Davies of Carpentaria pointed out a surprising situation: the Aborigines were now requesting that a mission be established at the Edward River. They had visited Mitchell River Mission and had even allowed some of their girls to live in the dormitory. He urged that the reserve should be offered to another religious organisation if ABM would not support it.[40]

In 1938 Chapman was allowed by the Munkan and Thaiore and ABM to reside permanently at Edward River. He remained there, often with very few supporting staff, until 1957. He managed to introduce the people at Edward River to English and to agriculture and to develop a mission village. Because of its late establishment, Edward River was the only ABM mission in which the dormitory system was not introduced. The parents were allowed to be parents.

Chapman had been at Mitchell River since 1914, for many years as superintendent, and was, typical of the age, authoritarian and paternalistic. At Edward River, he had to make himself accepted by the people even while he was developing an alternative lifestyle for them within their midst. His acceptance was demonstrated when he was initiated by the Aboriginal elders. Such acceptance did not imply unqualified approval or a failure to acknowledge the inevitable warts in Chapman's personality.[41] He retired in 1957 to Mitchell River Mission and died there in 1966. His record of forty-two years of Anglican missionary service to the Aborigines is second only to that of Ernest Gribble.

Edward River Mission was the last of the five ABM supported industrial missions to be established. All exist today as Aboriginal communities. The Queensland Department of Community Services administers Yarrabah, Mitchell River Mission (now known as Kowanyama), Lockhart River and Edward River Mission (now known as Pormpuraaw). Under the Deeds of Grant in Trust legislation a great deal of the day-to-day control and decision making has been transferred to the elected community councils.[42] The Anglican Church is still the only religious denomination established in each of these communities although members of other Christian churches make occasional visits.[43] The missions have become parish churches whose active congregational support varies from community to community and from time to time. Forrest River Mission is now the Aboriginal community, Oombulgurri, which rose Phoenix-like out of the ashes of the dead and buried mission.

5.

An Expanding Perspective 1900–1950

What are you going to do for us — you who
live in my mother country?

Despite the colonial holocaust Aboriginal people were known to be experiencing, there was little enough Christian charity about, and apart from grotesquely inadequate government efforts and occasional individual responses, the Christianity of the churches was virtually all Aborigines could expect to get from the white settler democracies that were occupying their land.

From 1900 to 1950 the ABM's major commitment of its human and financial resources within Australia was to the five missions it had established in association with the related dioceses. It was not, however, its only commitment. It came to support a handful of chaplaincies to Aboriginal communities, a number of these in association with either the Queensland, Western Australian, or Commonwealth governments. It also eventually became concerned at the condition of Aborigines of mixed descent, 'half-castes' as they were then termed, when they were brought to its notice. Finally, the board found itself being drawn into broader issues of Aboriginal Advancement either on its own or in conjunction with Protestant missionary organisations.

As we have seen, ABM had provided limited financial support for a chaplaincy to Lake Tyers, in the nineteenth century even before it supported the establishment of an Aboriginal mission. Chaplaincies could consist of a visit, once a week, once a month, or as the opportunity occurred or occasion demanded, or be of a full-time residential nature. Their expense could vary from an honorarium and/or travel expenses to a yearly stipend, accommodation, and expenses commensurate with running a rural parish.

The cost of the most expensive chaplaincy was small, however, compared with that of establishing and running an industrial mission.

Colonial governments, especially the Queensland Government, were only too willing for missions to exercise control over concentrations of Aboriginal people, and to provide education, training and social welfare appropriate to their perceived status as an inferior caste.[1] Even Christian politicians believed Aborigines to be a more appropriate challenge to Christian charity than to government. There were, however, situations not being met by the churches where destitute Aborigines in need were providing problems for the colonists or were living in such deplorable conditions that they were an affront to the settlers. The governments then created reserves to remove the Aborigines from the developing colonial society and to subject them to a lifestyle aimed at destroying their Aboriginality through an enforced pseudo-Europeanisation which would also confirm their low caste status. Colonial authorities believed that chaplaincies could play a useful part in the process by sanctifying European values, morals, and dominance.

It was in 1918, at the Western Australian Government's Moore River Native Settlement, near the railway siding of Mogumber, that ABM first entered into a working partnership with a government administration based on chaplaincy. From the early years of the twentieth century the Western Australian Government was anti-mission, a stance which was accentuated under the administration of AO Neville who was in charge of Aboriginal administration from 1915 to 1940.[2] Two government-run settlements, Carrolup and Moore River, were established in the south west of Western Australia to be a receptacle for Aborigines the administration deemed to have no satisfactory place within the developing society. It was Neville's ambition, never to be fulfilled, to isolate all of the Aborigines of the south west in these two settlements. The more attractive of the two sites, Carrolup, was closed in 1922 and the land subdivided for sale.[3] Moore River, 125 kilometres by rail north of Perth, was to persist as a bleak, cruel place of confinement, little different from a prison in the eyes of the Aboriginal 'inmates'. The threat of exile to Moore River hung over the heads of the Aborigines of the south west as an intimidating, ever present reality even when they were not confined there. An Aboriginal, Irene Farrell, recalls:

> There was a lot of tension between the people in the camps and the white people. The Superintendents were all the same, nasty, and they were the lord and master of everything — rations, hidings, everything. We felt like they really owned us and there wasn't much we could do about it...It wasn't much different from being in jail.[4]

The Anglican Church had been asked to 'minister to...the spiritual needs' of the Aboriginal 'inmates' of Moore River. In 1918, a Miss Kent was appointed as missionary to the reserve; in 1919 a Miss CM Hill replaced her. A number of reports in *A.B.M. Review* described her role. She conducted morning and evening services on Sunday when she was assisted by a choir of twenty-four voices. There were sixty adults and twenty-four children in attendance at services in 1920. The position had been initially described as a teacher of religious education which indeed occupied most of her time. She took religious education classes for men, women, and children in preparation for baptism and confirmation and took two and later three half-hour scripture lessons per week in the government school. Once a month the local parish priest from Gingin visited to administer Holy Communion to the confirmed and to baptise those who were considered adequately prepared. The government provided the resident missionary with accommodation and food while ABM paid her salary of £50 per year.[5]

In the early years, white visitors to Moore River were impressed at the impact the church was able to have working within the framework of a government settlement. One wrote:

> It is surely blasphemy to say that God does not care for the blacks [sic]. Because he cares, so should we. If we in our Christian charity are conscious only of our superiority to these children of the bush, let us not forget that the Christianity which began ages ago to leaven the minds of our heathen forefathers is largely responsible for any superiority we may possess.[6]

Indeed, the Secretary of the Western Australian committee of ABM, the Rev. A. Burton, believed that more resources should be diverted to Moore River and compared its cost effectiveness very favourably with Forrest River Mission:

> At Forrest River Mission we spend £2000 a year to evangelise two hundred, more or less, and we are loaded with much responsibility, and at least ten workers on the field, as well as many elsewhere, are largely occupied in the work. Why should we not do a little more than spend £50 a year for 250 natives, for whose temporal responsibility, a kindly Government assumes full responsibility and leaves us free to bring the blessings of the Gospel? Is it that distance lends a romantic glamour to the one work and not to the other?[7]

Burton wanted very little else: a chapel set aside exclusively for the church, instead of the existing multi-purpose hall, with perhaps a vestry attached. The 'kindly government' and the church were clearly relaxed about the situation at Moore River.

The churches had lower expectations of what constituted satisfactory living conditions for Aboriginal people than the 'inmates' of Moore River. The Anglican Church's chief concern at this time was the intrusion of the Roman Catholic Church. The Benedictines of New Norcia, about sixty kilometres away, had 'penetrated the settlement' to minister to the Roman Catholic 'inmates'. Football and cricket teams from New Norcia had even visited to play Moore River teams. Burton informed his Anglican readers and any others who chanced upon the *A.B.M. Review*: 'The more we occupy the field the less chance is there for these intruders to gain a footing, and I am not without hopes that the Chief Protector may be able soon to say those who are Roman Catholics may go to New Norcia if they like, or stay at Moore River and be content with the Church's ministry there'.[8]

Burton had good reason for stating publicly that he understood the mind of the Chief Protector. Neville was not only a Freemason and a scion of the Western Australian establishment, he was also a prominent Anglican layman, 'a true Churchman desirous that religion should enter the lives of the inmates and always ready to set a good example and support our workers there'.[9] It was while he was transferred to the newly constituted North-West Department that the Roman Catholic inroads had occurred. Once he was again in charge of the southwest as well, he chided his fellow Anglicans for their lack of effort at Moore River. Neville's well deserved reputation of being anti-mission did not derive from an anti-Christian bias but from a desire to bring all of the Aborigines in the settled parts of Western Australia as much as he could under government control so that he could develop his vision for the future of Western Australia's Aboriginal population. In this the churches were to play a minor supporting role.[10]

By 1938, the resident ABM missionary, Eileen Heath, had become very unhappy with the situation at Moore River. The superintendents had ceased to encourage attendance at church services; the supervision was incompetent, there was low staff morale, high staff turnover, and no training of the Aborigines for work outside Moore River; the health situation seemed to be deteriorating; and gambling was rife.[11] Heath made her concerns known to the government privately without effecting any improvement and then was encouraged by the Dean of Perth to make them public by presenting them in a report to the Synod. When it was widely reported in the press, the Native Affairs Department demanded her removal after ten years of dedicated service. The Anglican Church was not able to replace her and subsequently the Methodist Church supplied the resident missionary. The Anglican Church's only connection with Moore River was the monthly visit of an Anglican priest as Chaplain.[12]

In 1948, a special commissioner, FE Bateman, reported to the Western Australian Government in even more damning terms, especially on its failure to promote Aboriginal welfare:

> A cursory inspection of Moore River will convince anyone that the outlook from an institutional viewpoint is absolutely hopeless. There can be no possible chance of success, and its continuance without a drastic change of policy represents a waste of money and effort.[13]

Eileen Heath was not reinstated.

The sectarianism noted at Moore River was to manifest itself in a more virulent form at Palm Island, the next chaplaincy where the Anglican Church worked in partnership with government.

The Queensland Government established a settlement at Palm Island in 1919 after its previous North Queensland Aboriginal reserve at Hull River near Tully was destroyed by a cyclone. In January 1925, the chaplain at Yarrabah, the Rev. AC Flint, made an exploratory visit to Palm Island and discovered that there were many Anglican families there from Yarrabah and the Torres Strait Islands, most of whom had been baptised and confirmed. More than thirty attended the first Anglican Communion service on Palm Island. There were others willing to be confirmed and children to be baptised. A woman from the Aboriginal Inland Mission, a Baptist orientated voluntary society, was already residing there when Flint arrived. At this time there was an Aboriginal population of 800. Flint recommended the appointment of a resident Anglican chaplain but it was not until 9 September 1930 that the veteran pioneer missionary, Ernest Gribble, arrived to take up permanent residence at Palm Island.[14]

Gribble had been dismissed from Forrest River in 1928 as unsuitable to be chaplain-superintendent of an established mission. Despite this blow to his considerable ego, he set about his new challenge at Palm Island with his usual enthusiasm and was delighted to find among this congregation Aboriginal converts from Yarrabah who had been exiled to Palm Island which was already being used, in part, as a penal colony. John Mitchell Barlow, the young son of 'King John' Menmunny of Yarrabah, the first adult convert of the Gunganjdji, the original inhabitants of Yarrabah, was there with his wife and two children. John Mitchell Barlow had been a lay reader at Yarrabah and had attended the Pan-Pacific Missionary Conference in Brisbane in 1925. Gribble soon had him assisting with the church services and he later became one of Palm Island's representatives to the Synod of the Diocese of North Queensland.

Peter Bendigo, who had accompanied Gribble on two of his expeditions to establish the Mitchell River Mission and remained there because it

*Menmunny was the first
Aboriginal adult converted
at Yarrabah; he was baptised
as John Barlow and made
King of Yarrabah by Gribble.*
Forty Years with the
Aborigines, *ER Gribble,
Angus and Robertson, 1930.*

was his home country, was at Palm Island to greet Gribble. Bendigo had
originally been consigned to Fraser Island, transferred to Yarrabah in
1905, and finally made his way back to the Mitchell River, via Gribble's
expeditions. Exiled once more, this time to Palm Island, he made three
successful attempts to escape from Palm Island, twice making his way
back to the Mitchell to his land and his children, a distance of over 700
kilometres. Once he escaped on a log to the mainland, almost forty
kilometres away — as Gribble remarked, 'no mean feat'.

Two other Mitchell River Aborigines who remembered Gribble's
expeditions were at Palm Island. Gribble's comment on the process of
internal exile used in Queensland to punish or control Aborigines on
government reserves and missions reflected his appreciation of Aborigines
as fellow human beings, although, in keeping with contemporary white
opinion, of an inferior racial caste. As a consequence, he used English
legal terms to describe the process — not euphemisms like 'removal' that

were usually applied to Aboriginal peoples: 'One feels for these exiles, whatever their offences may have been, and it is hoped that they will be able to return to their own land after serving their sentence of banishment for a term'.[15] In Gribble's eyes what would be 'exile' and 'banishment' for whites, were equally 'exile' and 'banishment' for Aborigines.

The usual system of chaplaincy was soon established: teaching religious education at the government school, preparing children and adults for baptism and confirmation, daily church services, ministering to the sick at home and in the hospital and to prisoners in the Palm Island jail, conducting marriage and funeral services, and visiting families in their homes. Gribble as well regularly visited the nearby Aboriginal leprosarium and infectious diseases hospital at Fantome Island, one of the Palm Island group, to minister to Anglicans confined there. In 1937 there were over 200 people living on Fantome Island, fifty of whom were Anglican communicants.

In 1949, Gribble reported with his customary respect for statistics: 'I am now in my twentieth year here, and have baptised altogether 996 persons; have had confirmed over 600; married 155 couples; and the number of burials during that period has been 43'.[16] The pioneer missionary of Yarrabah, Forrest River Mission, and Palm Island considered the work entrusted to him at Palm Island as his most difficult challenge.[17] In 1931, the first church to be built on Palm Island was completed. Gribble reported proudly, 'The building has been erected by the people in their own time and at their own expense, of plaited coconut palm branches with grass roof; the women made the grass for the floor. The altar, bishop's chair, and processional cross were made by two Aborigines'.[18]

A report published in the *A.B.M. Review* in 1941 indicated the nature of the work of the 73-year-old Gribble:

> Canon Gribble writes that he is very busy at Palm Island. He says that on the preceding Sunday he had celebrated Holy Communion at St George's at 7.15 a.m. with 76 communicants, then after an hour's run by launch to the Lazaret another Celebration at St Lukes with 25 communicants; then on to the Lock Hospital to visit a dying woman, and back to St George's for Evensong. The next day he had to read the Burial Service, walking five miles to the cemetery and back. The Canon has three churches, and another is to be erected at the north end of the island when sufficient money is available. At St Luke's Church in the Leper Lazaret, Ellison Obah, who was a child at Yarrabah during Canon Gribble's superintendency, is now working under him as a lay reader. There is a Sung Eucharist in this church every Sunday. A new arrival among the lepers is a pretty little halfcaste girl of nine years from

a Government settlement in the south. Her bandaged wrists are the only sign she shows of the fell disease.[19]

At Yarrabah, Gribble had encouraged an Aboriginal leadership to emerge from within the mission structure to take such roles as evangelists, lay readers, and lay preachers, and in the secular sphere as members of the mission council and law court. He also used Aboriginal volunteers as missionaries, the most famous being James Noble who, as has been noted, became a prominent Christian leader in the early days of Yarrabah and went with Gribble on his exploratory missionary expedition to Mitchell River, assisted in the foundation of the CMS Roper River Mission in the Northern Territory in 1908, and soon joined Gribble at the Forrest River Mission where he remained for nineteen years. In 1925, James Noble became the first Aboriginal deacon in the Anglican Church. The next Aboriginal was not ordained until 1973. Soon after Gribble moved to Palm Island he sent for Noble to join him. James Noble was not allowed to live at the settlement and resided on the nearby Esk Island. By this time he and Gribble were both showing the effects of age, but Noble much more than Gribble. The constant travelling from Esk Island to Palm Island proved too much for him, his health further deteriorated, and in 1937 he returned to Yarrabah after twenty-three years' absence.

Brass band of the Aboriginal Christian Mission, Yarrabah, 1906. Courtesy Reverend Frederick Charles Hall Collection, James Cook University.

In 1945, the James Noble Memorial Scholarships were established at Gribble's request to enable Aboriginal children to attend secondary schools to develop Aboriginal leadership within the church. The education standard Aborigines attained at government reserve and mission schools was equivalent to grade four in white schools, the education of a ten-year-old child. In 1949 Gribble reported the first fruits of this scheme. Allan Polgen, a Gribble protégé from Palm Island who had spent several years at the Anglican Church Army Training College, had graduated as a Church Army Officer and been appointed evangelist by the Archbishop of Brisbane. As Captain Allan Polgen he was the first Church Army Aboriginal Evangelist.[20]

The leadership Gribble encouraged was always limited by the overarching white dominance. Even Noble was always some white person's assistant. However, prior to 1950 Gribble far outstripped his fellow missionaries in his ability to promote Aboriginal leadership within the Anglican Church. That he was able to do this at Palm Island, where his authority was limited to church affairs and the conditions in other ways were more difficult than he had encountered before, speaks volumes for the remarkable empathy he had with Aboriginal people. Yet he continued to believe that the future of Aboriginal people should be segregation from white society.

As early as 1931, Gribble was able to report that his first church committee of ten Aboriginal men had been elected and that they had carried on the church services and classes while he was absent for almost three weeks. He thought his absences were 'somewhat of a blessing in disguise, for it helps the people to rely on themselves and keep things going'.[21]

A Roman Catholic priest, Fr Molony, took up residence on Palm Island six months after Gribble's arrival. Gribble had been quite nonchalant about the presence of the Aboriginal Inland Mission, no doubt because it was Protestant but also because, in his own words, it did 'not cut much ice'.[22] The Roman Catholic Church was obviously determined to cut ice.

Gribble's father had enrolled Ernest at the age of ten in the Orange League, which was dedicated to the fight against Rome, the Antichrist in the eyes of many Protestants. On Palm Island, Gribble found himself at last confronting the ancient enemy of his faith. In October 1932, Bishop Feetham of North Queensland had reported to ABM 'that Gribble's influence on Palm Island was supreme'; however, after temporarily withdrawing after a religious controversy that was reported in the press, Molony returned, 'with seven other devils worse than himself', presumably the nuns who were going to work at the Roman Catholic school and the leprosarium on Fantome Island.[23] The Roman Catholic complement in

1945 had grown to two priests and fourteen nuns on Palm Island and Fantome Island, and two Torres Strait Islander couples. The Roman Catholic school had an associated boys' dormitory and girls' dormitory and ran, as well, the one school at Fantome Island.

The Roman Catholic priests and nuns believed that it was as important to convert Aboriginal Anglicans to their faith as it was to baptise pagans and made every attempt to do so whenever the opportunity occurred. Gribble rose to the challenge like a warhorse to the sound of battle and was vigorously supported by Bishop Feetham and by ABM.[24] Never had black souls seemed so precious. Arrayed against what Feetham termed 'the might of Rome' was Gribble, sometimes assisted by another priest for brief periods, an Aboriginal lay reader, Ellison Obah, at Fantome Island, and from 1936 a Church Army sister.

The double burial service given in 1947 to the woman, Kaim, a leper at Fantome Island, encapsulates the nature and the intensity of the struggle. Fr Foster claimed that Kaim had made a deathbed conversion from Anglicanism to Catholicism and he had given her a Roman Catholic burial service. As Gribble had given her communion just prior to the alleged conversion, Gribble refused to believe it, rushed over to Fantome Island, and read the Anglican burial service over her grave. When accosted by Gribble and some Anglican Aboriginal supporters, Fr Foster gave his version of the story and commented with patronising kindness:

> I know what you Anglicans hold and I am ready to believe that you really believe in your Opinion as regards your Church, and you must give me credit for the belief I hold regarding my Church and that is that she is 'THE CHURCH THERE IS NO OTHER' and Anglicans, Presbyterians etc. and pagans, are souls to be won into THE CHURCH.[25]

ABM's first effort in supporting Gribble and Bishop Feetham was in 1933 when it agreed to the bishop's request that James Noble be sent to Palm Island. The Bishop wrote:

> Rome has been greatly taken aback by the extraordinary success that Gribble had with these people, and they'll do anything they can to spoil his work. The presence of James Noble with the Natives, one of their own in Deacon's orders on the island, would immensely strengthen our position there.[26]

Before Noble's health deteriorated, Feetham had even been willing to ordain Noble to the priesthood to assist in what ABM officially described in 1936 as 'the long struggle against Rome'.[27] As indicated the 'struggle' continued unabated to the 1950s.

In 1933 John Barlow and five other Anglican Aborigines were sufficiently disturbed by Roman Catholic proselytising to present a petition to the North Queensland Synod requesting relief from attempts 'to turn them from their faith'. In this they were strongly encouraged and no doubt guided by Bishop Feetham. A determined attempt was being made on Palm Island to perpetuate western sectarianism among recent Aboriginal converts.

At the Moore River Native Settlement in Western Australia, the Anglican Church had received substantial support from the Anglican Chief Protector, AO Neville. At Palm Island the situation was reversed as senior officials and government ministers were supportive of the Roman Catholic cause.[28]

Gribble had an impact on Palm Island totally out of proportion to his role; that of a chaplain on a government reserve. Queensland Government officials greeted his arrival with some trepidation. His reputation for outspokenness had been enhanced nationally by his stand in revealing the Forrest River massacre in 1926, the subsequent Royal Commission, and the trial of the two white policemen involved in 1927. For his first three years on Palm Island, he had not been allowed to live in the village with his congregation, indeed had not spent one night there, and had to leave Palm Island at least one day a fortnight. Gribble soon proved the officials' fears well grounded as he campaigned against sexual promiscuity and the disgraceful living conditions on Palm Island. In this he was strongly supported by Dr Raphael Cilento, the chief government medical officer, an Anglican, who had the confidence of Feetham. Cilento informed Feetham: 'The place is worse than useless, it is a scandal, the ill-fame of it has reached London'. Gribble's agitation so worried the Home Office officials that they allowed him to live in a rectory in the village.[29]

In a decade Gribble had built up a congregation of about 300 Aboriginal communicants on Palm and Fantome islands. Feetham extolled Gribble's success, pointing out that this was 'a larger Native congregation than exists anywhere else in Australia. Many of these people have been raised from great degradation by Gribble's marvellous work...St George's is now the social and religious centre of the Island'.[30] By the late 1940s, a trickle of Anglican Palm Islanders was being encouraged by ABM and the Queensland Government to go on to Anglican boarding schools for secondary education.[31] By 1950, from the Anglican church's perspective, the labours of the aging Gribble seemed to have produced an abundant harvest and were promising even greater yields for the future.

The Roman Catholic community on Palm Island had grown and stabilised, centred, as it was elsewhere in Australia around the convent school, the church, the Catholic hospital, and religious orders. The Aboriginal Inland Mission, the Christian pioneers at Palm Island, had cut some ice after all and was still offering its Baptist oriented ministry. Indeed, the presence of two schools, two hospitals, and three competing established churches, none of whom could exercise the Christian dominance found on missions, might have led a reflective Palm Islander to conclude that, while white sectarianism disgraced the faith the missionaries proclaimed, it was not totally without its blessings.

* * * * *

In a casual way from its earliest years ABM had sometimes distinguished between 'full-blood Aborigines' and 'half-castes'. The terms were used with no appreciation that they might be offensive. In 1925, the board minutes record the presence of James Noble and the offer of 'George Singleton, a half caste at Yarrabah...for missionary service'.[32] The terms will be used at this point to allow an explanation of the developments described.

In 1925, the Federal Government asked the Anglican Church to take over a government hostel for 'half-castes' at Alice Springs in the Northern Territory. Its main function was to provide a refuge for children deemed in need of protection and to prepare them for employment, the girls as domestics and the boys as pastoral workers.[33] Although ABM refused to accept responsibility for an institution that was in reality a convenience from which the children could be sent at any time to unknown employers, the Anglican Church exercised a pastoral ministry in cooperation with committed Anglican Church staff members. The *A.B.M. Review* noted with satisfaction that most of the children at the Half-Caste Hostel, more than seventy, had been baptised Anglicans despite the visits by Roman Catholic and other missionaries.[34]

In 1945, the Federal Government provided buildings at a nominal cost for the Anglican Church to establish St Mary's Hostel, a 'welfare centre' for half-castes in Alice Springs. Initially ABM paid only the stipend of the matron who was to also act as welfare worker.[35] This was complemented in 1946 when ABM funded the purchase of a property in Adelaide to establish St Francis House, the Church of England Home for Inland Children.[36] St Mary's was a large property for half-caste boys and girls on the bank of the Todd River, six kilometres from Alice Springs. As well as supervised hostel accommodation, it provided religious and moral education for the children who attended a government school in Alice Springs. The most promising boys were sent to St Francis House for secondary technical education or to take up apprenticeships. Here, in

1947, a dozen or so boys lived under the supervision of the Rev. P Smith and his wife. The commonwealth generously subsidised these institutions, provided capital for improvements and specifically referred to them in its policy statement for Aborigines and half-castes in their solution for 'the half caste problem'.[37] These two hostels were the last institutions to be established by ABM between 1900 and 1950, a period that had also seen establishment of the Mitchell River, Forrest River, Lockhart River, and Edward River missions and placement of resident missionaries in the government reserves at Moore River Native Settlement and Palm Island.

ABM continued intermittently to support the chaplaincy to Lake Tyers Aborigines in Victoria and in 1928 began contributing to the expenses of the chaplain visiting Woorabinda Aboriginal Reserve in Queensland approximately 170 kilometres by road from Rockhampton. By 1930, the Rockhampton Diocese had been given permission to build a church, and regular visits ensued.[38]

The Lake Tyers chaplaincy confronted ABM with a challenge that nagged at them for over thirty years. Most of the Aborigines were openly dissatisfied with their lot, and made it clear that they were aware that white Australia had been developed at their expense. The Rev. GA Hancock reported in 1933 with some exasperation: 'The half-caste problem is particularly difficult; they are well looked after by the state, but the more they get the more they expect'.[39] In his 1934 report, Hancock developed the themes further: 'All philanthropy, even all religious endeavours, are regarded by the natives as just a mere pittance of what is due to them... they "patronise" all religious and social efforts'. At the same time, Hancock reported with evident satisfaction that '[t]he Church is coming to mean something real to many of the people, something more than an interesting spectacle: it is their own institution'.[40]

The Lake Tyers people soon demonstrated their religious autonomy. In 1938, a Pentecostal Aboriginal evangelist gained access to the mission and won fifty converts. The number of confirmation candidates shrank from eighteen to four. Hancock attributed the success of this Pentecostal 'sect' to its novelty and the superficial challenge it made to its adherents' lifestyles. It was only 'religious hysteria', huffed the representative of the one true English faith. Spiritual work among 'half-castes' was hampered because 80 per cent were 'thoroughly spoiled [and]...generally indulged'. It is clear that Hancock and the board that published his report believed that life was meant to be hard and harrowing for Aborigines and 'half-castes' so that they were compliant and grateful for the Christian charity offered to them.[41] As late as 1952, the Lake Tyers chaplain, Albert Clark, was complaining that 'there is a spirit of discontent...they are becoming disgruntled and dissatisfied' and a prey to outside agitation 'that they are not getting quite a square deal from the Government'. The chaplain found this lack of satisfaction 'a very unhealthy undercurrent'.[42] It was actually a healthy response to generations of oppression and deprivation. At the 1951 North Queensland Synod, an Aboriginal representative had challenged his church: 'What are you going to do for us — you who live in my mother country?'[43] Whether this emerging political consciousness found expression within the Anglican Church or outside of it would be a challenge for the second half of the twentieth century.

The Conscience of the Church

Outside of the scope of its missions and chaplaincies, ABM became the conscience of the Anglican Church as far as Aborigines were concerned and to a much lesser extent a conscience of the nation. Thus in 1929 it was asked to report on the plight of the 'half-castes' at Cape Barren Island and in 1930 on the desperate situation of the 'half-caste' population of southwest Western Australia. It submitted reports to the Tasmanian and Western Australian governments, receiving sympathetic responses in each case.[44] At first the Western Australian Government agreed to ABM's request that the Carrolup Reserve be reopened to provide a refuge for those who couldn't or wouldn't reside at Moore River; however, opposition from the white settlers soon caused the decision to be reversed. In this the government was supported for different reasons by the prominent Western Australian Aboriginal activist, William Harris, and the United Aborigines Missions who believed that there had to be a better solution than replicating Moore River. The Anglican Church accepted the time honoured response of segregation on yet another reserve. Carrolup was eventually re-opened in 1940 and, as Haebich notes, 'it simply duplicated the appalling institutional setting of Moore River settlement'.[45]

There were several other occasions during this period when concerned Christians brought the suffering of Aborigines in New South Wales and in the Northern Territory to ABM's notice. ABM responded by bringing the situations to the attention of the relevant government and urging action.[46]

The reports submitted by John Needham in 1930 on the situation in southwest Western Australia and on Cape Barren Island in Bass Strait provide interesting insights. Canon John Needham, chairman of ABM from 1922 to 1942, was a tall, hearty man, a gentleman who offered as much support as he could to his missionaries from his office in Sydney and on his forays into the field. In the nineteenth century in Perth he had worked among the Indians and Japanese and had subsequently committed most of his life to missionary work either as a missionary (in Perth and as Superintendent at Yarrabah for two years) or as an organising secretary for Queensland, a board member, and finally as the longest serving chairman of ABM. He was an urbane, kindly man with an encyclopaedic knowledge of Christian missions in Australia and throughout the world who could enthuse young people he encountered to support or become missionaries. In a tribute to Needham after his death in 1942, the board affirmed: 'John Needham was a saint and a great lover of souls, especially of the souls of those for whom the world has little time...especially as the friend of the Aborigines'.[47] He was, however, very much a man of his age.

The problem of the Aborigines and 'half-castes' in southwest Western Australia was easily solved: open up and develop Carrolup 'similar to the Moore River Mission' where the aged, the indigent, the sick, and expectant mothers could go for confinement, and the children be educated, and the adults instructed 'in useful vocations'. They would also be taught religion and morality and their marital arrangements regularised. Needham must have been aware that Moore River did none of these well, and some not at all. What it did do was exercise an oppressive jail-like control over Aborigines who were not wanted by white Australian society, as Palm Island, Woorabinda, Cherbourg, and to a lesser extent, Yarrabah did in Queensland. Needham, other members of the board, and most people who were at this time involved in the situation believed that Christian missions performed the caring and education functions much better than government institutions. Indeed the Chief Secretary of Western Australia wanted ABM to manage Carrolup with financial support from the government. Chief Protector Neville would have vigorously opposed this had Carrolup been re-opened at that time.

At the request of Tasmania's Attorney General, Needham visited Cape Barren Island Reserve to decide whether ABM would establish a mission there 'where the (so-called) half-castes of Tasmania have their homes'. He concluded that there were 'no real half-castes left — the last died two years ago'. The 250 residents 'have considerably more white than black blood, but the black strain affects the character to a pronounced degree'. As with the Lake Tyers people, Needham believed the Cape Barren Islanders to be indolent and discontented. Each had a three-acre (1.2 hectare) block and the right to lease another fifty acres (twenty hectares) but instead of working their holdings they lived off the mutton bird harvest which occupied them for six to eight weeks a year. He concluded that for them segregation was a great mistake and that the sooner they were absorbed into the white community the better. While they remained on the reserve, 'they ought to be subject to discipline. Idleness ought to be made impossible. It is a most inconsistent position altogether. All the adults have votes and yet — if they remain on the Reservation — need to be treated as minors'.[48]

A number of points are clear. Needham was paternalistic and racist. The prospect of Cape Barren Islanders' continuing to live as Australian citizens while they lived a subsistence lifestyle maintained by only two months' intensive labour a year provoked an almost fascist response. It was not so interpreted by his audience, the board of ABM, because the people for whom he was willing to recommend forced labour were believed to be dehumanised by an allegedly inconspicuous 'black strain'. There is no indication that anyone on the board disagreed with his assumptions or his conclusions. Indeed, there is no reason to believe Needham was not a white Australian of the highest character, the best available for the role of chairman of the board. His reputation was accepted well beyond the Anglican Church. Yet, clearly he had very low expectations of Aboriginal people and contempt for their traditional way of life. This was the dominant view in the church in the half century in which the greatest missionary expansion occurred. The first half of the twentieth century was, like the nineteenth century, a time when white supremacist thought combined with white power in economics, politics, and administration to subjugate effortlessly and almost unconsciously the colonised people of empire. Good men, like John Needham, were agents in this process.

Given this shared framework of European thought, it is not surprising that, throughout this period, state and federal governments used missionary organisations and that missionary organisations believed they needed to cooperate with governments whenever possible. This closeness and its missionary experience allowed ABM to act as a respected lobbyist in an area where few other white Australians, besides missionary organisations and anthropologists, could offer any advice at all.

Very early in the history of the Australian nation, ABM was confronted by the difficulties imposed on it and Aborigines by the federal structure. In August 1910 the General Secretary, Archdeacon Lefroy, urged that 'all responsibility for safe-guarding the human and civil rights of the Aborigines should be undertaken by the Federal Government alone'.[49] The next month a special meeting was called to consider the idea of 'federalising' the Aborigines and a decision made to seek the support of diocesan bishops, other religious bodies, and leading citizens, including Sir William McGregor, the governor of Queensland.[50] The proposal to transfer responsibility for Aborigines from the states to the Federal Government was vigorously raised on a number of occasions during this period, especially at times when amendments to the constitution were being considered.[51] Aborigines who moved from the Northern Territory to Queensland or to Western Australia or vice versa could find themselves working under different conditions of employment or different systems of control and welfare services. Moreover in this period Queensland and Western Australia, who had the heaviest administrative and financial responsibilities, were among the least developed and least wealthy states. Despite the poor commonwealth record in the Northern Territory before the Second World War, ABM believed that it would have to give more attention to Aboriginal affairs if its authority extended throughout the nation. Like the states and for the same reasons, the Commonwealth Government was keen to involve the missionary organisations in its Aboriginal policy and administration.[52] The commonwealth had to wait until the 1967 Referendum was passed before it could legislate on behalf of Aborigines; and, in 2006, Queensland still maintained its own administration and legislation for its seventeen Aboriginal Communities, the title now given to the old government reserves and Christian missions.

Throughout this period, the amount of finance supplied by the Queensland Government to missions was inadequate to provide capital to develop mission industries, to provide western style employment or to provide satisfactory essential services of housing, education, health, sanitation, water, and roads and bridges. In 1940, Needham reported to the board on the support provided by the federal and state governments. The amount provided by the Western Australian Government was almost non-existent. The Queensland Government gave £8050 to assist its thirteen Aboriginal missions and another £350 to missions in the Torres Strait; the Western Australian Government gave £752 to its six Aboriginal missions; the Commonwealth Government gave £2510 to the nine Aboriginal missions in the Northern Territory; and the South Australian Government gave £200 to its two mission stations.[53] Until well after the Second World War, white Australians, even those working closely with Aboriginal people, considered that Aborigines did not need or deserve living conditions anywhere near those in the general Australian community. Consequently, in comparison, the paltry sum expended by Queensland was considered reasonable. In 1938 the National Missionary Council, an ecumenical committee representing ABM, CMS, and the missionary agencies of the Presbyterian and Methodist churches, reported that 'Queensland does subsidise missions in something like a fair and just manner'.[54] Indeed, from 1886 when there was renewed interest in establishing missions, the Queensland Government had made grants to missions which were by contemporary standards quite substantial. As has been already noted with regard to the Anglican missions, Western Australia's reputation of being anti-missions was well earned. 'Practically no help comes from the Western Australian Government', the ABM treasurer lamented in presenting his 1935 budget.[55] There can be little doubt that lack of government support contributed greatly to the problems that constantly beset Forrest River Mission. In 1938, Yarrabah received £2750 in government subsidy, Lockhart River £500, and Mitchell River and its outpost at Edward River £600, while Forrest River received £14 from the Western Australian Government.[56] Yet in administering its own reserves, the Queensland Government resourced them on a scale that was lavish compared with the missions. When Alice Hann, a very experienced Anglican missionary who had worked at Forrest River, Moa Island in the Torres Strait, and Lockhart River Mission, visited Cherbourg in 1950, she was astonished at the resources in buildings, equipment, staffing, and medical and educational facilities available compared with Yarrabah and Lockhart River. When she returned to Lockhart River, the Aborigines had been sent out fishing and hunting because the mission was out of flour and rice.[57] Yet in the 1960s, when I first visited Palm Island, I was shocked at the third-world conditions in which I found the Aborigines living.[58]

The Queensland Government not only gave an annual grant to each mission, it also provided special purpose funds to purchase such items as cattle, the materials to build a hospital at Lockhart River, fencing wire, agricultural implements, and boats.[59] By 1950, the Queensland Government found itself providing ever larger funding to the missions to enable them to survive and thus prevent the Aborigines making much greater demands on the Queensland Treasury if the government had to assume full control and responsibility. In 1951, the government wiped out Yarrabah's accumulated debt of £11,000 and increased its annual grant for 1951–52 to £20,000. By this time, it had insisted that the superintendent of Palm Island be on the Townsville-based Yarrabah Commission committee as the government's representative who had to be consulted in all major decisions.[60] Earlier that year the government had purchased, for the Diocese of Carpentaria, a large ketch so the diocese could more effectively supply its missions in Cape York Peninsula and in the Torres Strait.[61] At approximately the same time, ABM had begun considering whether it would have to ask the Western Australian Government to take over full responsibility for Forrest River Mission because of its failure to get adequate government funding.[62]

The Queensland and Western Australian governments had always considered they had the right to make their views known to the missionary societies if there was something they did not approve of. At various times they had brought pressure to bear to effect some change. In 1910 the Queensland Government became so dissatisfied with the administration and financial management of Yarrabah that it threatened to take it over from the church and put it under government control. The government had made Yarrabah an industrial school in 1900 and sent Aborigines to it expecting that it would provide suitable education and work opportunities inside and outside the mission through the development of a strong industrial base. It was also unhappy that a Sydney committee of ABM supervised a Queensland mission. ABM set up a committee to supervise the administration of Yarrabah in Brisbane. The Queensland Government increased its subsidy to Yarrabah by £200 per annum to £720, an increase of almost 40 per cent, partly as a result of this and partly to meet ABM's valid criticisms that the government was sending it increasing numbers of needy and ill Aborigines and those otherwise unwanted in the developing Queensland society. The missionaries were not opposed to the concept of an industrial mission that would provide vocational training to prepare Aborigines for labouring and semi-skilled occupations in the pastoral industry, agriculture, or domestic service; however, their main aim was to produce moral, worshipping Christians living in the Christian mission community. In theory, the missionaries considered the industrial a means to this spiritual end; in practice, at Yarrabah and elsewhere on the mission field, the industrial side of the mission often dominated. Nevertheless, in 1910, several antagonistic government officials considered Yarrabah gave too much time and effort to religious development and too little to vocational training. Under threat of dismissal, the Anglican Church asked for title to the land. This was firmly rejected by the Home Secretary, who like his public servants, was unsympathetic to missions. Intermittently, from this time until it took over secular control of Yarrabah in 1960, the Queensland Government maintained a watching brief, at times coming to the mission's aid with increased financial support and equipment, and at other times severely critical of Yarrabah's performance and its inability to become self-supporting. Yet the state used Yarrabah as a prison, reformatory, orphanage, old age home, refuge for those incapable of supporting themselves, and as a poor-house, while providing only a fraction of the support it gave to its own institutions performing these tasks.[63] In 1950, the Minister for Health and Home Affairs was still not satisfied with Yarrabah or its prospects of improvement but did not wish to take over responsibility for another 600 Aboriginal dependants. The board was incapable of providing the resources necessary. As the Director of Native Affairs, O'Leary remarked: 'The Board has given Yarrabah an extra £600. What's the use of that? It needs £60,000'.[64] But the government did not supply it even though they recognised the need.

By this time, ABM had come to realise that, across the board, 'the welfare of the Aborigines on the material side is the Government's responsibility'.[65] The concept that Aborigines were primarily objects of Christian charity was at last being challenged. The executive officer of ABM, Canon Warren, informed the board in 1948 'we must depend more and more on Government finance if our Aboriginal work is to be done effectively...The Financial conditions of the future will force this upon us, and if such Government assistance is not forthcoming we shall be obliged to curtail our activities.[66] The Alice Springs and Adelaide half-caste homes were good examples of church activity, which could not and, in Warren's opinion, should not be maintained from ABM resources. He stressed: 'We must insist that any co-operation must be almost entirely at the expense of the Government. I should, in fact, think it more important to **fail** to make an arrangement for co-operation at **their** expense than to **succeed at our own**'.[67]

In effect, ABM was hoist by its own petard of 'success'. The mission populations had been steadily increasing with the decreased death rate, the attraction of Aboriginal groups to the missions, and the state government's policy of sending destitute Aborigines, especially children, to the missions. This contributed greatly to the growth of Yarrabah and, to a lesser extent, Forrest River. In effect Lockhart River Mission had been created at the urging of the Queensland Government primarily as a refuge for the Aborigines of the eastern Cape York Peninsula. In 1950, Yarrabah had a population of 634, Mitchell River Mission (now Kowanyama) 687, Edward River Mission (now Pormpuraaw) 301, and Lockhart River Mission 298. Forrest River Mission limped along with a population, in 1958, of 171.[68] Thus in 1950 ABM, through the dioceses, was supporting five villages with a combined population of over 2000 permanent residents, providing them with a basic, if completely inadequate, infrastructure of housing, health, secular education, communication, capital equipment, industrial expertise and management, a local, state and national administrative structure, and a religious education and ministry that was to permeate each Christian village.

In the Anglican Church the reality of support for missions has never matched the rhetoric and, with the passing years, ABM could not keep pace with the increasing numbers of Aborigines they were ministering to on the missions and in their various chaplaincies and institutions. The increased expenses associated with the expected infrastructure of their five missionary villages, resulting from the industrial and technological changes of the twentieth century, would prove too great a challenge.

The east coast line south of the 'old Lockhart' mission settlement.
Photograph by Leonard J Webb, courtesy AIATSIS Collection, No. 123139/9.

A World in Crisis

During the Great Depression of the 1930s, and the two world wars, enormous demands were made upon the suddenly depleted resources of ABM. Yet, in effect, these challenges were met after temporary setbacks. Indeed, each war resulted in an increased supply of people volunteering for mission service. The routine of their lives had been changed utterly by their war service. Some could not return to their pre-war mundane existence.

The Great Depression did not leave ABM unscathed. Its income dropped from £41,550 in 1929 to £34,282 in 1930, to £29,080 in 1931, a drop of 30 per cent in two years. Some missionaries were retrenched within Australia and administrative costs reduced by 20 per cent. The grant to the New Guinea Mission was reduced from £12,000 to £8,400 and that to the other South Pacific missions by 20 per cent. For some time, ABM had to withdraw all of its financial support for its missions in South Tokyo and its two missionaries in Shantung Province in China although funding from other sources was found to keep these missionaries in the field.[69] Yet despite these drastic economies, the work of ABM went on with a surprising degree of apparent normalcy in the face of the greatest economic crisis of the twentieth century.

The impact of the two world wars was not what one might have expected. They certainly posed problems by diverting some mission personnel and potential mission personnel to the armed forces; and while there was a fear of Japanese invasions in 1942, as many white staff as possible, especially women, were evacuated from Forrest River Mission. However, in a global way Australia's involvement in the two world wars stimulated support for ABM which flowed on though less strongly, to the Aboriginal missions. During the First World War there was a steady increase in contributions, which rose from £11,988 for the 1913–14 financial year to £19,946 for the 1917–18 financial year, the largest increases occurring in the last three years of the war.[70] While encouraged and grateful at the support shown throughout the war, the chairman, John Jones, stressed the urgent and growing needs in the old established overseas mission fields in New Guinea and Melanesia and the newer ones in China and Japan. The war had also made Australians much more aware of its part in the Christian world. The Australian Army's role in the fighting in Palestine was seen as a Christian challenge to support the mission to Jerusalem and the Middle East. In ABM's eyes 'the liberation of Palestine' offered a God-given opportunity.[71] The enthusiasm for overseas mission reflected unfavourably on the Anglican Church's missionary initiatives for Aborigines. In 1919, ABM was supporting Yarrabah, Mitchell River and Forrest River Missions; the CMS had established the Roper River Mission. ABM also supported the Diocese of Carpentaria's Torres Strait Island Mission. As the chairman, John Jones remarked: 'The above-named Missions represent the efforts of the Anglican Church to care for the despised blackfellows of the North... The Church as a whole does not display any great zeal in the task of caring for "the remnant that is left"'.[72] This lack of enthusiasm for Aboriginal missions, especially of white personnel to work in them, was an ever present reality for ABM and the relevant dioceses.

In the enthusiasm for a new beginning following the First World War, Jones advocated Bishop White's plan for a network of missions across Northern Australia supported by the Queensland, Western Australian and Commonwealth governments. It was not until another world war had elapsed that such governmental involvement occurred.

The Second World War had more profound and more long-term effects on Aboriginal people and ABM than either the First World War or the Great Depression. The increase in donations to the missionary organisations noted for the First World War occurred again. For ABM, after an initial drop in 1939 and 1940, there was a very dramatic increase from 1941 to 1944 such that the contributions for 1944 were 85 per cent greater than for 1940 and 62 per cent greater than for 1938.[73] There was, as well, an increase in the number of Australians offering for missionary service despite the fact that there was a total mobilisation for war service. The challenge of war made many Christians look to the fundamental values underpinning their lives. For some, increased giving to missions or offering for missionary service seemed the appropriate response. The suffering of the missionaries and Indigenous people especially in Melanesia and New Guinea, the witness of the young churches in these areas, the courage of the missionaries in remaining at their posts and the subsequent execution by the Japanese of eleven Anglicans and a greater number from other denominations in New Guinea and New Britain sharpened the awareness of Australian Christians.[74] Missions were no longer just a meagre, dutiful token put occasionally in the collection plate. The loyalty of the peoples of the Southwest Pacific to the Allied cause was another factor. New Guineans were no longer head hunters and savages but 'fuzzy wuzzy angels' who brought the wounded back to safety along the Kokoda Trail. Two of the Anglican 'New Guinea Martyrs' were Papuan evangelists. Giving to ABM and CMS and offering for service was 'at a standard never before known in the history of the Church in Australia'.[75]

During the war, especially after 1940, at the institutional level, ABM took a worldwide view. Overseas missions were reported on in great detail, CMS activities overseas were mentioned in the chairman's report as well as in the usual summary of CMS activities. The chairman's reports also dealt frequently with the worldwide situation of the mission movement. This was partly due to its increased involvement in missions overseas and in the isolation of Europe from the mission field. It was also reflected in some publications placed before the Literature Committee, such as, *Should Missions Go On?*

During the Second World War, ABM again attempted to place pressure on governments, especially the Commonwealth Government, to be involved with its work with and concern for Aborigines.[76] In part, this was a justification of its own role; in part, it reflected the increased expenses of Aboriginal missions; in part, it reflected a slowly growing awareness that Aborigines should not still be regarded as an optional extra call upon Christian charity but an inescapable responsibility of the church, the state and the nation. ABM also enunciated a new respect for Aboriginal culture as it planned to provide missions with workers not only 'zealous for the propagation of the Gospel' but also 'trained in the languages and culture of the people...and pledged to serve...for a useful term of years'.[77] This aim was stimulated by prominent Anglican academics, the anthropologist Professor AP Elkin, and the linguist, Dr A. Capell, both ordained priests whom ABM consulted extensively. The unpopularity of working in the Aboriginal mission field was to render this idealism stillborn.

In 1942, when a Japanese invasion was expected in northern Australia, the defence forces evacuated most of the white mission staff at Thursday Island and Forrest River. For the critical period in which invasion was feared, the Bishop of Carpentaria had to supervise his diocese, which then included the Northern Territory as well as far North Queensland, from Townsville.[78] For a time, John Best was not only chaplain superintendent of Forrest River, but also schoolteacher, works foreman, captain of the mission boat, nurse, medical officer, and mystified mechanic.[79] Staff were reduced everywhere, even at the government settlement of Palm Island where the nursing staff of the hospital were transferred south. So too were a number of Palm Island Aborigines. The Anglican Church Army nurse, Sister Johnson, volunteered for service at the hospital.[80] Aborigines visiting Thursday Island or living at Palm Island, Lockhart River, Mitchell River and Forrest River found themselves living alongside military camps, which enlarged their understanding of the world outside their mission.

Some Aborigines from all of the ABM supported missions and chaplaincies had been used as sources of labour outside the missions from the very earliest years, the men in the pastoral, pearl shelling, trochus and bêche-de-mer industries, and in harvesting crops; the women as domestic servants, cooking, cleaning and providing child care. The war expanded and diversified the use of their labour. In June 1942, the fiftieth jubilee celebrations of the founding of Yarrabah were postponed because of the war. The men were harvesting sugarcane, maize and peanuts, 'the normal supply of labour being so much reduced owing to the war'.[81] Lockhart River men were sent in gangs to the Atherton Tableland harvesting peanuts and timber getting; others went as crew for luggers, while Yarrabah was sometimes used as a staging post for the distribution of Lockhart River labour.[82]

The war disturbed, excited, and varied life on even the remote Mitchell River Mission. Although a very large station running approximately 6000 head of cattle had been developed at the mission, most of the men and many women, approximately two hundred in all, worked as cheap labour on North Queensland cattle stations.[83] During the war their labour was even more in demand, often more than could be supplied. Those remaining on the mission found the routine of mission work interrupted when an American aeroplane ran out of fuel and came down, twenty-seven kilometres from the mission. To rescue the aircrew, Mitchell River Aborigines built a road to the plane in a week by voluntary labour, using shovels, picks and bare hands. They then built a landing strip 1100 metres long in five days to allow the plane to take off. The workers refused payment, the missionary reported. 'It was a case of the native showing the Yanks how to work'.[84]

Similar examples of Aboriginal enterprise were reported in other parts of the North Australian war zone to show the loyalty of the Aborigines. As the *A.B.M. Review* noted: 'Reports indicate that the loyalty and devotion shown by Aboriginals is no less commendable than that of Papuans'.[85] Clearly white Australians had to be convinced that the colonised first Australians were as patriotic as the colonised Papuans.

The end of the war heralded the dawning of a new age of missions. This was demonstrated in part by some of the issues that confronted ABM. The growing realisation that the state and federal governments had a responsibility to provide funds to meet the secular needs of Aborigines on mission communities brought with it the realisation that the privation endured by generations of missionaries and Aborigines had in fact resulted from the perception by church and state that Aborigines were objects of Christian charity, that they were not an intrinsic part of Australian society. The churches had contributed markedly to this perception and indeed had been quite possessive about their responsibility for 'their Aborigines'. They now became incensed at the load they were bearing because of the refusal of governments to fund what they had accepted as church responsibilities. In 1948, the board declared it 'does not desire its missionaries at Forrest River to continue working under the conditions that now exist...the board makes it clear that it does not consider it to be its duty to provide from its funds — even if the funds were available — large sums of money to cover expenditure which should be borne by Governments'.[86] The Aboriginal people at Forrest River were of course living under worse conditions than the missionaries.

There never had been enough funds for ABM, or any other missionary society, to create their desired league of village theocracies. It had not only imposed hardships upon the missionaries, it had created an unnatural way of life for the Aborigines whom it made 'inmates' of peculiar, if caring, institutions, for most for the term of their natural life. In 1950, ABM like the other major missionary organisations had not been able to envisage an alternative. The European mind had been imprisoned by its perception of its own race and culture as uniquely important with gifts the rest of the world had to accept to be fully human. To the rest of the world, this was the ultimate in arrogance.

The Second World War had not only shown the lie to this claim to superiority, it had revealed the political vulnerability of the European empires and the moral bankruptcy of such concepts as manifest destiny and the white man's burden with which they had explained and sustained their domination. The political process of decolonisation in Asia and Africa had begun to liberate the European mind. In 1948, the chairman of ABM, Bishop GH Cranswick, encapsulated the challenge to the white man's Christian domination in a report, 'The Church and Changing World Relations'. He also demonstrated the European ambivalence to this emerging situation. While he acknowledged the increased nationalism in developing countries as good and necessary, and saw the drive towards industrialisation and secularisation as a reaction to European and American economic exploitation, he 'feared' the people of the Pacific would follow. Although he deplored the racism that whites were now conscious of, he could not advocate the relaxation of immigration controls. The Church had to 'show itself to be a universal society' and be 'local and domestic everywhere'. He enunciated this new widespread awareness:

> The Church in its missionary character in Asia and Africa and in other lands has been and often is terribly foreign looking [as the Europeans] have naturally built up churches of a kind that they knew! But all that is undergoing a vast change now. In great indigenous churches in the lands of Asia and Africa and round Australia native symbolism and culture are taking the place of western with increasing rapidity.[87]

He told his board that the poor churches in the new nations should be offered financial help but allowed complete freedom to decide how to spend it. He pointed to the 'huge challenge of today...of first class urgency...to see that the native church is really native, living the life of the people, seeming to the people of the country to be expressing the authentic voice of God, speaking in the accent of the country'.[88] It was to be a generation before reality approached this idealism in the Southwest Pacific. Indeed, at an Anglican Mission Agency Conference in Brisbane in 1986, church leaders from Asia, Africa, and the Southwest Pacific were still complaining of the dominance and lack of sensitivity of the white churches and missionary societies. They were accused of living off their glorious past, winning support from their members by highlighting the needs of the churches and peoples in the developing world, but then treating them as dependents rather than 'Partners in Mission'.[89]

It is doubtful if the Board in 1948 considered the brave words uttered by Bishop Cranswick had any relevance at all to Aboriginal Australians.

For this colonised people, the church was preparing to move from a one-hundred-year-old policy of segregation and paternalistic domination to one of assimilation, a policy that denied the possibility of 'the authentic voice of God, speaking in the accent of the country' for Aboriginal people.

Another Jubilee

In 1946, ABM began planning for its centenary in 1950. It aimed to attract fifty new missionaries and to raise £10,000 in a special appeal to create new missionary dioceses and to establish memorials in the mission fields to those who had served and died in the Second World War. Contributions amounting to £108,000 were raised and more than fifty people came forward to be missionaries. As a later Chairman, Canon Robert Butterss, remarked: '1950 was a high point in the history of ABM'.[90] The jubilee marked a fitting finale to fifty years of steady expansion into new missionary areas in Australia and overseas.

6.

Of Massacres, Missionaries, Myths and History Wars

[Gribble] treats them as the equal of whites. He continually puffs up blacks and has been a source of great mischief in the Wyndham district. That is why he is so cordially hated by those amongst whom he has lived for thirteen years.

The Missionary as Hero

In June 1926, a Western Australian police patrol of thirteen—twelve men and one woman — led by two young police constables, Graham St Jack and Denis Regan, set out to capture the Aborigines who, they believed, had killed Fred Hay, the soldier settler, co-owner of Nulla Nulla cattle station. Accompanying them were two special constables, sworn in for this patrol, three Aboriginal police trackers, two Aboriginal trackers added specially, Leopold Overheu, the soldier settler partner of Hay, as well as a friend of Hay, two other Aboriginal pastoral workers, and the wife of one of these men. The six white men were armed with .44 Winchester rifles and approximately five hundred rounds of ammunition, and the seven Aboriginal men with shotguns. The white members of the party also had side-arms.

Hay had, in fact, been killed by one Aboriginal, Lumbia, who was captured after an extensive search and tried, found guilty, and sentenced to death. Subsequently his sentence was commuted to life imprisonment after ABM had argued strongly that the sentence be reduced. Hay had actually provoked the attack. He was given permission to have sex with one of Lumbia's wives and had then tried to take her back to Nulla Nulla.

In the fight that ensued Hay was speared. His body was subsequently found, naked except for a pair of boots. Green refers to Hay's action as rape.[1]

In the months following the arrest of Lumbia, Ernest Gribble heard from Aborigines on the Marndoc Reserve, of which the Forrest River Mission was a small part, that the police party had murdered Aborigines. The rumours were recorded, when they were received, in the mission diary along with the mundane incidentals of life on the mission.[2] On 6 July, lay missionary John Thomson recorded that there had been an eyewitness account by an Aboriginal girl, Loorabane, of one brutal massacre of men, women and children. A local Aboriginal, Lily Johnson, translated her account for Thomson. Loorabane claimed the gunshot wound in her leg was from a police bullet as she and her brother fled the scene. In 1986, Lily Johnson told the story, as she remembered it, to Christine Halse, almost sixty years after Gribble had left Forrest River Mission.

> ...the police got all those Aborigines from the Kular tribe that lived from the coast to the mission...they put the men on one chain and the women with their children and their kids on another chain. Some of those women had babes at the breast...they killed the men. They just lined them up and shot them one by one...the women had to watch those men being shot...their husbands and brothers and relatives... the men had to collect wood first. They didn't know why they had to collect that wood but they had to get a big pile of it...They lined them up and shot them...then they cut them up into pieces, you know, a leg, an arm, just like that and those bits of body were thrown on the wood...and burnt there...the women were taken to another place just a bit away...and had to stand on the river bank but it was dry that time of year and they were shot there so their bodies just fell into the river... they bashed the brains out of the babies and threw them into the river with their mothers and burnt the lot...there's a lot of bodies. It took a long time to burn...With the women was a mother and her two kids... they had bush names. They couldn't speak English...The boy's name [was] Numbunnung (Kangaloo) and the girl was Loorabane...the boy spoke to his sister in language and told her that when that chain came off to grab mum and head for the bush...they were at the end of the chain...but [when they ran away] the police shot at them...they killed the mother and the girl got shot in the leg there [pointing]...they hid in the roots of the pandanus grass in the Forrest River. They hid under water and breathed through a bit of pandanus grass, you know, it's hollow, like a straw...the police looked for them everywhere but they just kept real still, not moving 'cause they were so scared...by evening, when they thought it was safe to leave, they moved out...swam across the Forrest River and travelled all the next day and then the day after

until the evening until they reached the mission where they knew they'd be safe...I was playing with the other girls...when Loorabane came...She was shaking with fright...She told us what happened and we told Mamma [Angelina Noble] and Mamma told Jim [Noble] and he told old Gribble.[3]

Kangaloo was able to name six Aborigines killed in this massacre, one of a number that occurred in the Marndoc Reserve. At each site the bodies were cut into small pieces, burnt, and any evidence carefully removed. This was how one Aboriginal remembered one of the massacres on the Marndoc Reserve sixty years after the event.

It was on 29 July 1926, two months after he heard the first rumours, that Gribble reported the matter to the Aboriginal inspector in Wyndham. He subsequently advised Western Australia's Chief Protector, AO Neville, the ABM secretary in Perth and the ABM chairman, John Needham, in Sydney.

The Rev. Ernest Gribble was a pioneer missionary who exposed the 1926 Forrest River massacres and was the spark that set the History Wars on fire. From A Despised Race: The vanishing Aboriginals of Australia, *ER Gribble, Australian Board of Missions, 1933.*

*The Rev. James Noble was a
pioneer missionary and the
first Indigenous Australian to
be ordained in the Anglican
Church. He assisted Gribble
in revealing the Forrest River
Massacres. From* A Despised
Race: The vanishing
Aboriginals of Australia, *ER Gribble, Australian
Board of Missions, 1933.*

The investigating police inspector, William Douglas, reported to the
police commissioner 'that sixteen natives were burned in three lots; one,
six and nine; only fragments [of] bone not larger than one inch remain'.
He also cautioned that it would be very difficult to convict anyone,
especially as Gribble was so universally hated by the whites of the east
Kimberley for his known antagonism towards them in general and the
police in particular.[4]

It was also widely believed that Gribble was a disruptive presence among
the Aborigines, as Walter Nairn, the lawyer representing the whites on the
patrol, later informed the subsequent Royal Commission, and through it
the press and public of Australia and overseas:

> [he] treats them as the equal of whites. He continually puffs up blacks
> and has been a source of great mischief in the Wyndham district. That
> is why he is so cordially hated by those amongst whom he has lived for
> thirteen years.[5]

Gribble's life was threatened on two occasions because of the passions he inflamed and the fact that whites were having to defend themselves against the charge of conducting a punitive expedition against Aborigines who were seen as a threat to the lives and property of the pastoralists. Gribble won the reluctant support of the Anglican Church in Western Australia and the wholehearted commitment of ABM's chairman, John Needham, after a cautious appraisal of the situation.

The ensuing publicity in the Australian press and overseas in England and America was almost certainly critical to the establishment of the Royal Commission in 1927.

Senior Stipendiary Magistrate George Wood was appointed commissioner on 26 January 1927. He was highly respected, with an impressive public service record which included a period as Government Resident in Broome. He was then familiar with the people of the Kimberley and could be expected to understand the problems of living on this remote frontier. The white members of the police patrol were represented by a competent lawyer, Walter Nairn, as a result of a public subscription strongly supported by the settlers of the East Kimberley. The Forrest River Aborigines, the department representing Aboriginal interests, the witnesses supporting the allegations of murder, including Gribble, James Noble, other staff of Forrest River Mission, and the Aboriginal witnesses who could give evidence, were not provided with legal counsel. Nor was Commissioner Wood provided with independent legal support to assist him in his inquiries. It looked like a Royal Commission on the cheap, a Royal Commission the government had to have.

Wood reported that there was 'a conspiracy of silence' in the Kimberley. Witnesses retracted previous statements or refused to testify, or disappeared from the scene. A key witness, Tommy, was never seen again after a meeting with his employer, Leopold Overheu, his alleged murderer. Wood concluded that the white members of the patrol, including St Jack and Regan, had lied and orchestrated their testimonies.

Nairn set about discrediting the evidence and character of Ernest Gribble, the main witness against his clients and the person who was left to produce most of the other witnesses. And, there is no doubt that, in this, he was very successful. No one tried to get evidence from the large number of Aborigines who might have witnessed the police attacks or be related to people who had been killed. The Royal Commission had been limited in its investigation to the circumstances of Tommy's disappearance and to three particular sites where it was alleged massacres had taken place, a restriction Wood pointed out that could limit his findings. Marndoc Reserve was very large. Most of the skeletal evidence collected at these sites was assessed by two medical witnesses in Perth to be not human, or not definitely human, although the medical officer in Wyndham had thought otherwise.

Wood submitted his report on 21 May 1927 to the Premier of Western Australia after having clearly taken into account all of the extensive evidence, including that specifically mentioned above. He concluded that the evidence of the whites in the patrol, including the journals of the constables, was fabricated. He reported that the police patrol had killed eleven Aborigines at the three sites his investigation was limited to, and then had burned the bodies. He concluded that there was no proof that Tommy had been murdered by Overheu. However, he specifically reported that four identified Aborigines had been murdered and burnt by the two police constables. Wood also warned that his conclusions were based on evidence he had considered during his four months' investigation. This was determined by 'the balance of probabilities', not 'beyond reasonable doubt', as would be required at a trial.

In 1968, Dr Helmut Reim of Karl Marx University in East Germany, now Leipzig University, interviewed three Aboriginal elders, and by an analysis of their testimonies, concluded that between eighty and one hundred Aborigines were killed in the massacres on the Marndoc Reserve. I have recently contacted Dr Reim who sent me the detailed transcript of the interview he gave in 1968 to Tony Thomas of the *West Australian*. I have attached this transcript as an appendix.

In 1968, Forrest River Aborigines reported that the massacres had occurred at five different sites. In his letter to me, Dr Reim referred to Peter Biskup's account in *Not Slaves, Not Citizens*, published by UQP in 1973, pp. 84–5, and to 'AO Neville's cautious statement (in his annual report to the Western Australian Parliament in 1927) on the findings of the Royal Commission: 'Anyone following the matter of these alleged murders carefully could only come to one conclusion, viz., that a number of natives had lost their lives in some untimely way'.' Untimely indeed.

In the same year, Neville Green interviewed Charles Overheu who claimed that his brother, Leopold, had informed him that the party had shot over three hundred Aborigines. Gribble claimed that thirty of the regular visitors to the Forrest River Mission had been murdered. In 1926, the Aborigines of the Marndoc Reserve believed a large number had been killed by the police patrol and that is still the belief in that area. The members of the police patrol, of course, never admitted publicly to killing anyone.[6] I could not hazard a guess as to the correct estimate. However, I am convinced a massacre occurred.

The Solicitor-General decided to charge St Jack and Regan with the murder of one Aboriginal, Boondung, presumably as a test case. They were tried in the Magistrate's Court in Perth on 12–13 July and 10

August 1927. The case was bound to fail as defense lawyer Walter Nairn pointed out: 'the evidence fails because there is no proof that Boondung, or anybody else, has been killed, nor is there any evidence from which that fact can be properly inferred'.

The magistrate discharged the accused because 'the evidence was insufficient to justify its being placed before a jury'.[7] No further investigations were made and no other charges laid. Many Aborigines living on Marndoc Reserve who might have been able to give evidence were not interviewed. The government clearly wanted the matter put to rest.

After the Royal Commission, Gribble received numerous letters of congratulations from people and organisations concerned for Aboriginal advancement. This continued after St Jack and Regan were discharged. The ABM contacted the Premier of Western Australia, Phillip Collier, to express the board's concern at the reinstatement of St Jack and Regan, and in the *A.B.M. Review*, 12 November 1927, publicly criticised this action and the court decision not to commit them for trial for murder. They had not been acquitted of the murder for which they had been charged, let alone the others.[8]

This story of the missionary as martyr became the faith of the Anglican Church, at least the few who were interested in Aborigines and Aboriginal missions, and of people throughout Australia interested in Aboriginal advancement. It was also accepted and promulgated by academics before the publication of Green's *The Forrest River Massacres* in 1995 and Halse's biography, *A Terribly Wild Man* in 2002.[9]

The Missionary as Monster

I thought I had completed my research on the Forrest River massacres almost a decade ago. I had wanted to explore how twentieth century Australians reacted to the well-publicised reality of contemporary frontier conflict leading to the imposition of white dominance and the dispossession of Aborigines who were standing in the way of 'progress', that is, Aborigines who were impeding colonisation. How did we white Australians, who were the passive beneficiaries of the violent dispossession of Aborigines in the nineteenth century, respond when the ugly reality that had produced our comfortable lifestyle re-emerged as a twentieth century reality? No longer was it a matter of a regrettable past, better forgotten, but a present reality again perpetrated on black Australian citizens. How did an aware Christian majority, in this case the Anglican Church, respond? More particularly, how did the conscience of this Christian majority committed to the welfare and souls of these black Australians respond, in this case ABM? As with the Mabo decision[10] and subsequent government decisions in the late twentieth and early twenty-first centuries, it was an opportunity to see how justice was done, or not done, to black Australians by Australia's power structure, its white democratically elected legislature, in this case, and its agencies of law and order, the police and the legal system.

An ABM missionary had generated a widespread concern that resulted in a Royal Commission into the alleged mistreatment of Aborigines by a government agency, the only one caused by a missionary in Australia's history. The resulting Royal Commission and trial led many to conclude that the police of Western Australia, with the passive support of the state government, had been involved in a cover-up to protect themselves from the well-earned criticism of influential, concerned people throughout Australia and overseas. The reputation of Western Australia was on the rack. Could it be that yet again a meddlesome priest was humiliating the sovereignty of the state?

Since my earlier research into the Forrest River massacres, Neville Green has published his detailed account of this incident and Christine Halse has published a biography of Ernest Gribble, each book being derived from their doctoral research. I have based my updated account of 'the missionary as hero' on their more recent analysis of the Forrest River massacres, as well as the primary sources I have consulted myself. Although Green and Halse differ somewhat in their descriptions of Ernest Gribble's character, they are in agreement in their accounts of the Forrest River massacres and in Gribble's role in revealing them.[11]

In 1999, Rod Moran, a Western Australian journalist, published *Massacre Myth*, the result of research begun in 1994, partly at the request of the son of Constable James Graham St Jack who died in 1993 without making any public comment on the Forrest River massacres. Neville Green had interviewed him some years before and these reminiscences with some later additions were made available to Moran. By this time, Moran had begun to find what he termed inconsistencies in the Royal Commission report. After intensive research he came to the conclusion that St Jack and Regan were completely innocent and that, in fact, no massacres had occurred at all. This conclusion was surprising enough. His corollary was even more astonishing: that the allegations of massacres had been generated by Ernest Gribble to divert attention from himself and to destroy the possibility that Constable St Jack would reveal that Gribble had been having sexual relations with an Aboriginal woman at Forrest River. This was an allegation St Jack had made in his unpublished reminiscences compiled sixty years after the 1927 Royal Commission and the subsequent hearing in the magistrate's court. The allegation, if known, was not used at that time by Walter Nairn. In her biography of Gribble, Christine Halse had emphatically claimed that Gribble had been dismissed from Yarrabah after fathering a child to an Aboriginal woman, Janie, employed there as matron of the girl's dormitory. Halse builds up a complex picture of a tortured man riven by guilt under accentuated sexual tension because he was separated from his wife for much of his life while working in remote areas with Aboriginal people. She believes this sexual tension persisted at Forrest River Mission but completely rejected Moran's assertion that Gribble was involved sexually with any Aboriginal woman at Forrest River. She and Green were aware that Dr AP Elkin had said that people in Wyndham referred to the mission as 'Gribble's stud farm'. Elkin made it clear that this referred to Gribble's practice of controlling the marriages and children of the couples living on the mission. Moran believed Elkin was naively mistaken. In a recent *Quadrant* article, Green examines and rejects the evidence Moran adduces to prove that Gribble was sexually involved with an Aboriginal woman at Forrest River. I also thought Moran was grasping at straws.[12]

Moran analysed the available evidence revealed at the Royal Commission and trial, and built up the case that Gribble had manipulated and orchestrated the submissions given by the mission staff and Aboriginal informants to implicate the police patrol. Royal Commissioner Wood was deemed incompetent because he had not analysed the evidence correctly. Not only were the police innocent, Ernest Gribble was a monster who would send two young men to the gallows to protect his position as missionary superintendent, his reputation as the saviour of Aboriginal people, and his enormous ego. Gribble had committed no crime and could not have been charged. It was all to save his professional and psychological skin. The state would at last be rid of its troublesome priest.

Or so it seemed. I have no vested interests in whether Gribble had sexual relations with Aborigines or not, or whether there was a massacre, or whether Gribble was the evil, scheming villain that Moran claims him to be. However, after reading *Massacre Myth* carefully, twice, and its corollary, *Sex Maiming and Murder*, I am convinced that Moran is wrong about the massacres and wrong about Gribble.[13]

There is no doubt that Gribble was sometimes a confused and confusing witness, and sometimes simply wrong. He was also an arrogant, paternalistic, autocratic, bullying, sometimes violent missionary who had a vision for his Aboriginal 'inmates' as a 'whitealised' child race, in need of isolation and protection from white society in perpetuity. He suffered periodically from psychological and physical health problems. He was an incompetent general manager who not only ran his missions into unsanctioned debt but often had disastrous working relations with his white staff and with his employers at ABM. They were considering dismissing him before the 1926 massacres and finally did so in 1929 because they thought he had outlived his usefulness, relations with his staff were impossible and that, under him, Forrest River Mission was a failure.[14]

I have no intention of going into a detailed analysis here of my inability to accept Moran's main conclusions. In brief, I think he believed so strongly in the innocence of the two policemen and the guilt of Gribble that he became the contemporary Walter Nairn who, as defence lawyer, attacked the credibility of the main prosecution witness, Gribble, his supporters, Aboriginal witnesses, and the evidence they produced, and upheld the testimony of the members of the police patrol. Moran repeated this procedure. Even more than Nairn, he attacked the competence of Royal Commissioner Wood. Wood concluded there was a conspiracy of silence by all associated with the police patrol. Moran argued strongly that there wasn't. Wood and Inspector Douglas, in his written report, believed St Jack and Regan had lied and fabricated parts of their journals. Moran didn't. I also find it difficult to accept that Gribble's influence on eyewitnesses and contemporaries persisted until 1968 when Reim interviewed them and 1986 when Halse recorded Loorabane's story.

Kate Auty has very cleverly explored the 'conspiracy of silence' alluded to by Royal Commissioner Wood. One crucial aspect of this was the insistence by the white members of the police patrol that they had stayed only one night at police campsite number two, known to the Aborigines as Youngada, and now known as Wodgil. A date carved into a tree at Wodgil indicates they stayed two nights, a fact supported initially by Aboriginal members of the party. If so, they would have had time to capture and kill Aborigines and to burn the bodies. A farcical story was fabricated to explain the carvings on two trees and why the 'wrong' date had been used. When the Royal Commission was established, it became imperative for the police patrol to prove that they had not made Wodgil a base for their operations as Gribble had alleged.

Auty suggests that a member of the police patrol had carved a memorial to Hay on the date when they claimed they had already left. They believed Hay had been killed by a group of Aborigines who were also known to be cattle killers destroying the viability of Nulla Nulla and neighbouring stations. Hay and the three volunteer members of the police patrol, including his soldier–settler partner Leopold Overheu, were Gallipoli veterans and could have become convinced that they were once again in a war situation where 'drastic action' was justified. Auty is convinced that Overheu did the carvings and discovered that the date was Overheu's birthday, one he was hardly going to forget. By orchestrating their evidence, they were able to make it impossible for their guilt to be established in a court of law. Auty's explanation is much more convincing than the one they concocted, at least to me.[15]

If the evidence against St Jack and Regan could not be accepted 'beyond reasonable doubt', the evidence Christine Halse produced to justify the claim that Gribble fathered a child at Yarrabah, upon which Moran built to support his conspiracy theory at Forrest River, seems flimsier, as Neville Green has pointed out. Halse's theory is largely derived from the reminiscences of an 84-year-old woman recounting that she had overheard the accusation made once seventy-six years previously. Another woman said that her mother had said that Gribble's alleged lover, Janie, had told her that Gribble was the father. There is no other evidence that Janie had told anyone else this story. It is not impossible that Gribble had an affair with an Aboriginal woman at Yarrabah but it is certainly not proven beyond reasonable doubt. Christine Halse and I have discussed this on a number of occasions and we amicably beg to differ.

There is no evidence that ABM dismissed Gribble from Yarrabah or from Forrest River because of scandal about his sexual exploits as Moran asserted. At both places relations with his white staff had become impossible, and his management had generally deteriorated. As well, at Yarrabah, he was extremely ill. He was employed in the Newcastle Diocese at Gosford for two years and then re-employed by ABM to establish Forrest River Mission. After his dismissal from Forrest River Mission, he was soon in their employ again as Chaplain at Palm Island where he remained for another twenty-seven years, a strange career for a man who was allegedly guilty of known sexual exploitation of women in his care and had been dismissed twice for it.[16] Stranger still that he was re-employed in the Diocese of North Queensland, which is responsible for both Yarrabah and Palm Island.

I do not believe it is necessary to demonise St Jack or Regan because they were involved in a punitive expedition, even though they were involved in the killing of innocent men, women and children. They were doing what they, and the other white participants, thought had to be done. The pastoralists in the region were facing insolvency because of the wholesale cattle killing and they felt themselves extremely vulnerable to attack by the large number of Aborigines in the East Kimberley. The death of Hay seemed to confirm this. At first, it was believed that he was killed by 'natives', not by one Aboriginal, Lumbia. Overheu wrote to his father that he had asked the police 'for a strong force to go out, and that the natives be dealt with drastically' so that he could be safe on his property.[17] If this interpretation is correct, Sergeant Buckland, the officer in charge of the Wyndham police, would have been aware of the purpose and likely consequences of his sending out such a large, heavily armed patrol. This was what the Royal Commissioner concluded from his investigation, carried out soon after the alleged massacres occurred. He also said that there was not enough evidence to convict anyone.[18] Nor was there. Nor is there.

In my Queensland research, there are many examples of Native Police Officers and ordinary police who were involved in 'raids' on Aboriginal camps and gatherings that resulted in Aboriginal people being killed. They were police, jury, judge and executioner of Aborigines on the expanding frontier. Some of these officers moved into other areas of the Queensland public service as officers in the regular police force, as mining wardens, and as magistrates. One, Sub Inspector Urquhart, who broke the resistance of the Kalkadoons in northwest Queensland, became police commissioner in Queensland and subsequently chief administrator of the Northern Territory. A few may have been monsters, most weren't, although they did things we today regard as monstrous. They were doing what was expected of them on the frontier if white people were to dispossess Aborigines and occupy their land. Though later in time, in the light of the research of these four authors I have concluded that the same challenge confronted the pastoralists and police of the East Kimberley. St Jack and Regan also went on to lead responsible and apparently blameless lives. They could have refused to lead a punitive expedition but the pressure of the circumstances in which they found themselves and the expectations of the white frontier culture, of which they were part, made them decide otherwise. The tragedy of St Jack and Regan is that they became by happenstance the agents of frontier expansion. There is no nice way to rob a people of their land.

The controversy demonstrated positive aspects of the mission policy of paternalistic protection. A courageous white missionary with the invaluable assistance of an Aboriginal missionary, James Noble, and local Aborigines had revealed a massacre, prevented more Aborigines being killed, and used all of the resources of British law to try to have the culprits brought to justice. After some initial caution, ABM had supported Gribble and pursued the cause of justice with the Western Australian Government even after the police were set free. The chairman, John Needham, had personally urged the Western Australian Government to take action against St Jack and Regan and pursued the matter until he believed his efforts had become counterproductive. The missionaries and ABM had offered protection against the brutality of the white colonising power for a people who otherwise would have been without advocates. Gribble and the Aboriginal people at Forrest River erected a tall iron cross emerging from a cairn covering the bones of some of the murdered innocents. It is still there today.[19] In 1950, the chairman of ABM, Canon CS Robertson, reported: 'Gribble is still living in their memory'.[20]

In 1929, ABM became peripherally involved in yet another massacre of Aborigines in a remote area of Australia, the last one known in Australia's history. ABM strongly supported the unsuccessful attempt by the Association for the Protection of Native Races to bring the police involved in the Coniston massacre in Central Australia to trial.[21] The age of violent colonial dispossession lingered on and the church was left with the responsibility of futilely expressing its humanitarian concern at the barbarity of the methods used. The white power structure once again closed ranks behind its frontier agents and accepted what were regarded as unavoidable excesses.

The History Wars

The controversy surrounding the Forrest River massacres and Ernest Gribble did not end here as a contested incident in Western Australia's history. When the conservative author, Keith Windschuttle, read Moran's *Massacre Myths*, it confirmed for him his suspicion that the academic historians exploring Aboriginal history were exaggerating, or even fabricating, the degree of violence used to dispossess Aboriginal people and the nature of the Aboriginal response. He then embarked upon a campaign to analyse the massacre stories and the nature of Aboriginal resistance found in the academic literature that began to appear from the 1970s and which has increased and diversified since. In the first of three articles published in the conservative journal, *Quadrant*, in 2000, he devoted the opening quotation and one-third of a long article to the Forrest River massacres and to Moran's revisionist analysis of the Royal Commission and the subsequent accounts that largely depended upon it. He strongly supported the kind of evidence Moran would accept. At the end of this section, he asserted:

> Historians should only accept evidence of violent deaths, Aboriginal or otherwise, where there is a minimum amount of direct evidence. This means that, at the very least, they need some reports by people who were either genuine eyewitnesses or who at least saw the bodies afterwards. Preferably, these reports should be independently corroborated by others who saw the same thing. Admissions of guilt, provided they are

recorded first-hand and are not hearsay, should also count as credible evidence.[22]

Professional historians, of course, use a much wider range of resources than this, which is really the evidence of the court. Such a narrow acceptance of historical sources would produce a whitewashed view of Australia's frontier history. Rarely were such witnesses available and willing to testify. I can, perhaps, illustrate this by responding to the criticism he made of me in 'Part II The fabrication of the Aboriginal death toll'.

In the 1970s, Henry Reynolds and I had collaborated to produce an article 'Aboriginal Resistance in Queensland'.[23] Among other things, Reynolds had asked me how many Aborigines had been killed in conflict by Europeans in my area of research, North Queensland. I replied that it was 'impossible to do anything but guess' but suggested at least ten times as many as the number of Europeans or their employees who were killed that I was tabulating as an incidental aspect of my early 1970s doctoral research, part of which was published by ANU Press in 1982 as *Invasion and Resistance*. Reynolds thought this a reasonable conclusion for his area, southern Queensland. Aborigines were killed not only for killing the colonisers but also sometimes for rushing their cattle, for killing their cattle, sheep and horses, for occupying the river valleys, for burning the grasslands, and sometimes simply because their presence near the stations and outstations frightened the colonists. The table of those I discovered killed as a result of Aboriginal resistance was published as an appendix to *Invasion and Resistance*. Windschuttle praises my empirical method at length:

> Ironically...Noel Loos has provided a good model in his study of whites killed by Aborigines in North Queensland between 1861 and 1897... He records the names, dates, locations, references and a number of other details about each incident. He also ranks the reliability of the reports, rating each as 'acceptable', 'probable' or 'possible'. He lists 381 deaths of whites in this period as subjects of acceptable reports, 30 as probable and 59 as possible. By providing full references for his sources, he allows other researchers the opportunity to check his claims for authenticity. This is the way an empirical historian should proceed.[24]

Apart from damning those historians exploring Aboriginal history, including me, with this faint praise, he might have concluded that I would have recorded Aborigines killed in frontier conflict in the same way if it had been at all possible. It wasn't then and it isn't now. However, by using an extensive array of sources, it was possible to draw the best and most honest conclusions I could of the impact of violence upon the

Aboriginal people of North Queensland. Subsequent research may modify my conclusions. That is the inevitable process of history.

Windschuttle makes much of a leftwing political bias he and his conservative supporters see in the Aboriginal history that has emerged since the 1970s, stressing violence to assert the rights of the Aborigines to recognition as the original owners of the land. He believes that this 'black armband history' has ignored the fact that Australia was founded by British Christians, children of the Enlightenment, determined to establish civilization and the rule of law and to assimilate Aborigines into their model of modernity. Needless to say this approach has to reject that Aborigines have a humanity and culture worthy of equal consideration. Windschuttle approves of my use of empirical methods but fails to notice that I was attempting to write a 'history from below', of a people on the receiving end of broad historical processes such as colonisation, the imposition of British law abroad, and the fate of the colonised people. I intended to write only one chapter in my doctoral thesis, submitted in 1975, on frontier contact. I was totally surprised by the nature and variety of frontier conflict in North Queensland and eventually wrote a chapter on each of four frontiers of contact: the pastoral, mining, rainforest and sea frontiers. In retrospect, I should have included my study of the first generation of missionaries to contact remote Aboriginal groups as a fifth. Most of my doctoral thesis, however, still focuses on how Aboriginal people were incorporated into the settler society after the period of frontier conflict. I included the highlights of these chapters into the final chapter of *Invasion and Resistance*, 'The Decent Disposal of the Native Inhabitants', and a quotation from the *North Queensland Register*, 11 October 1893, which found no difficulty in acknowledging the dispossession.

Windschuttle has published his revisionist history of Tasmania. Four books edited or written by professional historians have responded to him and one by a conservative author, John Dawson, has defended Windschuttle's history of Tasmania.[25] As well there have been numerous journal articles, public debates between Windschuttle and some of his main opponents, such as Henry Reynolds and Robert Manne, radio and television coverage, and extensive debates in the broadsheet Australian newspapers. The controversy has also been given coverage overseas.

Bain Attwood's *Telling the Truth about Aboriginal History* probably best presents this extensive literature and public debate. While rejecting what he terms the 'new conservative' revisionist history of Windschuttle and similar public intellectuals, he produces quite a respectful picture of Windschuttle, the man. Indeed I felt not only embarrassed for Windschuttle but also a kind of pity that he was making such a public spectacle of himself in his search for truth and certainty and in his naive defence of the values and practices of Australia's colonial society.[26]

Attwood points out how the Labor Party under Paul Keating enthusiastically accepted the new understanding of Aboriginal history as a central part of Australia's history with its consequences of Native Title and recognition of Aborigines as the original owners and occupiers of the land. His successor, John Howard, has argued against what Geoffrey Blainey termed this 'black armband view of Australia's history'. Howard stressed the worth of the settlers' core values and their achievements. In this he has been supported by a number of important conservative public intellectuals. Windschuttle has become their battering ram to break down their imagined edifice of Aboriginal history. The campaign has attracted enormous publicity and gives solace to those who want to continue to believe in the earlier view of the colonisation of Australia. Despite this, Attwood concluded Windschuttle 'was ill equipped for the work of a scholarly historian especially in the field that Aboriginal history has become...the allegations Windschuttle and other Howard intellectuals had levelled depended on badly flawed assumptions and assertions rather than soundly based arguments'. Elsewhere, Attwood notes: 'Windschuttle's interpretation of settler violence, however, does not rest only on the so-called historical record. It is determined primarily by his historical method, which is seriously defective'.[27] Most professional historians would agree with Attwood's conclusions. I suspect that the History Wars are not over yet. We await Windschuttle's two volumes on mainland Australia's Aboriginal history.

The focus on massacres, the nature of Aboriginal resistance and the numbers of Aborigines killed has diverted attention from the main point. To dispossess Aboriginal people, as much violence was used as the colonists thought necessary, whether it was little or a great deal. Australia was not a colony of settlement, a terra nullius, but an English-settler colony of conquest like the United States, Canada, and New Zealand. Aboriginal and Torres Strait Islander people have never accepted their dispossession. They are not just other Australians to be awarded citizenship but a people whose Native Title has to be acknowledged. Conservative Australians clearly find this difficult to accept. In *Recognizing Aboriginal Title*, the distinguished Canadian academic, Peter Russell, has stressed the necessity in these four English-settled societies for the settlers and the Indigenous people to reach mutually acceptable agreements that acknowledge the right of **both** groups to live in their nations in justice and harmony. In Canada, he has actually been involved in the process as an envoy of the

Canadian Government.[28] This does not seem very 'left wing' to me. Not imposed by statute or law court, but mutually acceptable.

Despite his not inconsiderable ego, Ernest Gribble would be amazed to find himself a central figure in the History Wars, the spark that set fire to Windschuttle's passion for truth, certainty, and the restoration of the reputation of Australia's founding fathers. Not only had Gribble instigated the only Royal Commission into a massacre of Aborigines in Australia's history, he had ignited Australia's greatest ever historical controversy. He had also been linked by Windschuttle with other missionaries who had sensationalised alleged atrocities committed against Aborigines for their own self aggrandisement.[29] The cairn embracing the bones of victims at Forrest River and the memories of Aborigines there and at Yarrabah, where Deacon James Noble retired, tell a different story, one in which missionaries are simply also there.

7.

The End of an Era

They do not take discipline easily and it is very hard to change a nation of people who have been almost slaves into a nation of free people. We gave them such a bad time in the early days, we have been giving them such a bad time since...

We are the cause of the apathy and penury of the people, and we ought to do something about it.

Although the second half of the twentieth century began confidently with the successful conclusion of the 1950 Jubilee Celebration, the seeds of change had already been sown. The ABM board realised that the government ought to be meeting the material needs of Aboriginal people on the existing missions, that Aborigines, as a people, should not be considered merely objects of charity. The churches could not supply the infrastructure necessary for a twentieth century Australian village, which increasingly was subjected to comparison by both black and white Australians with facilities available to the rest of the Australian community, and was increasingly under the gaze of the international community. There was also the recognition, at least at the conceptual level, that paternalistic control was self-defeating. There had been a radical change in commonwealth government policy, which had been clearly communicated to missionary agencies by the Minister for Territories, Paul Hasluck: assimilation was to be the goal set for Aborigines and Torres Strait Islanders.[1] Although it was not realised at the time, the post-missionary age was dawning for Australian Aborigines.

The assimilation policy was developed before the Second World War in the Northern Territory administration and promoted by the then Minister for Territories, John McEwen, and the Professor of Anthropology at

Sydney University, AP Elkin. Its implementation was delayed until 1951 by the war and by Labor governments from 1941 to 1949 that showed little interest in Aboriginal welfare.[2] Elkin later claimed that initially assimilation was not meant to be interpreted as a social engineering process in which Aborigines would be expected to turn away from their own language and culture to adopt what was then seen as a monochrome white Australian culture. That may have been his understanding, yet there is no mistaking Hasluck's passionate zeal in his directions to the missionary organisations in 1953:

> We have a two-fold task of providing the means and the opportunity by which these people can live at the higher standard and of helping to awaken in them a belief that the change is not only possible but is worth an effort on their part. It is a matter of changing the hearts of men and women as well as of changing the circumstances in which they live. The pace of social change is set by the hearts of men, both those who try to do the lifting and those who are being lifted...
>
> Beyond these practical tasks [the provision of satisfactory health services, housing, education, diet, and a western style family life] there is the even more important need to communicate ideas and to give hope and encouragement to the native people who were making the effort of change, for we not only need to change the house in which a man lives but also the man himself.

Hasluck concluded his address to missionary organisations by identifying commonwealth government policy not only with the claimed civilising effect of mission practice, but also with the Christian faith itself:

> In approaching these tasks in the Northern Territory the Government values the part being played by the Christian missions. On the practical side they are helping us to carry out those daily tasks of health, education, and social improvement to which I have referred above. They are also helping to give to the native people that feeling of brotherhood and acceptance which is so necessary for their encouragement. Even more important than these, they are sowing in their minds those Christian ideas which are the foundation of a good life.[3]

The missionaries charged with providing the one foundation of a good life could have been forgiven for concluding that the only important aspect of their heritage their Aboriginal 'inmates' should be left with was their black skins.

There were some indications that ABM had independently been considering changes in mission policy and practice. As early as 1945 the chairman, Bishop GH Cranswick, stated they were going to ask missionaries to learn and use the local Aboriginal language.[4] Considering the difficulty of finding staff for Aboriginal missions and the lack of commitment to the education of missionary candidates, it is hardly surprising that this idea was stillborn. There was also some expectation that missionary control would be less rigid and that the Aboriginal 'inmates' would be more involved in decision making. However, the regime on each mission still depended upon the superintendent of the day and any changes were marginal indeed.[5]

Yet the missions, with the exception of Edward River, were past the pioneering or foundation stage. They were isolated, village theocracies in which Aborigines had been subject to lifelong Christian influence and teaching at a Sunday School level for two or three generations.[6] As Professor Elkin noted: 'The work in hand is to run an institution of a peculiar kind — the building up of a community'.[7]

The Aboriginal Christian Co-operative Movement

Despite this growing awareness, the adoption of co-operatives as ABM's strategy for empowering Aboriginal and Torres Strait Islander people to participate more equitably in Australian society comes as quite a shock to anyone studying the ABM's history.

Before the Second World War, those Anglicans who stressed that the church should be involved in social issues were a small, ignored minority. After the Second World War, there was a greater concern among Australians generally for a more just, peaceful world order, a concern that was reflected in the Anglican Church to the extent that those committed to social justice and structural change were heard, if rarely heeded.[8] The adoption of co-operatives associated with the empowerment of the working class, as a mission strategy and the appointment in 1957 of the Rev. Frank Coaldrake, a prominent conscientious objector during the Second World War, as chairman of ABM, were two indications of this increased awareness.

I have analysed the Aboriginal Christian Co-operative Movement elsewhere and will deal with it briefly here.[9] After the Second World War, two Anglican priests, James Benson and Alf Clint, had begun developing co-operatives to assist Papua New Guineans to regain control over their own land and resources and to make them financially independent of white plantation owners. The Anglican Bishop of New Guinea supported the innovation and appointed Clint as Priest Warden of Christian Cooperatives.[10] In 1950, Clint was afflicted with a severe form of dermatitis which forced him to leave New Guinea.

Clint persuaded the board of ABM, to adopt the co-operative movement as a strategy for its future work with Aborigines and Torres Strait Islanders.

In 1952, Clint was appointed director of ABM Co-operatives and initially provided with £1250. As he was not allowed to appeal to traditional ABM sources, Clint turned to the trade unions, right and left wing, and to the secular co-operative movement for additional support.[11] At Lockhart River, Clint found a profit-sharing operation based on trochus shell, developed by the superintendent, John Warby. He realised that this successful initiative made Lockhart River the most promising base from which to launch the ABM co-operative movement.[12]

Warby had developed a co-partnership system in which crew and mission shared in the profits. Elected Aboriginal councillors managed the work of their cutter, the *Cape Grey*.[13] Warby's vision for the mission catapulted them unawares into an informal co-operative enterprise. The Aboriginal crew became more proficient and committed to their work so a second, larger boat, *Yola*, was purchased. In 1953, an adult education program was introduced in which the men studied boat management and a number of general educational subjects. After extensive consultation with Clint, the Aboriginal workers decided to form the first Aboriginal co-operative in Australia: The Lockhart River Aboriginal Christian Co-operative. It was registered under the Queensland Co-operative Societies Act, its board of directors consisting of seven Aboriginal men, five elected by the men and women members of the co-operative and two appointed by the bishop. John Warby was the non-voting supervisor and his wife, Bunty, the non-voting treasurer. Frank O'Brien was elected president of the board and Peter Creek, secretary, and subsequently the co-operative store manager. Over the years other prominent Aboriginal members of the board were John Butcher, David Marrott, Charlie Claremont, Jimmy Doctor, Furry Short, Alick Sandy, and Daniel Hobson.[14]

A third boat, *Francis Pritt*, was purchased. Forty-five men out of a total population of approximately four hundred and an able-bodied adult male population of approximately 110 were employed by the co-operative. In 1955, virtually every able-bodied Lockhart man was employed in cooperative or mission activities.[15] Warby reported on the metamorphosis this had produced:

> They have at last arrived at a position where they operate their own boats from their own mission... Family life is improved and the people are happier; self respect has been raised to a marked degree. The people are more self reliant and initiative, previously subjugated, is increasing day by day.[16]

The board of directors even overruled a major recommendation Warby had made regarding its membership.[17]

The first Board of Directors of the Lockhart River Aboriginal Christian Co-operative. Standing L–R: Frank O'Brien, Alf Clint, Alec Sandy, John Goodman and David Marriott. Sitting L–R: John Butcher, Peter Creek and Charlie Claremont. Photography by John Warby, Noel Loos Collection.

Warby did not state the obvious: that, for over thirty years, the Anglican Church had been the subjugating agent.

By 1956, the ABM 'pilot program' at Lockhart was well under way. The co-operative was operating three boats in the trochus shell industry with further plans to diversify into agricultural and pastoral ventures. Discussions were held with the Queensland Department of Agriculture to ascertain the suitability of the region to produce such crops as cotton, palm oil, and coffee. Concurrently, mission staff were undertaking correspondence courses to upgrade their technical knowledge. The first audit for the period, August 1954 to 30 June 1956, revealed a profit of £5369, which allowed a dividend of 7.5 per cent to each member additional to any wages earned, plus a bonus. This success stimulated increased contributions to share capital.[18]

In 1956, a Christian co-operative was initiated for Moa Island in the Torres Strait. The fledgling co-operative planned to incorporate wolfram mining, crayfishing, agriculture, and a bakery; however, two years passed before the Moa Island Christian Co-operative had its first meeting, partly due to some tardiness on Clint's behalf and partly due to a painfully slow government response.[19] Around this time, tentative moves were made to establish co-operatives on the Edward River and Mitchell River Missions.

The importance of adult education was underlined by the developments and plans at Lockhart River and Moa. Clint's efforts to establish a Co-operative Training College in Cape York Peninsula foundered because of insufficient financial support and because of his immediate need to train a qualified baker for the fledgling Moa Island Co-operative. He sought an alternative site in Sydney and was given 'Tranby', a mansion in Glebe, by Father John Hope of Christchurch, St Laurence. Hope had introduced the young Clint to Christian Socialism and led him to ordination. In 1958 Tranby commenced the training of two Aboriginal students sponsored by ABM's co-operative fund. The annual summer schools soon established Tranby's reputation as the leader in Aboriginal training for self-management, twenty years before the concept was seriously considered at the federal or state levels.[20]

Ironically, the co-operatives were by then confronting mounting difficulties. The development of plastics caused the collapse of the trochus shell industry at Lockhart River and then the pearlshell industry to which Warby had turned. Many members of the Co-operative were again unemployed. ABM was unable to supply the finance and staff to allow diversification and the new Bishop of Carpentaria, John Matthews, was not committed to mission co-operatives.[21] Neither the Aboriginal and Islander people nor the mission had the legal claim to the land to attract financial capital to explore the mission's mining potential or to develop the cotton industry beyond the trial stage.[22] All that remained was the co-operative retail store. The community was once again heavily dependent on church and government funds. Recognising the demoralising effect of unemployment on the Aborigines and its increased financial burden on the church, ABM recommended a reversal of Warby's policy of keeping men employed on the mission with their families and again actively encouraged them to take outside work.[23] The clock had been turned back a decade.

Clint was criticised for not attending to routine tasks, for the lack of progress, for building up unrealistic expectations among the Aborigines and Islanders, and was accused of financial incompetence.[24] Bishop Ian Shevill of North Queensland had also accused Clint of being a Communist.[25] Shevill was supported by Dr Noble, the Liberal Party Minister for Health and Home Affairs. The Nicklin Coalition Government had taken office in August 1957 when the Gair Government had split into the Australian Labor Party and Queensland Labor Party factions. This was the first time in twenty-five years that there was a non-Labor government in Queensland

and only the second time since 1915.[26] On two separate occasions, Noble alleged that Church officials were being 'used by the Communists' to disseminate Russian propaganda against Australia and against Liberal governments. Russia had embarrassed Australia at the United Nations over its treatment of Aborigines on matters published by the trade union movement. He referred to 'missionary people', obviously Clint, spending hours with Communist-dominated trades and labour councils. When Noble visited Lockhart River, he likened the co-operative's plans for farming to the Russian collective farm.[27] Warby, perhaps, plumbed a greater depth: 'There seems little question that they are afraid of the co-operative idea, as they consider it will bind the Aboriginal people together and make them too strong'.[28] An apparently subversive process in which missions were not meant to be involved.

The new Bishop of Carpentaria, John Matthews, and senior Carpentaria mission staff were now openly critical of the co-operative approach. Clint was seen as a destabilising influence and forbidden entry to any Aboriginal or Torres Strait Island missions in the Diocese of Carpentaria, a decision that was supported by the Queensland Government. Matthews was concerned that co-operative members had gained the false impression that their legal status had changed, that they were free from mission and government control.[29] In Queensland in the 1960s, the idea that black Australians might think they were free deeply disturbed the whites controlling them. The concept of empowerment of the poor enshrined in the co-operative model was blamed for this disquiet. The bishop was also concerned that he was left out of the lines of authority in co-operative matters, especially in relation to finance and staff.[30]

On 29 March 1963, the Lockhart River Co-operative was voluntarily wound up. The Aboriginal members opted to cut their losses and turn their backs on the co-operative way which, by now, seemed unprofitable, unsupported by any mission officials, and burdened by the white people's bookkeeping and fiscal mysteries.[31]

Denied access to ABM supported missions in the dioceses of Carpentaria and North Queensland, Clint could only communicate with these communities by letter or through the students they sent to Tranby. He turned his attention to Aboriginal people in New South Wales and was instrumental in forming the farming-based Numbahging Co-operative in 1959 at Cabbage Tree Island, which was functioning into the 1980s. In 1967, under the energetic chairman, Jacob Abednego, Moa Island Co-operative established its bakery, which survived for a number of years with only token support from the diocese and no support from the Queensland Government.[32] Other Aboriginal groups considering co-operatives in New

South Wales, Queensland, South Australia and Western Australia sought Clint's advice.[33] Some, such as those at the Anglican missions at Forrest River and Mitchell River, were stillborn but others, such as the Yarrabah Co-operative Bakery, were established. In 1974 Percy Neal, the baker and manager at Yarrabah, completed his apprenticeship in Sydney through Tranby and won a cup and first prize at East Sydney Technical College for baking wholemeal bread. In the same year, the Clump Point Co-operative near Tully in North Queensland was awaiting government approval to commence operations.[34] Clint and Tranby had played a formative role here as well.

In May 1962, ABM terminated its Co-operative Department. From December 1962, the ABM Christian Community Co-operative Ltd moved towards independence and autonomy. Its name was changed to Co-operatives for Aborigines Ltd and subsequently the body assumed full responsibility for the operation of Tranby Co-operative College and other co-operative endeavours. The Anglican Church had distanced itself from the co-operative movement it had endorsed so enthusiastically less than a decade previously.

Around the same time responsibility for settlement management was transferred to the Queensland Department of Aboriginal and Islander Affairs, commencing in 1960 with Yarrabah and followed in 1967 by Edward River, Mitchell River and Lockhart River. In 1968, the Forrest River Mission was closed. At the 1966 General Synod, the board amended its constitution to make clear its responsibility not only to those on remote communities, but also to all Aborigines in Australia.[35] Thus freed of old mission-oriented policy restrictions and their associated financial burdens, by 1967 the ABM board found it had to enter a new stage in its relationship with Aboriginal Australians. These developments will be explored later in this chapter. ABM's venture into the co-operative movement was, in retrospect, the first step in its withdrawal from the control of Aboriginal communities.

The amazing thing is not that the Anglican co-operative movement failed but that it was introduced at all in Queensland in the 1950s and that Tranby still exists as an instrument for the Aboriginal and Islander empowerment that the Aboriginal Christian Co-operative Movement hoped to achieve. It was an acknowledgement by a few enlightened missionaries of the failure of the previous paternalistic mission policy to meet the needs of Aboriginal and Islander people.

The End of Missionary Domination

Although the board, at the national office in Sydney, periodically reflected seriously upon the implications of its continued administration of the

Aboriginal communities created by its missions, the decisions to end this state of affairs were taken in the remote dioceses responsible for their day-to-day running. There the decisions were based on insufficient funds, inadequate government support, and the difficulty of staffing the various mission villages. In the case of Forrest River, supervised by now by a subcommittee in Perth, the conclusion was reached that, after over fifty years, the results were not worth the effort. Indeed, ABM's inability to institute major changes in mission philosophy and practice, as indicated by the failure of the Aboriginal Christian Co-operative Movement, stands in sharp contrast to the growth in social awareness that was evident in Sydney.

Bishop GH Cranswick, chairman from 1942 to 1949, is nowhere near as dominant a figure in the history of ABM as his predecessor, Canon Needham. However, his comments about the historical experience of Aborigines and the responsibilities resting upon white Australians for their future, as was mentioned earlier in this chapter, suggested that the 'new age' in mission history he referred to had dawned, even for Aborigines.[36] In Cranswick's instructions to the new chaplain-superintendent at Forrest River, the Rev. Keith Coaldrake, he attacked negative stereotypes, elaborated upon the richness of Aboriginal culture and the poor treatment they had previously received. He suggested surprising models, the camps organised for Aborigines by the army in the Northern Territory. Here they experienced 'security and fellowship, community life, and attention to diet and health' in contrast to their previous existence on missions and government settlements. Cranswick insisted: 'It is for the natives to choose whether they will accept...a better way and truer belief...or will modify their own codes and belief, or will build up some blend both Christian and native'. The missionary had to be 'fulfillers and not destroyers of the ancient law of the Aborigine' to help 'these men and women left over from the stone age to survive and prosper in that contact with our advanced civilisation that has now become inevitable'.[37] Although these instructions are still clearly daubed with ideas from the past, there is no escaping the more enlightened vision. While still maintaining the importance of the missionary role, he admitted mistakes had been made in the past and that methods had sometimes been unsatisfactory. His lengthy 'Instructions' codified as 'The Aim and Policy of the Australian Board of Missions' concluded with the challenge that all involved in the missionary task had to ask from year to year: 'What is it we are really trying to do?'

The experience of Keith Coaldrake clearly illustrates the conflict between the idealism emanating from Sydney and the reality of the mission field. Although, no more authoritarian or puritanical than many of his predecessors, and certainly dedicated to the missionary task, he could not develop the empathy to work co-operatively with Aboriginal people. His own upbringing in white Australia and the mission's history of total white dominance worked against him and in 1954 he was replaced as superintendent.[38] Under new management, Forrest River Mission's population remained very low, while the costs and debt increased. It staggered from crisis to crisis until September 1968 when the Perth committee responsible for its administration closed it. Most of the Aborigines moved to Wyndham where they were unhappy with the slum conditions they were expected to endure and the social problems that confronted them as refugees. In 1972 thirty adults and children moved back to the old mission site and re-established themselves as the autonomous Aboriginal community of Oombulgurri. They received extensive financial and administrative support from the federal government and the population of the new community grew.[39]

There were many other examples of the growing social awareness in Sydney of the problems confronting Aboriginal people in Australian society. Archdeacon Robertson, ABM chairman from 1949 to 1956, was clearly aware that missions had to contend with an Aboriginal response that was at least in part conditioned by colonisation. He wrote to Sister Delaney soon after her arrival at Mitchell River Mission:

> They do not take discipline easily and it is very hard to change a nation of people who have been almost slaves into a nation of free people. We gave them such a bad time in the early days, we have been giving them such a bad time since...[40]

In 1966 Canon Frank Coaldrake, chairman from 1957 to 1967, challenged his board and supporters of ABM to support the struggle for Aboriginal citizenship rights. 'The citizen's rights of the Aborigines and Torres Strait Islanders in the State of Queensland have long been defective...The Church in Australia should not ignore the fact that so many Australian Anglicans are being kept in a condition of bondage'.[41] Earlier, in 1960, he had informed the Board that the 6000 Torres Strait Islanders were 'Anglicans in poverty — Anglicans in bondage'.[42] The church, of course, had been a willing agent in imposing the bondage.

By 1961, ABM, in association with the Diocese of Carpentaria, had unsuccessfully sought permanent tenure of reserve lands, not only at Lockhart River for the co-operative, but also at Mitchell River where the diocese was developing the Carpentaria Aboriginal Pastoral Company. The Queensland Government even rejected a proposal to allow Aborigines on Anglican missions to buy and own their own homes because it suggested a permanent Aboriginal presence that the government could not contemplate.[43] Increasingly, ABM found that its plans for Aboriginal people on its missions were in conflict with Queensland Government policy: 'To be in control of himself, his family and his property he [the Aboriginal] must be exempted from the Act'. But if he gained exemption he was not allowed to live on an Aboriginal reserve or mission 'among his own people, in his own country'.[44] ABM found itself caught up with other churches, especially those involved in Aboriginal missions, in an exploration of what legal right Aborigines had to their land, an investigation that resulted in the Australian Council of Churches' support for land rights and compensation for the loss of land.[45]

There was also an awareness of internal contradictions in mission policy and practice. From the beginning a caste system had been created of white missionaries and Aboriginal people that was manifested in the siting of the missionary residences apart from those of the Aboriginal Christians within the mission compound. The camp for visiting Aborigines and those who had not accepted mission authority or been accepted into it was completely outside of the compound at a distance where each group could maintain separate existences with a minimum of disturbance, one from the other. While the missionaries thought of themselves as the ones who were being shielded from the noise and lifestyle of the camp, it is equally clear that the camp Aborigines derived a similar benefit.[46]

The caste system, however, extended well beyond the geographical placement of the living quarters. The quality and size of the missionaries' living quarters, while often extremely primitive compared to what was the norm in white Australia, reflected the superior caste the whites assumed within the mission community.

A number of reports were made about the perpetually troubled Forrest River Mission in the late 1940s and 1950s when closing the mission was being seriously considered. They emphasised the contradictions posed by the caste system within missions. In 1947, the Rev. RB Cranswick pointed out that the ration system of payment not only made mission 'inmates' into beggars, but also acted as a disincentive to working harder than they had to. They were obviously passively resisting the 'prison-like dis-cipline, which seemed to be enforced for its own sake and with little apparent reason'.

In his most damning assessment of the church's long mission to Aborigines, Cranswick concluded that it was on the spiritual side that the mission had been able to do least because of this 'guard–inmate' situation and that the Aborigines 'have seen little of what Christianity is, and therefore are not attracted'. They were made to feel their inferiority not only at every meal, but even on a picnic, as one at Forrest River dramatically demonstrated:

> They see white people keeping all the best for themselves and have become accustomed to expect it of us. Scraps of food left on the plates of the staff are eagerly sought for. During the first week of my visit to the mission we went to Camera pool. At meal time they made our fire, got us improvised seats and saw us sit down to turkey and tinned fruit, having already carried everything necessary all the way. They then went away elsewhere to a meal of damper and tea. There seems to be a very definite feeling of inferiority on their part.

He pointed out that 'the prison-like discipline' had created 'an atmosphere of suspicion and mistrust in which it is impossible to do much Christian work', and that 'Corporal punishment, chaining of natives and punishments which show a complete lack of respect for native customs, seem to have been the rule back to the early days of the mission'. The 'chaining of natives' referred to the chaining of Aborigines found guilty of a serious misdemeanour to a tree and so combining imprisonment with public humiliation — the equivalent of putting someone in the stocks.

This regime had been so internalised that Aborigines who were given some authority thought this was the only way to run a mission. One said: 'I owe what I am to the thrashings Mr...gave me'. In the 1970s and 1980s, some older Aborigines told me about the 'civilising', Christianising effects of the dormitory system at Yarrabah. In 1947 Cranswick was able to point to the ultimate contradiction in mission policy. It aimed at creating a new spiritual understanding by denigrating and disallowing the expression of Aboriginal spirituality: 'The native customs seem to provide endless opportunities on which to build Christian teaching, but we have shown a lack of respect for these'.[47]

There was also an awareness, by the end of the Second World War, that the missions were going nowhere. With the exception of Edward River, the first stages of what was then believed to be the evangelisation process had been completed. All Aborigines in the mission compound were now baptised and, if old enough, confirmed as Anglican Christians. Their understanding and commitment to their faith varied probably as much as that within any parish in the suburbs. Keith Coaldrake had felt the need to state this in his report to the Board and to his Perth committee:

> The exact nature of the spiritual work here is, I think, not understood by most people. Briefly, the period of its foundation is now part of the history of this Mission, the place functions more as an isolated country settlement today. Likewise, the period of purely evangelical preaching and teaching on a very elementary level, and the proselytising of heathen

primitives has passed and we now deal with natives who have most had lifelong Christian teaching and influence. Most of the teaching is on the Sunday School level.[48]

Professor Elkin, an ordained Anglican priest himself, was nowhere near as complacent about this level of achievement: 'Our Church services and bell-ringing are all of a piece with the general routine we have introduced. The Compound is a boarding-school from which only death, or perhaps old age, will release its inhabitants'.[49] The boarding-school label could be applied to all missions and government reserves where entry and departure were controlled. In 1946, Elkin pointed to the self-perpetuating apathy these closed institutions had generated:

> The young men of 1928 are still lining up daily to be allotted their tasks, having become specialists in nothing, having no sense of independence, having no money or other exchange-economy through which to express themselves in satisfying physical and mental needs. And all they can look forward to is a parasitic old age, probably out in the Camp...when they should be in their prime, as leaders of social groups, they are leading an aimless existence; unpaid workers on a Mission which, outwardly at least, gets nowhere...

He said of Forrest River, but it applied to nearly all missions and government reserves at this time, and for decades after: 'We are the cause of the apathy and penury of the people, and we ought to do something about it'.[50]

Elkin's solution was starkly simple and reflected his own limited expectations for Aboriginal people. The church should learn from the Queensland Government and, as a consequence, provide a much more expensive infrastructure and spend a great deal more each year. As he pointed out: 'The work in hand is to run an institution of a peculiar kind — the building up of a community'.[51]

Consequently, by the 1950s, the Board had been confronted by the sociological and religious contradictions and problems inherent in governing Aboriginal communities as its executive officer, the Rev. M.A. Warren said, 'to maintain a work which only in its minor aspects could be called evangelistic'.[52]

* * * *

Yarrabah, like Forrest River Mission, was beset with administrative problems from its inception but there was soon a great deal more to show for it. A sizeable mission village of over 800 people developed to which the Queensland Government was only too happy to send Aborigines it considered in need of such confinement, more so than to any other Queensland mission. As was pointed out in the previous chapter, there was conflict with the Queensland Government because it considered the church gave too little attention to the industrial side of the mission and too much to the religious, especially because of its failure to make the mission anywhere near self-supporting. The government was also drawn into the conflict within the Anglican Church over the administrative control of Yarrabah.

Although within the Diocese of North Queensland, Yarrabah had been administered from its beginning in 1892 by ABM's Sydney based executive council because North Queensland was unable or unwilling to assume responsibility. The Bishop of North Queensland was responsible for overseeing its spiritual life. Like the Diocese of North West Australia, North Queensland was a poor, struggling diocese in a vast, sparsely populated region. In 1910, when the Queensland Government objected to dealing with a New South Wales committee, an administrative committee was set up in Brisbane with the Archbishop as chairman. This situation persisted until 1937 when Bishop John Oliver Feetham of North Queensland gained administrative control for his diocese after a bitter struggle with the ABM board that began in 1929.[53] The correspondence contains serious allegations by Feetham of poor management and some agreement from ABM that it was in need of improvement. Subsequent events suggest that the North Queensland diocese was even less capable of meeting the challenges implicit in governing a mission community.

From 1948, the Queensland Government put pressure on the Yarrabah committee to improve living conditions on its mission and was in turn challenged to provide more adequate financial support because the church was doing government work. Even after receiving a grant of £25,000, the Yarrabah Committee considered it would have to hand over the reserve to the government unless it received more adequate support.

The government met all Yarrabah's accumulated debt in return for a position on the committee. It was still much cheaper to retain church involvement than to take on full responsibility.[54]

The difficulty of finding and retaining suitable staff had always been a problem at Yarrabah, as at all of ABM's Aboriginal missions. In 1952, the decision was made to employ Anglican Church Army officers as superintendents. Their discipline, training, and commitment to evangelism and service led them to set high standards for themselves and to aim at a similar response in the people to whom they ministered. This had proved attractive to some Aboriginal people at Palm Island and Yarrabah and a small number entered the Church Army training college at Newcastle. Some of these graduated and eventually worked among their people. Bishop Arthur Malcolm and Sister Muriel Stanley of Yarrabah and the Rev.s Alan and Norman Polgen of Palm Island owed their Christian formation to the Church Army example and training.[55] However, many Yarrabah Aborigines objected to the greater demands the Church Army officers made upon the labour force and to the increased penalties they imposed upon those offending against mission rules. Eventually, in 1957, the Yarrabah Aborigines staged a strike to protest against their inadequate rations, poor working conditions, and the autocratic rule of the superintendent.

In retrospect, it seems that the Church Army Officers, at that time unfamiliar with the aspirations and problems confronting Aboriginal people, were trying to impose the strategies of the 1930s and 1940s upon a people who were increasingly aware of what was normal and acceptable. In 1956, eighty-six men and women were employed outside of the mission. By this time, contact had been made with the trade union movement and some union officials were becoming concerned at the living conditions in Aboriginal communities. The development of vast bauxite deposits at Weipa, a Presbyterian mission, inevitably focused the attention of the relevant trade unions on the Cape York Peninsula mission.[56]

The Superintendent, Captain Wilcox, with the support of the Queensland Government, expelled three leaders of the strike. Approximately two hundred residents of Yarrabah, many of them supporters of the strike, were quickly given exemption from the Queensland legislation controlling Aborigines as wards of the state and left the mission over the next two years. This massive increase in exemptions was publicly justified as part of the policy of assimilation. The hypocrisy escaped comment and Yarrabah seemed to settle down. A social welfare committee, similar to those on government settlements, was formed to involve staff and Aboriginal residents; rations were increased; more attention was given to health; more trained teachers were employed; and farming was expanded with the assistance of the Department of Native Affairs.[57] However, when the Minister, Dr Noble, and the senior officers of the Department of Native Affairs, Con O'Leary and Pat Killoran, visited Yarrabah in late 1959, they were shocked at the condition it was in. They confided to John Warby when they moved on to Lockhart River that Yarrabah was a 'headache'. They needed to spend £250,000 on improvements and would not commit such a large outlay on a non-government settlement. Perhaps, even more worrying was the rowdy resentment expressed at a community meeting that lasted until 2.00 a.m. that O'Leary and Killoran attended. The Aboriginal residents kept 'interrupting and shouting out that the Superintendent was a liar etc etc'. Noble was also concerned at the conditions the people at nearby Bessie Point were living under, many of whom had left Yarrabah in the previous two years. Noble considered the treatment of the Bessie Point people 'a disgrace'. They were at last forced to consider proposing to Bishop Shevill that the Queensland Government take over administration of Yarrabah.[58]

By this time, the Townsville committee and the ABM had had enough, even though the government was by then contributing £50,000 per year to Yarrabah's upkeep. The Superintendent reported in the diocesan yearbook: 'The Church at Yarrabah is no longer running a mission but a large Social Service project beyond the financial and manpower resources of the Church'.[59] After a decade of propping up the mission to avoid the inevitable, the Queensland Government took over administrative and financial responsibility on 1 July 1960, even paying the chaplain's salary. The Church of England was guaranteed that no other religious denomination would be allowed access to Yarrabah. Until there was a schism among Aboriginal Christians in 1990, St Alban's Anglican Church was the only one in the community.

In 1960, no one expressed the view that the Diocese of Carpentaria missions should also be handed over to the government. After a special visit to the three Aboriginal missions in which he saw the desperately poor conditions under which the Aborigines and missionaries lived, the chairman, Frank Coaldrake, was still optimistic for the future. He had confidence in the diocese, the wealth of natural resources of the region, and the goodwill of the Aborigines at Lockhart, Mitchell, and Edward River Missions. If ABM had been able to draw more upon the resources of the Queensland Government or had the capital of multinational companies like Comalco or BHP, Coaldrake's optimism might have been justified.[60]

The new bishop, John Matthews, had earlier visited the diocese and was appalled at the state of the missions. He had then taken up a senior appointment in Carpentaria before being consecrated bishop. In 1961 he reported that the three missions were 'almost at the point of disintegrating' because of lack of staff and the pressure on those working there. 'It does not look as if the Church in Australia is vitally interested in this work', he wrote, echoing the cry missionaries had uttered during the previous hundred years.[61]

The first indication that the Bishop of Carpentaria might seek a radical solution to the problems confronting his missions surfaced the same year when he suggested moving Lockhart River Mission fifty kilometres to be closer to Portland Roads wharf and Iron Range aerodrome, a plan the government was ready to agree to. This plan was then abandoned. With the collapse of the Lockhart River Aboriginal Christian Co-operative, the future of the mission looked so difficult that in 1962 consideration was given to moving the whole community to Edward River and Mitchell River missions, provided 'the consent of the people concerned is freely given'.[62] After discussions with the Queensland Government in which he had requested greatly increased government subsidies to Carpentaria missions, Coaldrake suggested that the people be moved to the government settlement of Bamaga at the tip of Cape York Peninsula where they would have much better food rations, educational and medical facilities, employment prospects and housing than the church could supply. They would thus have become the government's administrative and financial responsibility. All of these suggested shifts were over distances of approximately three hundred kilometres. Fifty people from Lockhart River were persuaded to move to a village at Bamaga which was given the Lockhart River name, Umagico. The rest of the community soon made it clear that they did not wish to move. The decision was then made to relocate the village in the mission reserve near Portland Road wharf and the airport, as first planned. There, in its present site, it was at least much easier to service.

By this time, Bishop Matthews had concluded he could not get adequate funding from the Queensland Government to run the missions satisfactorily. Aboriginal people and missionaries would have had to continue to exist in deplorable, degrading conditions with substandard services beyond the means of the diocese or ABM to improve. Consequently, with the support of ABM, he decided to transfer all the Aboriginal missions in Cape York Peninsula to Queensland Government administration. The takeover of Lockhart River, Mitchell River, and Edward River Missions occurred on 1 May 1967.[63]

When the removal of Lockhart people was considered in 1962, Coaldrake emphasised that all associated costs would have to be borne by the Queensland Government and that, in the new situation, the church would only exercise a pastoral ministry. The Yarrabah model was fresh in his mind.[64]

There were a number of other factors that supported the conclusion that the administration of the missions should be transferred to the Queensland Government. Diocesan concern extended well beyond the bishop. As well as the government reports referred to in Chapter 2, a number of church reports in the early 1960s had indicated how deplorably inadequate the communities were in terms of food, housing, clothing, sanitation, mission development and maintenance. One report submitted to the board by the superintendent of Edward River, Gordon Green, finished with a section headed in bold capitals: 'THE CONTINUING DISGRACE OF ABORIGINAL LIVING STANDARDS AND

LACK OF REASONABLE IMPROVEMENTS ON ABORIGINAL MISSIONS'. Green urged the church to 'make public the scandalous conditions on these missions' unless the government quickly remedied their secular aspects. However, he sheeted home the responsibility to the church for being so pusillanimous in its dealings with the government.[65]

In addition, by 1966, church and government administrators had accepted the inevitability and the logic of the transfer. In February 1964, cyclone Dora had destroyed Edward River and Mitchell River missions. The government had accepted the responsibility of rebuilding the two townships at standards comparable to government settlements, a task clearly beyond the Anglican Church. ABM began a special appeal reaching out ecumenically beyond the Anglican Church within Australia and overseas through inter-church aid, raising a 'generous' $84,000, which was enough at least to rebuild the church in each community. Thus the government was involved in rebuilding all the Anglican missions in the Diocese of Carpentaria and resiting Lockhart River Mission. By this time, the 'goodwill' of the Aborigines on these three missions was wearing thin. Many now worked outside the missions and were increasingly aware of how poor their conditions were and how bleak their future. The chairman reported in 1966: 'In these two areas [Cape York Aboriginal missions and the Torres Strait mission] there has been much unrest as the people's expectations rise'. ABM was unable to meet the expectations or to persuade the government of their urgency. The government's response to ABM's request that it take responsibility for the schools had been met with a slow and hesitant agreement. Finally, ABM accepted the impossibility of staffing the Cape York missions. There were always important positions vacant and a rapid turnover. Few staff lasted longer than the initial two-year term, many not even that long. Where ABM could expect a missionary to serve five or ten years in other places, in Carpentaria they could be burnt out in two years, thus magnifying greatly the recruitment problem. 'There is no greater challenge to sacrificial services anywhere in the Church', the Chairman, Frank Coaldrake, lamented. It was part of the challenge that finally had beaten the church.[66]

On 15 September 1966, the Queensland Minister for Education and Aboriginal Affairs, Jack Pizzey, met with the Bishop of Carpentaria and the chairman of ABM and agreed that the transfer of the three Cape York Anglican missions should occur as soon as practicable to make available greater resources for their management. The bishop and the minister agreed 'that this would be a transfer of management but that Church and Government would continue in partnership to serve the interests of the Aboriginal people'. The Anglican Church was left with its religious monopoly of the three missions for at least the next ten years.

The board and the missionaries in Cape York were very much aware that, when the Queensland Government had taken over the Presbyterian mission at Mapoon in 1963, it had been closed down and the people moved, some by force, to Bamaga. In 1966, Weipa was taken over by the government and a large part of the Aboriginal reserve was cancelled and thrown open for bauxite mining by Comalco. The bishop was assured that the government would maintain the three Anglican Aboriginal reserves at their existing extent and that the cattle, stock and plant would be vested in the Aboriginal Welfare Trust, thus assuring ABM that profits from the very large herds of cattle that the diocese had built up would not be used instead of government expenditure. The board noted that the transfer was part of a 'general trend to transfer missions to Government control throughout Australia'.[67] In Queensland, beginning with discussions over Yarrabah in 1960, the ABM missions had initiated the trend with a reluctant government.

The concept that underpinned all of the negotiations was assimilation, sometimes expressed with such frankness that it seemed to be assimilation gone mad. The degree of social engineering that was contemplated with well-intentioned equanimity was breathtaking. 'The training of Aborigines in the development of skills which will enable them to take their place in the general community is the avowed aim of government programmes', Frank Coaldrake observed in 1962. 'This must mean the eventual movement of Aborigines from Cape York into southern townships and rural areas', except for the aged and incapacitated who would be institutionalised in their mission locality and a small number who could find employment in the few projects being developed in the Peninsula, most associated with mining. Consequently, it was seen to be no great hardship for most Lockhart River or Yarrabah people to be transferred to other areas if that was necessary. Coaldrake believed that eventually two hundred of the three hundred Lockhart people 'could be ready for absorption into the general community in the South'.

It is clear that at this time, for the government and the Anglican Church, the rebuilding of Edward and Mitchell River communities and the re-siting and rebuilding of Lockhart River Mission were but temporary expedients until Aboriginal reserves ceased to be needed. By 1967, confronted with the reality of the closure of Mapoon and the transfer of its people, and the reduction of Weipa Reserve to a fraction of its original size, the Anglican Church had realised that the rights and wishes of the Aborigines deserved greater consideration.

The board had formulated its policy with regard to Aboriginal reserve land in 1959 in association with the ecumenical National Missionary Council. It stipulated 'security of land tenure for residence and economic enterprise must be provided for Aborigines and Missions in Reserves'; and

> Australia's honour demands that Aborigines be considered for preferential treatment concerning any use of reserve lands...In the case of unexempted, or backward persons, such rights should vest in trustees or guardians on their behalf. Such provisions are an integral part of any assimilation process.

The stand was clear despite the ethnocentric paternalism starkly evident in its expression. As the Anglican Church prepared to divest itself with, in retrospect, a somewhat indecent haste, Coaldrake asked his board:

> [S]hould the Church respect the people's wishes and uphold them, even if the Church is convinced of the ultimate need for the things planned by the Government?[68]

To its credit, the answer was given in the affirmative.

By allowing the government to take over the four missions in North Queensland in the 1960s, the church performed an extraordinary miracle, a twentieth century example of the loaves and fishes. Resources for which it had begged for so long began instantly to appear. Plans were made to completely rehouse the residents of Yarrabah in 120 new houses. Twenty were occupied within a year of the takeover, part of a massive building program that would transform Yarrabah. Milk and vitamins were provided for the children and trained teachers improved the standard of schooling. Trained staff worked in maternal and child welfare clinics, and hygiene, education, nutrition, indoor plumbing, and sanitation programs were developed to make Yarrabah a healthier place. Powdered milk, Farex™, Baby Rice, Vegemite™, peanut paste, cheese, Hypol™ and fruit, common enough in Cairns but luxuries in Yarrabah, were made available to young children. Electricity was introduced; Yarrabah was fully electrified by 1965. A new primary school was constructed and taken over by the Queensland Education Department in 1962.[69] At Edward River and Mitchell River, the extensive rebuilding programs had begun in 1964 after cyclone Dora. After the takeover in 1967 the provision of services and amenities was similar to that at Yarrabah. At all missions a cash economy replaced the previous ration and mixture of ration and cash economies that the missions had used.[70]

The miracle the church had wrought was, of course, the necessary effort and expenditure the government needed to bring these communities up to the same standard as the other Aboriginal reserves at Bamaga, Palm Island, Cherbourg, and Woorabinda. The effort devoted to hygiene, sanitation, diet, reticulated water, and community health programs reflected the need to raise the health of the community. The government was attempting to meet the minimum standards on Yarrabah and the other missions now that it, and not the church, was responsible. Yet, as noted in Chapter 2, the consistently poor standards of housing, diet, clothing, education, and community health were well known from government inspections. In the 1920s 90 per cent of Yarrabah Aborigines had been infected with hookworm; and 80 per cent were reported to be suffering from skin diseases in the 1930s. In 1938, the anthropologist, Norman Tindale, had reported the rations were 'only enough to prevent starvation'. In 1935 Dr Raphael Cilento, a government medical officer, had reported the diet 'entirely lacking in vitamins...and represents an actual menace to healthy development'. The government had criticised the dormitory system and the close supervision of girls and unmarried women although similar supervision existed at Palm Island. Yarrabah's education standards were poor even in comparison with the low standards expected and accepted on government reserves.[71]

Yet, there was a good deal of justification in Bishop Shevill's angry protest when the Minister for Aboriginal Affairs, Dr Noble, informed the press in 1959 that Yarrabah Mission 'lacks all facilities'.[72]

'Of course, we want housing, a new school, a new hospital, and an airstrip. For these things we have been battling for seven years', the bishop retorted. He pointed out that each year they had estimated the costs of servicing the community and each year their requests had been 'cut to the bone by the Government of Queensland'. By 1967 the government's cheap ride at the expense of the Anglican Church and to the cruel detriment of the Aboriginal people was over.

By 1968, the post-missionary age had dawned for the Aborigines on ABM supported missions. The theological significance of that was probably lost on the Aborigines. One set of administrators who had been given authority over their communities was replaced by another; the Department of Aboriginal and Islander Affairs. The Anglican Church moved from its central role in the secular activities of each community, to which it had devoted such a great deal of its efforts, to the periphery. For many Aborigines the religious trappings of the mission years lost their significance. The move from mission to church meant that the senior advocate of culture change was now the government. Aborigines were keen to accept many innovations from the white intruders while wishing to maintain basic cultural values. As John Taylor said of the Edward River people, they bound themselves to Europeans 'in a culture-donor/culture-recipient relationship'. Once the missionaries withdrew from this central role, they turned to the Department of Aboriginal and Islander Advancement.[73]

Acceptance

In 1967, ABM developed a new policy which Frank Coaldrake entitled 'Acceptance: The Next Step Forward'. Its goal was the acceptance of Aborigines as Aborigines by white Australians and the acceptance of white Australians by Aborigines. It accommodated the missionary situation ABM was in by emphasising the responsibility of the dioceses and parishes to minister to Aborigines within their geographic area of responsibility, something, as we have noted, they had lamentably failed to do except in isolated cases. The acceptance of Aborigines as inferiors living in an inferior culture that needed to be replaced was an artefact of colonisation. This had not only blamed the victims, it had also absolved most white Christians from having to confront their participation in the process. Their understanding and expression of their Christian faith developed within the suffocating shroud of European power and domination.

Coaldrake observed in 1961:

> The first reaction to a parish Aboriginal problem seems to be the suggestion that this is a work for the A.B.M. While this is flattering to the Board, it is a shallow appreciation of the nature of the problem in the parish.[74]

ABM promised to support such initiatives financially and, if necessary, in locating suitable staff.

ABM would continue to support through the relevant dioceses, chaplaincies and welfare work at Yarrabah, Palm Island, Mitchell River, Edward River, Lockhart River, Woorabinda, Lake Tyers and St Mary's Hostel in Alice Springs. It was also associated with state missionary bodies in supporting such work at Point Pierce in South Australia and Forrest River in Western Australia. The ABM board agreed to accept further requests for such support.

Throughout the policy statement there is an awareness that a new, young 'aggressive and by ordinary standards, rough and radical' Aboriginal leadership was emerging. Consequently, the policy aimed not only at understanding such leadership but also at assisting in the development of new leaders at Tranby or other educational institutions. The board also offered to meet the full cost of a theological college course for any Aboriginal accepted by a bishop as a candidate for ordination to the priesthood. The policy statement envisaged the appointment to the national office of a full-time officer for Aboriginal Advancement 'to assist the Aborigines, the Community or the Church, in promoting the mutual acceptance of Aboriginal and European peoples'. It was envisaged that an Aboriginal would occupy this very challenging position, one that would be important if the board were to be directly involved in a ministry to Aboriginal people. In effect, it was an attempt by ABM to remain significant in the Anglican Church's association with Aboriginal people.

More important, perhaps, than the details spelt out by the policy statement was the change in philosophy. Although still framed within the current federal policy of assimilation and still envisaging a continuance of the partnership between the state and federal governments and ABM, it considerably modified the policy to include the concept of pluralism:

> Acceptance is what Aborigines feel they need. Acceptance — without a demand for alteration and conformity — is an idea which the European people in the community will need to accept.[75]

Indeed, it challenged the Ministers' Welfare Council to refine its policy envisaging 'a Single Australian Community' so as not to deny 'the possibility of pluralism ethnically and culturally'.

This was a time of ferment in Aboriginal advancement. The Aboriginal protest movement of the 1960s had raised the awareness of many white Australians. Aboriginal leaders such as Don Brady, Margaret Valadian, Charles Perkins and Chicka Dixon could command attention; the ability of Aborigines to exercise influence through such organisations as the Federal Council for the Advancement of Aborigines and Torres Strait Islanders (FCAATSI) and a multitude of other Aboriginal organisations and committees, many of them short lived, had increased. Influential politicians like the Liberal, Bill Wentworth, and the Labor front bencher, Gordon Bryant, were working with Aboriginal people and gradually raising the awareness of their parties. Academics like Charles Rowley, WEH Stanner, John Mulvaney, Lorna Lippman, and Colin Tatz were influencing students and younger academics to reconsider Australian history, sociology, anthropology and politics to include an analysis of the place of Aborigines within Australian society. In 1967, referenda had been passed with huge majorities to allow the Aborigines and Torres Strait Islanders to be counted in the Australian census and the federal government to pass legislation and to provide services for them. Previously, the Australian constitution had restricted such responsibility to the states.

Alongside of this activity the policy of 'Acceptance' might seem very small beer, but its adoption by a conservative church, ahead of government policy and general community thinking, was in fact its great leap forward. It also pointed to future major developments within the church that would attempt to establish a respectful working relationship between black and white Anglicans. Some Indigenous Australians, like some non-

Indigenous Australians, would see the church as central to their life, or at least as important.

At this time, Aboriginal land rights was a political issue that divided the nation. A cautious statement in 'Acceptance' reflected this divisiveness and probably the difference of opinion at board level:

> The Board is aware of the problem of Aboriginal land rights and will continue to study the issues involved in the light of a policy of acceptance.[76]

The policy statement had been widely circulated for comment, although only among white Australians with experience in Aboriginal missions, gaining general approval except that the secretary of the Methodist Overseas Mission, the Rev. A Ellemor, favoured a stronger statement on land rights.[77] As the policy aimed at mutual acceptance of Aborigines and white Australians, the half-heartedness of the statement on land rights was clearly aimed at gaining approval from the dominant group in the church. As there was little likelihood Aboriginal Anglicans would read it, Coaldrake may have considered this a price he had to pay.

The policy statement had recommended that the board employ an 'officer for Aboriginal advancement' to promote Aboriginal advancement and to foster the mutual acceptance of Aboriginal and white Australians in the community or the church. Although it was apparently not realised at the time, this appointment was to become the sole strategy ABM was left with for maintaining a direct involvement with Aboriginal people. After 1967, ABM became more and more a funding agency for projects and ministries involving Aboriginal people. It also remained involved with recruiting staff for the dioceses although, as often as not, the dioceses acted independently. The board minutes contain impressive statements of concern and analyses of the Anglican Church's desired relationship with Aboriginal people, but any implementation was left to the dioceses.

Increasingly the dioceses with Aboriginal ministries evolved their own plans of action to meet the needs as they saw them and then turned for support to ABM or the other relevant Anglican funding agencies, the National Home Mission Fund and CMS. Thus in 1971 the National Home Mission Fund took over the church's share of the funding of St Mary's in Alice Springs. In 1980, the then chairman, Bob Butterss, reviewed the work of ABM in the 1970s and analysed its role with regard to Aboriginal people. While affirming that the welfare of the Aboriginal people 'is a high priority for mission', he noted: 'The Board does not work in its own name among the aboriginal [sic] people, but through the Church which is already in that place'. The board now saw its role as giving leadership to Australian Anglicans 'concerning the best thought and action with regard to the well-being of the aboriginal [sic] people'.[78] A very difficult role indeed.

It was not until May 1968 that the decision was made to go ahead with the appointment, for a five-year term commencing in January 1969, of the 'Representative in Aboriginal Affairs', the position previously referred to as the 'officer for Aboriginal advancement'. The board considered there was no suitable Anglican applicant for the challenging task, an extraordinary admission of past failure, and appointed Pastor Frank Roberts, an Aboriginal Church of Christ minister from New South Wales.[79]

A great deal was expected from the new appointment. The chairman, Frank Coaldrake, confessed his and the board's ignorance of the next steps to be taken by ABM to assist Aborigines in 'the new stages of their development'. They would 'have to be discovered' by the board's Representative in Aboriginal Affairs.[80] Roberts submitted regular reports to the board. They are clearly and impressively written, at times even eloquent, but quite depressing to read. He took up his challenge with enormous enthusiasm and high ideals. Working from within the parameters of the policy of 'Acceptance', he tried to use the potential outreach of the Anglican Church structure to establish a nationwide program bringing together Aboriginal people and white churchgoers at a parish and diocesan level to meet spiritual and socio-economic needs. He communicated with Aboriginal and multi-racial community groups and organisations; church groups, congregations and mission agencies; government departments, government ministers and members of parliament, and local government bodies; youth, student and university groups; and women's groups. He attended conferences and seminars. He led deputations to government ministers and relevant opposition members and gave interviews to the media. He travelled extensively, although mainly in New South Wales. Wherever he went he tried to meet the local Anglican bishop because he realised they were 'the key to what may transpire in the establishment of a work programme on a regional or diocesan basis'. He was obviously received politely by the bishops and clergy he met and listened to with enough sympathy for him to be optimistic about a wholehearted Anglican response. But, such was not to eventuate. Anglicans were, and are, accustomed to giving individual expressions of sympathy to worthy causes while reserving their resources for existing needs. In his reports some dioceses were identified as committed to action. Yet, in October, 1971, Roberts noted:

> I sense there is a reluctance in some Anglican quarters for me to come
> face to face with their congregations, perhaps because it presents a
> challenge, an abrupt awakening to an invitation for the Church to
> speak out and do things in a concrete manner.[81]

Alf Clint had met this reservation of traditional church resources to
traditional affairs at a formal level. Frank Roberts was meeting it without
its ever being expressed. Despite the policy of 'Acceptance' Aborigines
were still considered aliens in their own land, to be recipients of resources
normally devoted to foreign missions. In the market place terminology of
the 1970s, they were still considered optional extras.

Throughout his reports, Roberts had stressed the spiritual or religious
nature of his task pointing out the numerous organisations and government agencies that focused on meeting secular needs. However, like
many Aboriginal Christians, he did not exclude issues of social justice and
human dignity from his conception of 'spiritual emancipation'. Thus in
his first annual report he suggested ABM support FCAATSI. Although
four members of the executive of this body were practising Christians
and its federal secretary, Jack Horner, a well-known white Australian
Anglican, FCAATSI was essentially a political pressure group.[82] While
most Aboriginal Christians accepted it as a valid expression of Christian
concern, most white Anglicans at this time who were aware of its existence
would have seen it as radical and secular because it pursued a black
agenda.

Roberts presented the board with problems perceived by the Aboriginal
community. Many believed that government agencies were not only
advocating birth control but, in the Northern Territory and New South
Wales, forcing Aboriginal women to accept it. Roberts believed this to
be an attack upon Aboriginal family life and communal values 'in line
with the government's policy of genocide'. He informed the board of a
new rent policy of the New South Wales Government that was causing
great distress because of the alarming rate of Aboriginal unemployment
and even greater lack of permanent employment. He outlined the degree
of racial prejudice Aborigines had to confront. He wanted the Anglican
Church to support a Royal Commission into the plight of Aborigines and
brought to the board's notice aspirations of Aboriginal people detailed
in the National Aboriginal Conference's declaration, issued at Ballina
on 15 August 1971. This demanded a Bill of Rights for Aborigines, a
declaration against racism in Australia, and the recognition of Aboriginal
land rights and cultural heritage. In addition, it made recommendations
on Aboriginal health, housing, education, legal aid, and training in
technical and business management. The National Aboriginal Conference

also demanded anti-discrimination legislation.[83] After years of having a loose oversight of the administration of remote Aboriginal communities, ABM was being confronted with the uncomfortable, real world of urban Aboriginal activism, which was inextricably part of the expression of their Aboriginal representative's Christianity.

Roberts had noted in his report:

> At the present time in New South Wales and generally throughout Australia, the church keeps itself aloof from the Aborigines and her committal to the field and work, whether in evangelism, social or moral programmes is almost nil. Seemingly the church as a whole is reluctant to engage in a spiritual and social work programme that would help uplift the Aboriginal to a spiritual and social level that is accepted as a norm of living by the church. I say this not in the spirit and tone of criticism, but on fact, for I am deeply concerned and perturbed that such apathy is so pronounced among the majority of churches.[84]

The Anglican Church as a whole did not rise to Roberts' challenge. Indeed, given the diocesan autonomy, it is hard to see how it could have done so. It had only achieved a national constitution and structure on 1 January 1962 and there was no likelihood that the commitment Roberts sought would be accepted. Most dioceses still saw Aborigines as a responsibility only for those remote dioceses where they existed in recognisable communities.

Frank Roberts formally brought it to the notice of the board and the relevant diocesan bishops that large communities now existed in the capital cities, especially Sydney, and that the Anglican Church had a responsibility to offer them ministry. In association with Bishop Reid of Sydney he was able to establish a ministry in Redfern. Another non-Anglican Aboriginal pastor, Ben Bird, a member of the Aboriginal Evangelical Fellowship who had previously worked for the Aboriginal Inland Mission, was appointed in April 1973 to work from St Paul's Community Centre. This was perhaps Roberts' most tangible achievement. By the time he had completed his five-year term, he was hopeful of a similar development in Adelaide. He was also able to report that Norman Polgen, an Aboriginal deacon from Palm Island, and an officer in the Anglican Church Army, was working in Western Australia among the Geraldton Aborigines, while another Church Army Officer, Captain Arthur Malcolm from Yarrabah, was engaged upon similar work at Brewarrina in New South Wales.[85] These were, however, diocesan initiatives.

In 1974 about thirty of the estimated 8000 Redfern Aborigines worshipped with Pastor Bird at Redfern. There were another 2000 Aborigines living in Housing Commission homes at Mount Druitt. The challenge to minister to the escalating population of urban Aborigines migrating to the capital cities in search of work, housing and educational opportunities was not adequately met by either ABM or the metropolitan dioceses. A survey by ABM of Aboriginal and Torres Strait Islander ministries conducted in 1990 revealed that the Anglican Church was still failing to offer effective ministry to the majority of Aborigines who now lived in the cities. The Anglican Church had not escaped from its legacy of associating Aboriginal and Torres Strait Islander people with overseas missions.[86]

An Aboriginal Affairs Advisory Committee was created in 1972 at Frank Roberts' suggestion.[87] When his five-year term was completed at the end of 1973, this committee was retained to allow ABM to consider its relationship with Aboriginal and Torres Strait Islander people.

The Rev. Fred Wandmaker, a white Australian, was appointed assistant to the chairman of ABM in 1978; one of his major tasks was 'to hear what Aboriginal people feel and want' and to communicate this to the Anglican Church. This he did until 1988 with great compassion, energy, and eloquence. This function was considered so important that it was transferred to the General Synod, the national Anglican office, in 1985, as the then chairman, Bishop Ken Mason said, 'to remove it from a 'party camp', that is, to place it above the doctrinal factionalism and loyalties split between ABM and CMS.[88] A detached observer could only wonder if their God cared.

At this time, the reassessment of the role of overseas missions throughout the world was in full swing and the paternalistic domination of the donor church or mission agency acknowledged. In an attempt to reflect the post-colonial, post-missionary age, the Anglican Church worldwide had enunciated policies that reconceptualised the concept of mission as a sharing among equals, between the materially wealthy churches of Great Britain and its transplanted 'white' colonies and the Anglican churches in the newly independent nations of Africa, Asia, and the South Pacific. By 1978 the new relationship was termed Partnership in Mission and mission was conceptualised as 'here and there'. The chairman, Canon Bob Butterss, had reported enthusiastically to his board on the contemporary approach to mission, which attempted to throw off the connotations of colonialism it had endured complacently for two centuries. He also acknowledged that the concept of Partnership in Mission reflected upon the Anglican Church's relationship with Aboriginal people:

> Whenever we talk about Aboriginal affairs we recognise our failure and our ignorance. Our partners in mission from overseas will judge our missionary integrity very much in terms of our understanding of the

> Aboriginal people of Australia and our recognition of the fact that the
> problem is a white problem rather than an Aboriginal problem.[89]

For ten years Fred Wandmaker was the conscience of the Anglican
Church communicating with black and white Australians to try to move
the Anglican Church from this realisation of failure towards a partnership
with Aboriginal people. After Wandmaker retired, his position was not
filled for several years. Initially it was argued that the General Synod's
Aboriginal Affairs Officer had to be an Aboriginal. However, increasingly developments in the dioceses of North Queensland, the Northern
Territory and Carpentaria had made the position redundant. In these
areas the Anglican Church had begun exploring ways to establish a new
relationship with the Aboriginal people to whom it had ministered for
generations.

And, more importantly, Aboriginal people had responded and were
speaking with their own voice.

8.

A Black Church: 'Let My People Go'

The face of Willie Ambryn, the South Sea Islander who helped the Gribbles found Yarrabah, glowed as he described to the Aborigines at the mission the Christian heaven that could be theirs. There was no sickness, no pain, no sorrow and, 'No white people there'. Seeing the 'surprise and consternation' on Gribble's face, he quickly added: 'Everybody will be the same there, all brothers'.[1]

In 1901, his Aboriginal audience may have found heaven more attractive if he hadn't caught Gribble's alarmed response. It is difficult to imagine Aborigines, not already committed to the new way of life, wanting to aspire to an eternity with the whites they had come to know, including these strange missionaries who wanted to take control of their lifestyle. Would they wish to share heaven with people who pressured them into surrendering their own children to be locked up in the mission compound in dormitories or in the school, who would not let them participate in life-giving ritual, or speak their own language, and even controlled whom they would marry? Sometimes, when Aborigines wanted to keep a captured kangaroo from escaping until they were ready to kill it, they broke its legs. These missionaries seemed to want to break the legs of Aboriginal culture. What sort of heaven could it be if you could not escape their all pervading, relentlessly loving domination?

Yet, even before Willie Ambryn's sermon, young Aboriginal men had followed the example of Alick Bybee, one of Gribble's young local Aboriginal assistants, and addressed Aborigines in camps near Yarrabah to witness to their new faith.[2] Gribble had also discovered by accident a group of young people willingly attending a prayer meeting Willie Ambryn had organised.[3] There were other very early examples of young Aborigines independently adopting Christian worship.[4] Indeed, the hostility at times expressed by Aboriginal elders was witness not only to the contempt they had for the whiteman culture but also to the danger they perceived to their way of life.[5]

In retrospect, it is surprising how quickly church-going communities emerged in the industrial missions and in chaplaincies such as Palm Island and Moore River. New Christians were generally young people not far advanced in tribal knowledge and status, or with limited or no contact with their Aboriginal roots. However, within a decade, the dormitory system was producing a steady stream of mission Aborigines who grew up and lived most or much of their life within the framework of activity and expectations the white missionaries had created with their Aboriginal, South Sea Islander, or Torres Strait Islander assistants. Especially significant were those local Aborigines who decided to commit themselves to the new, very different way of life. Within a generation, for many Aborigines the mission was home, punctuated possibly for men by periods of work on stations as ringers or as crews on pearlshell, bêche-de-mer or trochus boats; and for women as cooks, domestic servants, or child care providers on stations, and occasionally elsewhere. On the missions there was a multitude of tasks to be involved in under mission control.

The more established Christian communities provided ABM and its associated dioceses with Aboriginal missionaries from the earliest years, although, with exceptions like James Noble, they were not recognised as evangelists. Ernest Gribble at Yarrabah and Nicholas Hey at Mapoon were two missionaries who understood in their nineteenth century pioneering days the valuable Christian witness of black assistants, especially local Aboriginal converts. More important than what they said to other Aborigines was what they did and what they were — models and catalysts of the changed way of life.[6] At Yarrabah by 1898 Aborigines like James Noble, George Christian, Menmunny, by now renamed John Barlow, and Pompo Katchewan (Patterson) had emerged to fulfill this function.[7] Subsequently Gribble took Yarrabah Aborigines with him to assist Gilbert White in finding a site for the Mitchell River Mission.

James and Angelina Noble and Horace Reid volunteered to serve at Roper River, the CMS mission in the Northern Territory. Here, from its foundation in 1908, Angelina Noble soon proved herself a gifted linguist. James and Angelina Noble joined Gribble at Forrest River Mission, at his request, in 1914 and served there for eighteen years. It is doubtful if Gribble could have survived in this remote mission without them. Indeed it was the tracking skill of Noble and local Aborigines that disclosed details of the Forrest River massacre. Angelina was the only woman missionary for the first six years, as she had been at Roper River for three years.[8] Because of the male domination of the Anglican Church during the nineteenth and twentieth centuries, Angelina's role was often overlooked. She has been seen as James Noble's support. She was much more than that. Missionary women as nurses, teachers, and housekeepers interacted generally at greater human depths with Aboriginal people than most male missionaries. And on all of the missions where Angelina worked, her linguistic ability and her intelligence were appreciated, if rarely commented on.

'Chappie' Chapman took a Mitchell River man, Hector, to help him found the Edward River Mission and was supported by Walker, a young local 'who rapidly learnt the new way of life'.[9] In earlier brief visits to Edward River, Chapman had been accompanied by three Mitchell River volunteers who had kinship links with Edward River Aborigines. In 1925 George Singleton had volunteered for missionary service at Forrest River, increasing the Yarrabah Aboriginal contingent on staff by joining Angelina and James Noble.[10]

Although Aboriginal Christians, like Jhinna Murga and Charlie Fourmile from Yarrabah, went on deputations to address meetings of missionary supporters and attended the diocesan synod, James Noble was the example placed most frequently and most emphatically before the eyes of white supporters, occasionally by his presence on deputations but much more frequently by references to him in reports in Anglican journals, as well as by photographs, sometimes in the company of Ernest Gribble.[11] James and Angelina Noble had gone to Palm Island to support Gribble before being forced to retire to Yarrabah because of James's ill health.[12] Palm Island had earned its name among its residents as 'a punishment place', being used by the Queensland Government more than any other reserve or mission as a place of secondary punishment for Aborigines who couldn't be controlled by the white officials, or who had committed an offence in the eyes of the white administration, and sometimes in the opinion of members of their original community. Here, as we have seen, Gribble soon gained a large congregation with locals, such as John Barlow, son of Menmunny, and Fred Brackenbridge, emerging to take on positions of responsibility in the St George congregation.[13] An interesting personality to emerge was a leper, Ellison Obah, who was a lay reader in the Church of St Luke on Fantome Island, the leprosarium close to Great Palm Island. Gribble appealed for years to ABM supporters for an harmonium, in the process giving an interesting, if patronising, vignette of the lives of some Aboriginal lepers:

> Our lay-reader there is an old Yarrabah boy [sic], of whose family I have baptized five generations. He, his wife and one son are lepers…Ellison Obah, the lay reader, is a good musician and was the organizer and conductor of our brass band here. We had a very old discarded organ

given to us six years ago, but it is now past repair, and an harmonium would be better suited as it could be moved if repairs were needed at anytime. I am visiting the Lazaret six times a month. It is an hour's run from here by our launch.[14]

In 1939 Muriel Stanley from Yarrabah went to the Anglican Church Army College to become an evangelist, decided to train as a nurse, and graduated in 1945, first in her class, from South Sydney Hospital, the first Aboriginal to become a fully trained nurse. As Matron of the Yarrabah Hospital and community health adviser, she became a living example to her own people of the possibilities of Aboriginal cultural change, as well as to white Anglicans she came into contact with, especially her own Church Army.[15] Today, she would be labeled an assimilationist but when she commenced her work in the Church Army, that was all that could be hoped for, a fair go in the whiteman's world.

The James Noble Memorial Fund established to send selected Aboriginal Anglicans to church secondary schools, soon bore fruit when Alan, Norman and Emma Polgen from Palm Island also went to the Church Army College. Emma died before she graduated but Alan and Norman remained Church Army officers for the rest of their lives, serving mainly in southern Australia, although Norman returned to Palm Island in 1980 to be chaplain there until his death in 1982.[16] Just before he died in 1978, Captain Alan Polgen recounted how the Anglican priest he was working for at the time refused to be his sponsor when he decided to seek Australian citizenship. 'We expect Aborigines to forget a lot of little hurts', *Church Scene* noted in a dramatic, if unintended, understatement.[17]

All of these people dating back to the earliest years of Yarrabah were Aboriginal missionaries to their own people. Using Barnett's model of innovation, as modified by Tippett and Whiteman, they were important innovators of cultural change; the missionaries were the advocates.[18] Many other Aborigines sincerely accepted the new faith and new way of life in their own way, many more than those referred to above. These names have been culled from white missionary records where they have generally been referred to in a patronising, if affectionate way, like promising children who have responded pleasingly to their superior teachers. The much larger number who practised the new faith, generally unknown to ABM or the readers of church journals, were well known within their mission communities as were those within government reserves where chaplaincies had been established. They still are today despite the low church attendance in all of these communities, except at Yarrabah. Even in the other communities there is a small core, often a very small core, of Anglican Aborigines who still find something relevant in the regular church worship they have known in their communities.

Since the church surrendered administrative control and ceased to be central in the daily activities of mission life, it has become apparent that the temporal activities in mission days bound most of the people to the church and established its relevance. The state took on responsibility for these activities, such as provision of housing, employment, health, education, and social welfare. Since the acceptance of the Queensland Deeds of Grant in Trust legislation in the late 1980s, the elected Aboriginal Council has taken on local government responsibilities and become the central integrating force in each community. The Anglican Church has consequently moved to the periphery of community life. Moreover, the increasing secularisation of the age is affecting Aboriginal communities as it has affected church affiliations in the rest of Australian society. Modern communications, radio, television, videocassettes, telephones, faxes, computers, email, the Internet and popular culture are now ever-present realities. All communities are linked by road for all or most of the year, and regular, often daily, flights link the communities with the outside world. On these communities Christian and traditional Aboriginal belief and ritual are challenged by the secular age, especially by its recreational drugs and alcohol.

The destructive effects of excessive alcohol consumption are tragically obvious in the effect on family life, community relationships, health, and uncontrollable violent conflict often resulting in death or serious injury, frequently directed at young women. Yet alcohol is clearly meeting the needs of many people in these communities in this period of rapid culture change. It provides release from tensions associated with the culture change, high density community life, unemployment, and the feeling of aimlessness and hopelessness of an Indigenous group in a land dominated by intruders who have swept away their satisfying old way of life, deprived them of their land and impoverished them materially and spiritually. For many, alcohol often seems tragically more central to community life than either the introduced religion or the old Aboriginal beliefs and practices which persist today as glowing embers of the spiritual fire that burned throughout Aboriginal society.

Today alcohol brings people together socially. It creates a temporary feeling of warmth, wellbeing and confidence. It permits the release of inhibitions, of pent up emotions and frustrations and lifts the individual above the mundane existence of community life. The Romans associated wine with the God, Bacchus. Many Aboriginal people today on these communities, like many white Australians, have set up a shrine in their lives to this seductive demon. Indeed, in Aboriginal communities, most people see alcohol and church affiliation as incompatible. With varying success many, especially at Yarrabah, have sought refuge from the destructive effects of alcohol in affirming their Christian faith. However, in the current circumstances on the Aboriginal communities examined in this study, it seems unlikely that the Anglican Church will really confront such a massive challenge until it is rooted thoroughly in the community, with Aboriginal people from these communities enunciating alternatives to alcohol abuse.

The Aboriginal Church

The term, Aboriginal Church, is used quite frequently by Aboriginal Christians and white Christians working with them as if it already has a definition and an existence. It no doubt means different things to different people. It seems to extend beyond merely an Aboriginal congregation, such as is found in many of the old missions. It implies at least Aboriginal leadership of Aboriginal congregations, 'with some real autonomy and acceptance as a cultural group in the Church, worshipping and practising their faith in their own way'. In the Anglican Church, at the local level, this means an Aboriginal priest with a local Aboriginal council to which he can relate. However, in the Uniting Church a separate synod, the Uniting Aboriginal and Islander Christian Congress, has been set up with an Aboriginal president.[19]

Within the Anglican Church, as we saw in Chapter 1, there has been progress towards developing separate Aboriginal and Torres Strait Islander bishoprics. Both assistant bishops are still subordinate to their diocesan Bishop of North Queensland. As mentioned previously, the Diocese of Carpentaria ceased to exist in 1996 when it was amalgamated with the Diocese of North Queensland.[20]

After the ordination of James Noble as deacon in 1925, it was forty-five years before the Anglican Church finally ordained an Aboriginal priest. This was Patrick Brisbane in the Diocese of Carpentaria, who was deaconed in 1969 and priested in 1970 by Bishop Eric Hawkey, thus becoming the first Aboriginal priest in the Anglican communion. He worked at Lockhart River and Cowal Creek until his death in 1974. As Alan Gill remarked at the time of his death: 'His ordination on October 29, 1970, was perhaps the most momentous — if least reported — event in Australian Anglican history'.[21] Neither Brisbane nor anyone else in the church acknowledged its significance. In November 1973 Gumbuli Wurramurra (Michael Gumbuli) was ordained to the priesthood by the first bishop of the Northern Territory, Ken Mason, at the old CMS mission at Roper River (Ngukurr), which James and Angelina Noble had helped to found. His successor, Bishop Clyde Wood, pursued a policy of ordaining to the priesthood, men from the local community approved by members of that community. A number of Aboriginal men and women were ordained as deacons or deaconesses in 1985; three of the men were ordained to the priesthood the same year.[22] Within each community a small core of committed Christians supported their priests and deacons in a form of 'shared ministry'. In 1987, Bishop Wood was able to report that all of his Aboriginal parishes were staffed with Aboriginal priests; only one of these was from outside the diocese, Wayne Connolly from Yarrabah.[23]

Associated with this Northern Territory initiative was the intention that the leaders ordained within their own communities and committed lay people would undertake courses in theological education and personal development through Nungalinya College in Darwin. Those ordained did a year's study that gave them a Certificate of Theology and a semester's start on the Diploma of Theology, which it was hoped they would complete.

Nungalinya was established in 1973 by the Uniting and Anglican churches to provide culturally relevant Christian education, from short-term courses through to a Diploma of Theology, for Aboriginal and Torres Strait Islander people. Nungalinya offered courses in four broad areas: Community Development Studies, Language Studies, Cultural Orientation, and Theological Studies; however, ordained Anglican priests and deacons in the Northern Territory and North Queensland at first, did not use it as systematically as did the clergy of the Uniting Church.[24]

Because so many students had come from Queensland, a branch was established in North Queensland, supported by the Anglican, Uniting and Roman Catholic churches, called Wontulp-Bi-Buya. In 1992, the Lutheran Church also decided to support it. The title reflects both its Aboriginal and Torres Strait Islander clientele. Wontulp is the Wik Munkan name for Mount White on Cape York Peninsula, a site associated with an Aboriginal myth that Christians have related to the power of their faith: Bi and Buya mean 'light' in the eastern and western languages of the Torres Strait respectively, referring to their Coming of the Light festival on 1 July which commemorates the arrival of Christianity in their islands in 1871. Wontulp-Bi-Buya: power and light. The Anglican Church in North Queensland is turning more to Wontulp-Bi-Buya, which has such potential to provide culturally relevant Christian education.[25] In 2003, most of Wontulp-Bi-Buya students were Anglican and Father Michael Connolly from Yarrabah, whom we met in Chapter 1, was its principal. Two of its graduates, James Leftwich and Saibo Mabo, are now bishops in the Diocese of North Queensland.

Consecration of Bishop James Leftwich at Yarrabah, 1 July 2002 with his wife, Lala, and retiring bishop, Arthur Malcolm. Courtesy Anglican Diocese of North Queensland Archives.

Looking back to these events, the ordination of Patrick Brisbane to the priesthood in 1970 seems to have been an isolated event, that of Gumbuli Wurramurra in 1973 the beginning of a movement which was temporarily interrupted. Yet developments within the then Diocese of Carpentaria around the time of Patrick Brisbane's ordination were in many ways promising a new era in that diocese although the promise was not to be fulfilled.

Bishop Donald Shearman, chairman of ABM from 1971 to 1973, reported exciting developments after a visit to the diocese. On the Aboriginal missions for a number of years after the Queensland Government takeover, there was a 'very strong feeling that the church had let them down and deserted them…there was now a new boss and they didn't have to go to church, nor could anyone force them to become Christian'.[26] The chaplains had welcomed this new understanding, Shearman wrote, but assured them that the church was still there to serve them. The people at Edward River (by then called Pormpuraaw) were fortunate to have Michael Martin, who had studied the Edward River and Mitchell River languages and the culture of the people. By 1972 he had been in the diocese for twelve years. Lockhart River was also fortunate from 1969 to 1977 in having David Thompson who made a systematic study of Lockhart River language and culture and even became an initiated member of the society. His searching analysis of Aboriginal religion at Lockhart River stressed 'a dynamic view of Aboriginal culture' showing that 'the Aboriginal world view differs from both European and Melanesian world views and is more akin to that of the early Israelites'.[27] He stressed the compatibility of the Aboriginal and Christian worldviews and their major religious rituals, 'bora' (referring here to the Lockhart initiation ceremonies) and church. Thompson saw Christianity as complementing Aboriginal religion and pointed confidently to 'those sincere Aboriginal Christians who find a harmonious identity through being active participants to both Bora and Church'.[28] Radical stuff in the 1970s for white Christianity.

With this new respect for Aboriginal religion went the realisation that the Christian Gospel could not be satisfactorily communicated to the Aboriginal people at Kowanyama (Mitchell River Mission), Pormpuraaw (Edward River Mission) and Lockhart River without major changes to the way in which it was communicated. Shearman referred to a 1969 survey at Kowanyama, the oldest of the three Carpentaria missions, which indicated that only 58 per cent of all English was understood and 'culturally divergent English' at much lower rates. 'Culturally divergent' presumably meant English that had not been rooted in the experience of Kowanyama people. The linguist, Bruce Sommer, gave an example of the difficulties confronting missionaries. Because they could not differentiate between the 'e' and 'a' vowel sounds in 'bless' and 'blaspheme', two of his most advanced informants thought these were the same word and that the 'pheme' ending was just another of English's nonsense syllables that was better ignored. The mind reels at the thought of how many times these two words had been used with the Kowanyama people in the sixty or more years since the mission was founded, or even how many times adults like the informants had heard them in their own lifetime and thought they understood.[29]

Shearman also pointed out other ways the Christian message was being ineffectively communicated. Sometimes the narratives were misunderstood. Sommer discovered that his Aboriginal informants believed that, when Christ was walking on water to his disciples in the storm at sea, he had cried out in fear for their safety whereas they had cried out thinking he was a ghost.[30] How many times had they heard or read that passage and placed upon the events their own logical analysis? Presumably they understood the story within the known frame of reference of Christ's miracles and resurrection, and his concern was a more compelling explanation than the disciples' surprise at yet another miracle.

Through the anthropologists, linguists, and chaplains he spoke to, Shearman learned how the first generations of Aboriginal Christians had come to understand the new religion by incorporating it into their own world view. At Kowanyama and Pormpuraaw, the Gospel Story had been identified in each place with a certain clan and with that clan's land. They thus 'owned' the Christian story and had responsibility for maintaining it by the introduced rituals of church services and maintenance of the church and everything associated with it. The other people felt only a secondary responsibility or none at all. At each of the two communities, according to Shearman, Christ was identified with 'an outsize giant with oversized genitals and a capacity to boot, but they had no trouble associating him or aligning him with the Christ of the Gospels'.[31] The anthropologist, John Taylor, has made a detailed study of Pormpuraaw society and investigated, among other things, the accommodation of Edward River people to the Christian ideology and the impact of the mission on them. He reported the identification of God with the mythic culture hero, Poonchr, as he was known in Kuuk Thaayorre, who lived in the sky world and occasionally visited earth in human form. He was often referred to as Poonchr-God and Poonchr significance often still remained when the term God was used by itself.

Taylor also detailed how ritual had been modified with changing circumstances. Increase ceremonies were no longer used or needed because the community store provided for daily needs while the bush is now a plentiful resource of game and fish to supplement the store diet or as a recreative escape from the pressures and tensions of community living. Surprising, at least to me, is the fact that initiation ceremonies were last performed in 1946, only eight years after the founding of the mission by Chapman. Admittedly they had become familiar with Mitchell River Mission before this and even allowed girls to go there to live in the dormitory. During the war years Chapman had no white support staff and was initiated into the tribe himself. They could have retained the initiation ceremonies if they had wanted to, or have revived them in later years as has occurred at Lockhart River. Others, such as the mortuary ceremonies, were retained or modified. John Taylor concluded with confidence:

> In brief, the Edward River cosmology has survived the challenge to its relevance and continued to function powerfully in the everyday life of the community. It has responded to changed needs and altered contexts by economically renovating beliefs and generating new rituals. While these renovations incorporate introduced elements, it has also maintained clear links with the past so that Edward River people can truly say, as they often do, 'We follow on from old custom'.[32]

Among the 'introduced elements' were substantial aspects of Christian ritual and belief that suggested Shearman was reaching conclusions that were too simplistic and, from his own Christian perspective, too pessimistic. Taylor detailed the impressive number of baptisms, confirmations, participation in communion services, marriages, and Christian burial services that had been performed before the 1967 Queensland Government takeover. He also noted that by 1968 church attendance had fallen away dramatically.[33] Weekly celebration of the Eucharist clearly did not touch the lives of most Edward River people although 'big days' such as Christmas still attracted large attendances. Baptism was still seen as an essential rite of passage. Edward River parents sought Christian baptism of their children; even Aboriginal adult newcomers who had come to live in Pormpuraaw sought baptism to show they were part of the community.[34] Christian burial was still an integral part of the mortuary ceremonies which have been modified by incorporating Torres Strait music and dance elements into the 'house opening' of the deceased's former dwelling, along with 'Old Paten' Aboriginal music and dance. The creative myth-making capacity of Aboriginal people, with its associated ritual, dance, music and its incorporation into an extended socially binding ceremony, was very clearly demonstrated.[35] The use of such Christian rituals as baptisms, funerals, and 'big day' church attendance is now voluntary and meets needs in Pormpuraaw society, and with some variations, in the Mitchell River and Lockhart River communities, as David Thompson has detailed in *Bora is like Church* and Philip Freier has described in his doctoral study of Kowanyama. All, or nearly all, of the residents of these three communities like those at Yarrabah still consider themselves Christian, nearly all identifying in varying degrees with the Anglican Church.

In 1972, referring to the Lockhart, Edward, and Mitchell River people, Shearman concluded 'there are only a few who have any real commitment to Jesus Christ and of these some appear to have retained some of their old beliefs'.[36] Twenty years later I heard similar judgments expressed of the Aboriginal response on communities in Cape York Peninsula and in Arnhem Land by church officials, anthropologists, linguists, and schoolteachers. Others like David Thompson, Philip Freier and Tony Hall-Matthews, then Bishop of Carpentaria Diocese, discovered more compatibility than incompatibility. When Jimmy Doctor and Stephen Giblet were made deacons at Lockhart River on 19 May 1985, Bishop Hall-Matthews encouraged the Aborigines to use a damper as the host in the communion ceremony which had previously been 'speared' as part of a traditional initiation ceremony.[37]

It would be a mistake to conclude that all Aboriginal Christians in these North Queensland communities founded by Anglicans had or have a uniform and unproblematic understanding of the merger of aspects of their traditional religion with their new understanding of Christianity brought to them by missionaries. There is no doubt a variety of responses. The research examined here refers to certain times and places. All refer to communities where, to varying degrees, there was then little expression of traditional ritual. Some of the more enlightened modern missionaries in the Diocese of Carpentaria were tentatively trying to incorporate Aboriginal people and Aboriginal ritual, where it was still important, in the expression of Christianity within those communities. Essentially they were trying to graft on to the white Christianity an Aboriginal presence and input that had been deliberately excluded previously.

The white Australian Christian confronting Aboriginal Christianity often asks: 'What is acceptable to the Christian faith in Aboriginal beliefs and practices and what is not?' By this the white Christian means 'acceptable to my understanding of western Christian faith and practice'. There are certainly Aboriginal Christians who have similar concerns, mainly it would seem learned from the Christian tradition they have come to know. However, left by accident or design with intellectual room to move, many Aboriginal Christians seem able to bypass this problem, as David Thompson has noted of the Lockhart River people:

> It is evident that Aborigines of Lockhart River did not see the acceptance of the Christian faith to be in conflict with the continuing performance of traditional ceremonies…In fact they detected real parallels between their ceremonies and the ceremonies of the Church. This is reflected in some of the English words used to describe the Bora to outsiders, e.g. godparents, godchild, baptism and confession.[38]

Other Aboriginal Christians, aware of the concerns Shearman and other white Christians raised, are beginning not only to reject this deficit model of Aboriginal spirituality but also to incorporate their old way as part of their response to the Christian Gospel. In doing so they are aware that they are rejecting the perspectives and teachings of generations of white missionaries, yet most express a magnanimity towards these ruthlessly loving cultural imperialists and an appreciation of the mission communities they brought into being as refuges against the ruthlessly unloving wave of secular colonial expansion that would otherwise have swamped them.

For me this perception of Aboriginal religion has been most clearly discussed in print by a Uniting Church minister, Djiniyini Gondarra.

Djiniyini Gondarra's book, *Let My People Go*, is composed of four theological reflections on Aboriginal theology.[39] Djiniyini was for seven years an ordained Uniting Church minister to his own people at Galiwin'ku (Elcho Island) and for two years a lecturer at Nungalinya College in Darwin before being appointed the first Aboriginal Moderator in the Uniting Church. Inevitably, for Djiniyini Gondarra, with his zeal for holistic evangelism, Aboriginal theology reflects on mission history, the place of Aborigines in Australian society and the issues confronting Aborigines today, such as 'housing, employment, training, community development, land rights, health and youth work'.[40] Djiniyini Gondarra studied theology in Papua New Guinea and has been influenced by third-world theologians such as the African, Charles Nyamites, who demands identification with the poor and oppressed. He likens the Noonkanbah oil explorations in sacred Aboriginal sites to a bulldozer's crushing of the Ark of the Covenant in the holiest of holy places in the temple of Jerusalem and quotes enthusiastically[41] Kath Walker's poem, 'Aboriginal Charter of Rights', which contains the lines:

> *Give us Christ, not crucifixion.*
> *Though baptized and blessed and Bibled*
> *We are still tabooed and libeled.*
> *You devout Salvation-sellers,*
> *Make us neighbours, not fringe dwellers;*
> *Make us mates, not poor relations,*
> *Citizens not serfs on stations.*

He notes:

> As Aboriginal Christians in Australia, we have adopted nearly all of the customs and ways of life of the early missionaries. This is very sad indeed, but the early missionaries in North Australia have been very successful in convincing the people that our ways of life, our culture and beliefs were seen as pagan, bad to be linked with the Christian faith. This is very damaging…[42]

Essentially he sees Christianity as the fulfillment of Aboriginal religion, regarding it as related to Christianity in much the same way as the Old Testament is to the New Testament. He explores with profound simplicity the Aboriginal Christianity of sacred sites, totemism, Aboriginal spirituality, and the Aboriginal contextualisation of religious expression. To his Aboriginal audience he stresses the defects not only of mission Christianity but also of contemporary western society and values, including its theology with its emphasis on individualism and rationalism. This is a development in Christian theology that challenges white Australian Christians, something which Djiniyini Gondarra believes is long overdue.[43] He states with confident faith:

> Black preachers and evangelists have preached many years to convert the white church — that Christ's power of resurrection is a power to set man free from the power of sin and death, and from the sin of domination over other people.[44]

It is tempting to imagine that a heavenly host of long gone missionaries will rejoice that they haven't been totally counter-productive; that, with all their limitations, Djiniyini Gondarra's theology, the Galiwin'ku revival movement and other autonomous Aboriginal responses could still take place.[45]

It is also important for other Australians to understand this development within Aboriginal culture if Christianity is now as central to the lives of many Aborigines as the Dreaming. Indeed, another of Djiniyini Gondarra's essays is entitled *Father You Gave Us the Dreaming*.[46] Consequently, understanding the role of the missionary as an advocate of culture change becomes more, not less important. Where the change has been anything more than superficial window-dressing, the innovators have always been Aboriginal people. Djiniyini Gondarra overtly, and John Taylor by implication, have demonstrated this.

In the old Carpentaria Diocese, the initiatives at Kowanyama and Lockhart River that Shearman described with enthusiasm in the 1970s failed to develop. Shearman had emphasised the importance of communicating the Gospel in the language of the people. He was present when David Thompson delivered a sermon in a Lockhart River language which he had prepared with his then churchwarden, Jimmy Doctor. Michael Martin at Edward River and David Thompson at Lockhart River seemed on the verge of introducing a language program; and at Mitchell River, the linguist, Bruce Sommer, had made a detailed study of Kunjen, one of the two major languages in the three tribal groups. Shearman believed it could be used as a bridging language to the whole community.[47] However, it became apparent that progress would depend upon staff members being allowed to concentrate full-time upon translation and literacy work. In 1974 David Thompson proposed that he resign as chaplain to concentrate on a community communication project but the offer was not taken up. If the spirit was willing, the Anglican Church body was weak.[48]

The Diocese of Carpentaria subsequently explored a variety of initiatives. Since 1976, the Melanesian Brothers had served at Edward River, Kowanyama and Lockhart River. The Melanesian Brothers is a religious order that was developed in the Anglican Church of Melanesia, which is situated in Vanuatu and the Solomon Islands. It is committed to primary and follow-up evangelism and is regarded as one of the Indigenous success stories of the Anglican Church in the South Pacific. Although well received, they made little impact on Aboriginal people, a conclusion the Melanesian Brothers readily acknowledged. Melanesian priests from Vanuatu and the Solomon Islands have also been employed as chaplains in the Aboriginal communities.[49] The Brothers and the priests were confronted with the challenge of working in a different culture that was just as great as it was for white Australians, perhaps even greater as they were initially unfamiliar with the historical situation and the social and political issues that concerned Aboriginal communities as they emerged from white domination. Moreover, Aboriginal communities in the 1980s were better resourced materially and more sophisticated in terms of the broader Australian culture than the regions the Melanesian Brothers came from. They were thus further culturally removed from Aboriginal communities than were white Australians, although in both cases the personality and ability of the individual, regardless of ethnic origin, was of greatest importance.

The Diocese of Carpentaria always found it difficult to staff its missions in Cape York Peninsula. Torres Strait Islander priests and other mission staff have been used sometimes to bridge the cultural gap between the Aboriginal people and the white Australian church; more often, it seems, because suitable white Australian priests could not be found to work in these communities, despite repeated appeals and advertisements in *A.B.M. Review*. There was always a ready supply of Torres Strait Islanders, and such people as William Namok, Poey Passi, Tom Savage, Kebisu and Kosia Ware, and Sailor Gabey established Anglican Christianity at Lockhart River with an enduring Torres Strait Islander form of expression especially in the hymn singing. They were always responsible to a white superintendent and of course, to a white bishop. They had the added advantage that they were cheaper to maintain than white missionaries.[50]

This diocese was, perhaps, the most difficult challenge facing the Australian Anglican church. It could not maintain itself from its own resources, yet the Anglican Church nationally would not give it the support it needed to meet the challenges confronting it. Eventually it would have to consider more radical organisational restructuring. It was dependent on grants from ABM and other missionary organisations and these are and always were, poorly supported. Impoverished dioceses, at home and abroad, it seemed, got what was left over from the rich man's feast.[51] Consequently, in the Diocese of Carpentaria desperate measures had been taken over the years to try to minister to the Aboriginal communities, which, for a variety of reasons, came to nothing. This included the attempt to foster local Aboriginal leadership.

After the death of Patrick Brisbane in 1974, a decade passed before Stephen Giblet and Jimmy Doctor were ordained deacons in a ceremony, on 19 May 1985 that included Aboriginal ritual participation.[52] Both assisted the chaplain at Lockhart River in the liturgical life of the church. Tragically Stephen Giblet died soon after his ordination and Jimmy Doctor, who was elderly when ordained, virtually retired in the late 1980s, and died in 1990. At Kowanyama (Mitchell River) the priest in charge, Philip Freier, fostered Aboriginal leadership in the church. This lead to Alma Wason and Nancy Dick becoming liturgical assistants; in 1987 Nancy Dick became the first Aboriginal woman to be ordained deacon, an event that was welcomed enthusiastically by the small regular church congregation and by the community as a whole. The Rev. Nancy Dick, assisted by Alma Wason, conducted church services in the priest's absence and led fellowship services in residents' homes once a week. When Philip Freier moved to a parish in Brisbane, Nancy Dick was the spiritual leader of the Anglican community. Once again a promising development was tragically cut short when Deacon Nancy Dick died on a visit to Papua New Guinea in 1991.[53] After this, the positions were occupied by Melanesian and Torres Strait Islander priests, assisted by the Melanesian Brothers at Lockhart River.

In these communities there were, at this time, elected Aboriginal councils with important local government responsibilities. Increasingly, Aboriginal people were managing their own service agencies and some were operating commercial enterprises. By the 1990s, they had for years been involved, in co-operation with other Queensland Aboriginal communities, in extensive and sophisticated debate with the Queensland Government over land rights and in assessing the significance of the Mabo decision with regard to Native Title to land, and the Goss Labor Government's Land Rights Act.[54] The lack of Aboriginal church leadership must inevitably be interpreted by the Aboriginal people on these communities as a statement to them, not of their failure to measure up to the challenge, but of the Anglican Church's irrelevance in their lives. Aborigines on those communities established by the Anglican Church interacted with Aboriginal people from communities where Aboriginal Christian leadership was a reality. There had already been some discussion among Torres Strait Islander priests of the possibility of a Torres Strait Islander Diocese within the Anglican Church, separate from Carpentaria,

The tombstone unveiling of the Rev. Nancy Dick, Deacon at Kowanyama, September 2000, presided over by Philip Freier, Bishop of Northern Territory. Photograph courtesy Joy Freier.

based on the Maori Aotearoa model.[55] The Torres Strait Islanders have had their own priests for over seventy years and their assistant bishop was consecrated in 1986. Despite this, a number of other Christian denominations with more flexible leadership structures have established themselves throughout the Torres Strait. Aboriginal Christians increasingly have become aware of the fact that they have other options. They may realise that the Anglican Church needs them to validate its role in the far north more than they need it.

9.

A New Beginning
A vision from Yarrabah

It's like scales fell from our eyes...Our people are starting to
see our Lord Jesus Christ in everything.

In the Diocese of North Queensland, as it existed prior to 1996, the situation was different in a number of ways. The people at Yarrabah and Palm Island had experienced much more contact with the outside world than the Aboriginal Anglican communities that had been missions in the Diocese of Carpentaria and the Northern Territory. North Queensland was also fortunate in having the gifted Aboriginal evangelist, Arthur Malcolm, who had left Yarrabah at the age of sixteen in 1952 to attend the Church Army College near Newcastle. In 1959, after three years of general education and four years theological education, he graduated as a Church Army officer. When Bishop Lewis was looking for a replacement, at Yarrabah for Father Cyril Brown, Yarrabah resident, Teresa Livingstone, suggested the two Church Army officers, Arthur and Colleen Malcolm. Lewis seized the opportunity to develop an Indigenous ministry.

There was only a handful of church attendees in 1974 and the first seven years were dry, difficult years for the Malcolms. However, a response was growing, especially among those who believed their lives had been severely affected by alcohol, marijuana, gambling, domestic violence, and sexual promiscuity.[1] Encouraged by the Malcolms, some residents turned to their old faith to find a new meaning or purpose in their lives, or at least a stability, this in what was now a secular community in which the church had become irrelevant or peripheral. For most there was no competing alternative. Many had conversion experiences which they referred to as being 'born again', a response central to the charismatic movement which has attracted large numbers of Christians, black and white, from a wide range of denominations. It would be easy to see the Yarrabah experience as part of the revival or renewal movement that has swept through Aboriginal communities in the Northern Territory since the 1970s.[2] The expression of Christian fervour at Yarrabah was, however, unique, deriving not only from the Aboriginal perception of a spirit-filled universe of which they were an integral part, but also from Yarrabah's Christian history.

The degree to which some members of the community had become Christ-centred manifested itself dramatically, beginning in June 1983, when people began to have visions, a response that Aboriginal people accepted as authentic to their traditional experience, visions of Christ in the familiar world of their community. One day, a group of children going to netball training saw various representations of Christ in a cloud formation which they described in detail to Arthur Malcolm and his assistant, Wayne Connolly, who accepted the validity of the children's vision. At that time few adults were attending church services and most, especially the white residents, thought the children were simply imagining things.

Two days later a preschool child, Carl Nicholas, was doing a 'butterfly' painting by splashing paint on paper and folding it in halves. When he flattened out the paper, the children and the teacher, Caroline Modee, saw a dramatic image of a bearded Christ, with crown of thorns and piercing eyes, staring directly at them from the painting. This image shocked many of the people and was accepted by adults as confirmation of Christ's presence among them. Other visions of Christ were then seen by Yarrabah adults: in a branch of a tree; in the form of a tree seen at dusk; in a scorch mark on an iron; in the folds of a curtain; and in the photograph of a child.[3] In an interview Wayne Connolly captured the significance of the visions when describing the transformation of the tree branch:

> [A] couple of months after this vision [of Christ in the painting] one of our men-folk was sitting on his steps at home and looking down towards the village [when] he noticed that one of the branches of a tree was in the form of our Lord Jesus Christ with his back bared like he was being whipped.
>
> It really shocked a lot of people here in Yarrabah because that tree has been there for 40 years and no one ever saw this vision before.
>
> It's like scales fell from our eyes and we became more spiritual here in Yarrabah. Our people are starting to see our Lord Jesus Christ in everything.[4]

The Christians at Yarrabah to whom I have spoken accept the validity of the visions and are unconcerned that white Australians will reject them

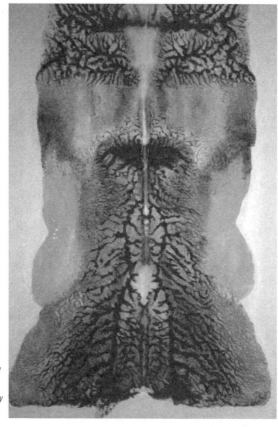

Christ with Crown of Thorns *(painting by Barbara Cheshire). The original butterfly painting by a child in Yarrabah revealed this vision of Christ. Courtesy Barbara Cheshire.*

or be sceptical. As Wayne Connolly said, 'That doesn't worry us really because we believe that the Lord is at work here and accept it'.[5] They link current visions with one James Noble had which led to a transformation in his life and to his decision to become a missionary. An 'old man' whom he identified with God asked Noble, who 'wasn't a good man' at the time, to help Gribble establish Mitchell River Mission. This site is referred to as Vision Creek and is close to Reeves Creek where the children reported the first vision.[6]

The emerging Aboriginal leadership believed that Yarrabah had an historic role to fulfil in keeping with its past:

> We believe that Yarrabah was chosen by God in the first place — to be a witness to our Aboriginal people.
>
> The first Aboriginal Deacon, James Noble, went out from Yarrabah. We believe we are a mother church to aboriginal people around Australia.[7]

They also believed they had a role to preach reconciliation to white Australians and to inspire in them a more wholehearted commitment to Christ.[8]

The renewed commitment to the Christian faith did not involve a rejection of their old Aboriginal spiritual beliefs, as Wayne Connolly pointed out in an article entitled 'Poor Fella — My Culture?' Some Yarrabah Christians believed they had to reject their traditional culture to be Christian. Connolly disagreed:

> [S]ome of our own people [who] think that when you have Jesus in your life, you must give up your culture, your old ways of worshipping tree spirits, water spirits, and a spirit who you know by name. Also corroboree, hunting, spear and shield making, knowing where to go for healing and tribe magic.[9]

Connolly argued that while there was much in the old religion inspired by Satan that should be rejected, there was much that could be retained as coming from God. It would be the responsibility of Yidinjdji and Gunganjdji Christian leaders to 'clean up our culture so that only the Godhead and the Good Spirits, Angels, remain with us giving worship to the True and living God'.[10] The debate about what aspects of Aboriginal culture could be incorporated into Christian worship occurred again when Connolly wanted to use traditional Aboriginal dance in the church service to tell Biblical stories.

He informed the 2004 North Queensland Synod that some of his congregation did not support his plan at first. A group of young male converts, who had all previously led dysfunctional lives, demonstrated to the Synod how electrifying such a presentation of a Christian story could be. No doubt the introduction of traditional Aboriginal ritual will produce a variety of Aboriginal responses in communities where it is attempted as it has elsewhere in Australia.[11] The enthusiastic commitment of the young Aboriginal men involved in the dance was clear to all, as was their confidence before this large conference of white, Aboriginal and Torres Strait Islander people.

In 2003, Connolly had informed the North Queensland Synod that Aboriginal people 'had the Gospel all the time'. The missionaries brought them the story of Jesus Christ. He believed that the spirit-filled world of the Aborigines made it easier for them to appreciate the Christian revelation:

> Think of Guyaala, the Good Spirit and Dumari, the Evil Spirit and you can easily see we always knew the Spirit world. But more importantly, good from evil.[12]

Connolly used the healing pool at King Beach, Yarrabah, to illustrate that Christ had been always with them, when they prayed to the Pool Spirit by breaking a green limb and hitting the water or ground three times.

There was now no need to travel to Medicine Water as Christ was within them 'Yeel-a-Muce-Kii in person, the God of all healing', as he had been at the Cleansing Pool near Jerusalem. If they chose to repeat the old ritual, Connolly told them, they should thank Jesus for the healing powers.

The transformation of church life at Yarrabah at this time astonished white Christians. Bishop Lewis remarked: 'Christian life in Yarrabah is like a page from the book of Acts. When they meet for worship here there is an air of joyous expectancy. They sing, clap, read and pray confident that the Lord is with them'. Midweek fellowship meetings drew congregations of over 250 people, up to 170 people took communion of a Sunday, and over one hundred young people were involved in church activities.[13] A number of men had sought ordination to the diaconate and the priesthood; the Mothers' Union and Girls Friendly Society had become integral parts of community life linking up with the rest of the diocese. Ordained men with their wives had served at such places as Palm Island, Wyndham/Oombulgurri (Forrest River), Oenpelli in the Northern Territory, Cherbourg, and Woorabinda, supporting each other as part of the James Noble Fellowship. Aboriginal church leaders, ordained and lay, had increasing links with their church at a diocesan state and national level, and links with other Aboriginal Christians through Nungalinya and Wontulp-Bi-Buya, and an increasing number of workshops, conferences and other ecumenical functions. There was an awareness of an Aboriginal Christian identity which was supportive in the face of the majority of Aboriginal people who were apathetic while a few on the community were, to varying degrees, hostile. While 'backsliding' of friends and relatives was a perennial concern of Aboriginal Christians at Yarrabah and elsewhere, the Christian round of worship, fellowship, clubs, societies, and meetings reinforced and supported the changed lives of newly committed Aboriginal Christians.

Hume's analysis of Aboriginal Christianity at Yarrabah concludes, 'In summary, the visions, prophecies and revelations, the Aboriginal [bishopric], and events leading up to them have created a 'new' Christianity at Yarrabah'. Throughout her article, she seems uncomfortable with some manifestations of Aboriginal Christianity and wonders whether it will support land rights. Yet Arthur Malcolm received a unanimous vote from an initially hostile North Queensland Synod. He informed members he would not be able to return to Yarrabah if the synod rejected the motion to support land rights.[14] Aboriginal Christians at Yarrabah sometimes state that their Christian faith is more important than land rights. Implicit in such a statement is an acceptance of land rights as a given, as becomes clear when land rights becomes an issue.

Yarrabah is a community very conscious of its history. Another historic day arrived on 9 November 1985 when the first Aboriginal Bishop, Arthur Malcolm, ordained two Aboriginal men priests and four as deacons and licensed another three men to be Eucharistic assistants, an extraordinary response from such a small community.[15]

In 1989, however, a serious rift had occurred within the James Noble Fellowship over a number of issues, including authority within the church structure, but the primary one was whether Aboriginal priests should drink alcohol socially. A number of the Aboriginal clergy wanted it to be a rule of the Fellowship that its members could not drink alcohol at all. When this was rejected because it was seen as a denial of the individual's freedom of conscience and unacceptable as a diocesan policy, four priests, Michael Connolly, Wayne Connolly, Leslie Baird and Conrad Yeatman, formed a breakaway congregation, called the Juyuga Ministries. Another proposal was the use of non-alcoholic wine in the Eucharist. The Juyuga Ministries attracted a large number of supporters, and eventually retained a following in the 1990s of fifty to sixty people, reducing the congregation at St Alban's that was, however, still regularly over one hundred. Recently there has been a complete reconciliation between the two ministries. Wayne Connolly is a canon of the cathedral of the Diocese of North Queensland and Michael Connolly, the Principal of Wontulp-Bi-Buya. Both have been outspoken and respected members of the Diocesan Synod.

The priests in the James Noble Fellowship replaced the mynah bird in their coat of arms with the sea eagle, a bird that has ancient totemic significance for Yarrabah people. The mynah bird is an exotic import to Australia from India and had Aboriginal significance only as part of Michael Connolly's prophecy. This change also quietly removed the notion of white Australian patronage from the coat of arms. The Aboriginal sea eagle rises triumphant from the crown of thorns, symbolic not only of Christ's humiliation and triumph but also of the small boy's butterfly painting, the vision that proclaimed Christ's presence to Yarrabah's Aboriginal Christians. The boomerangs now unmistakably embrace a black Australian's cross.

The question of a Christian's attitude to the consumption of alcohol is of the greatest importance in Aboriginal communities where many have

Bishop Arthur Malcolm with Archbishop of Canterbury, Robert Runcie at the 1988 Lambeth Conference. Courtesy Anglican Diocese of North Queensland Archives.

experienced the devastating effects of alcohol in their personal, family, social and religious life. Nearly all Aboriginal Christians at Yarrabah voluntarily turn their backs on it. Nearly all of the ordained clergy have done this emphatically. The debate really hinged on whether it had to be accepted as a rule of life. All of the priests who remained with St Alban's signed a statement and posted it on the notice board in the church indicating that they would not consume alcohol while on an Aboriginal community, but asserted that this was a matter of individual conscience.[16] In the context of Aboriginal Christianity, each side of the debate deserved great respect. The breakaway group did not at that time accept the structure and decision making of the Anglican Church in North Queensland as final in such an important matter of conscience. What is also clear and seemingly overlooked, is that the dispute is a measure of the importance of the 'new Christianity' in the lives of the parties in dispute. Both congregations offered a challenging Christian witness in Yarrabah.[17]

At the Yarrabah Centenary celebrations on 17 June 1992, members of the Juyuga Ministries took communion with St Alban's congregation and delayed the opening of their worship centre until after the celebrations, out of respect for Bishop Malcolm, Father Kevin Baird, and the others involved with the Anglican Church. I spoke briefly to Wayne Connolly and asked him what his future held. He worked at his brother's shop, he said, and he still had a ministry to fifty or sixty people.

'Do you still see yourself as Anglican?' I asked.

'They still call me Father', he replied.

Since the reconciliation between the two congregations, he once again functions as a priest of the Diocese of North Queensland.

And there was not a black arm band in sight, although that had been suggested by those who were going to indicate their opposition to the celebrations commemorating the foundation of the mission. Everyone participated, along with the many visitors, in the celebrations which commemorated the creation of an Aboriginal community and the beginning of ABM's work with Aboriginal people. There was a remarkable display of harmony despite the friction within the community caused by the new Queensland Government Land Act.

At Palm Island, by 1988, Bishop Malcolm and Wayne Connolly had developed an Indigenous ministry from the small congregation when Valentine Clumpoint and Dudley Bostock were ordained priests.[18] There was still an Aboriginal Inland Mission presence and a strong Roman Catholic ministry, but the old hostilities had long since faded. Indeed, in 1976 Bishop Lewis had considered a joint ministry at Palm Island with the Roman Catholic Church but not proceeded with it.[19] In 2006, there was no resident priest and only a small handful of worshipping Anglicans, where once, in Gribble's time, there had been hundreds.

Throughout the rest of the Anglican Church in Australia there was some attempt at ministry to Aboriginal people through the Bush Church Aid Society and the Home Mission Fund, while CMS continued its involvement in the Northern Territory. In Sydney, Brisbane and Adelaide ordained Aborigines were ministering to a tiny percentage of the urban Aboriginal population. Elsewhere throughout Australia there was a minute sprinkling of Aborigines in the congregations. If John Harris's estimate is accurate, and I suspect it is, by the 1930s, 'the proportion of Aboriginal people who were Christians was much higher than the proportion of white Australians who were Christians', most were still not attending mainline churches, except in their mission communities. Throughout southern Australia most belonged to congregations developed in rural reserves by the Aboriginal Inland Mission and the United Aborigines Mission.[20]

Throughout much of the twentieth century, the white Christians of the capital cities and other large urban centers were unaware that, when they were worshipping their Saviour who, they dutifully repeated, brought good news to the poor, one or two hours' drive away in the country Aboriginal Christians gave thanks that he had. Indeed, even in fringe camps near urban centres where Aborigines lived in galvanised iron shacks with earth floor and no running water, there was often an Aboriginal Inland Mission, a United Aborigines Mission, or an Assemblies of God presence. Aboriginal students of mine have described such Christian communities at Townsville and Ingham, communities that white Christians referred to with distaste as 'Blacks' Camps', and averted their eyes. In such surroundings, some Aboriginal Christians were teaching Sunday School.

The Centre of Gravity Moves North

During the nineteenth century and the first decades of the twentieth century, while the Aboriginal holocaust swept through Aboriginal Australia like an unchecked bushfire, white Anglicans had formed committees and subcommittees to discuss the appropriate Christian response to the continuing presence of Aboriginal people in the land that British people had colonised. They had passed resolutions and framed policies and appealed to the Christian majority affiliated with the Church of England to support their work among Aboriginal people. It was presented as an appropriate call upon Christian charity. Lazarus was sitting in great need at their gate and, if Christians did not respond, it was clear that the needs of most Aborigines would be ignored. In the late twentieth century, when churches had no role in meeting the temporal needs of Aboriginal people but were trying to support their spiritual needs, ironically Aboriginal people have found themselves snared by the same Anglican decision-making process and the same cumbersome structure.

Within the Anglican Church, since 1967 the development of ministry to Aboriginal and Torres Strait Islander people has depended upon diocesan initiatives with the possibilities of funding from ABM, the National Home Mission Fund, or the Bush Church Aid Society. For most of this time, ABM's role has been remote with its major funding contribution to the Diocese of Carpentaria and, after amalgamation in 1996, the Diocese of North Queensland. In effect the Anglican Church was still geared to its colonialist past as Aborigines were rarely ministered to by the normal parish structure.

ABM's Aboriginal Advisory Committee was reactivated, including Arthur Malcolm in its membership, and receiving inputs from Kevin Cook, the Aboriginal administrator of Tranby College. From this Aboriginal Advisory Committee emerged a proposal to establish a National Aboriginal Anglican Council. ABM subsequently sponsored a conference, in February 1992, of sixteen Aboriginal and Islander Anglicans and four white observers to formulate a proposal. This was enthusiastically accepted by the General Synod in July 1992. Its aims were ambitious, the first one being 'to celebrate Aboriginal culture, language and lifestyle within the Anglican Church'. The overall purpose was to 'go...into the world making disciples of all nations'. Another aim was 'to work towards self-determination and development of Aboriginal ministries, within the Anglican Church of Australia'. Optimistically, it stressed that the Anglican Church would listen to the recommendations of the National Aboriginal Anglican Council. It expected having the support of the church to combat racism and prejudice. The motion also requested the synod to continue Anglican involvement in the Aboriginal and Islander Commission of the Australian Council of Churches, in this way reaching out to the emerging black church in other denominations.[21]

The proposal encapsulated the concerns of the emerging Aboriginal Church, the need for Aboriginal people to be allowed to develop their own spiritual response to the Christian Gospel, unhindered by the western church but not separate from it. And quite deliberately the evangelistic outreach was not limited to Aboriginal Australians.

ABM headlined the proposal in its newsletter, *Partners*: 'Whisper becomes a shout'. The old missionary body had a right to feel elated. The acceptance at General Synod and the reports in the national Anglican weekly, *Church Scene*, underlined the importance of the creation of the National Aboriginal Anglican Council. The main speech in support of the proposal was printed in full, using a comment by the proposer, Bishop Wood of North Queensland, as the headline:

> We are, I believe, seeing a gradual emergence of Aboriginal congregations throughout Australia.[22]

The emergence was in reality the recognition by the white mainline churches that there were groups of Aboriginal people who had once belonged to their denomination or been associated with it, who were worshipping elsewhere or not at all. Such groups needed Aboriginal leadership and a great deal of autonomy to become part of 'the Aboriginal Church'.

The Roman Catholic Church in Queensland had been providing a ministry to Aboriginal people for two decades and in September 1991 had formed the national Aboriginal and Islander Catholic Council. The Uniting Church had begun creating a national body, the Uniting Aboriginal and Islander Christian Congress, in 1980 after the Rev. Charles Harris of Townsville encountered Maori Christians taking control of their own Christian destiny. The congress was formally established in 1983 and Charles Harris became the first president.[23] Aboriginal Inland Mission and United Aborigines Mission congregations had been dotted throughout southern Australia for generations[24] and, in 1971, the Aboriginal Evangelical Fellowship was formed, a completely Aboriginal organisation, to state clearly to all Australian Christians who would listen that Aboriginal Christians were no longer willing to accept white domination, no matter how well intentioned.[25]

* * * *

The proposal to create Aboriginal and Torres Strait Islander bishoprics was an attempt to provide Aboriginal autonomy within the structure and ethos of the Anglican Church. The same could be said for the National Aboriginal Anglican Council.

It is much too early to comment on the prospect of this body. It will depend on its being listened to at a national level by the General Synod and ABM and such voluntary societies as CMS, Bush Church Aid and the Church Army, but more importantly, by the response it receives from the individual dioceses and local entities which can pursue its aims at the grassroots level.

In 1998 Anglican parishes in the Torres Strait Region joined the renamed National Aboriginal and Torres Strait Islander Anglican Council (NATSIAC). The council had met annually since its inauguration and aimed at having a representative from each diocese in Australia by 2000. There were only two dioceses that did not have representatives — Tasmania and Wangaratta — and in 2003 that was still the case.[26] The membership has a very heavy representation from the far north of Australia. In reality, this does not reflect adequately how much the centre of gravity for black Anglican Christians is in the north, remote from the white power bases in the southern capital cities.

The coming together to discuss and participate in common issues gave NATSIAC the confidence to assert that 'we as people of faith, and with many gifts, have much to offer to the Anglican Church of Australia'. The Anglican Church was referred to as 'our Church'.[27]

The acceptance of NATSIAC by the Anglican Church was demonstrated in typically Anglican ways. In 1998, a canon (church legislation) was passed spelling out in ample detail its composition, functions and relations to the federal governing body, General Synod. In 1995, NATSIAC had participated in the opening church service of General Synod. Two prayers proposed by NATSIAC were included in the children's worship book, *A Prayer Book for Australia*. Traditional Smoking Ceremonies had been used at the opening of the 1995 General Synod, at the National Anglican Conference and during the visit of the Archbishop of Canterbury to the Diocese of Newcastle in 1997. These were symbolic contributions to 'our Church'.

More important, perhaps, were the items NATSIAC placed on the Anglican Church's agenda, such as the protection of Aboriginal and Torres Strait Islander sacred sites. In 2000, NATSIAC requested and received the support of General Synod for ongoing support for the process of reconciliation. NATSIAC also focused on the racist bias in sentencing in the criminal law of the Northern Territory and Western Australia and the disappointing response by the federal government to the Stolen Generations report. Bishop Arthur Malcolm urged all Australian Anglicans to support Indigenous people who had been hurt by the inadequate response:

> As far as the Aboriginal people are concerned, almost every person in this country will believe that they have been touched in one way or another by the Stolen Generations issue. This is because almost every Aboriginal person would have come in contact personally or with the aftermath of what happened.[28]

NATSIAC places great emphasis on encouraging Indigenous Australians 'to tell their stories of both pain and joy' and for other Australians to listen to them as part of the process of reconciliation. It is doubtful if many non-Indigenous Australians would have realised how important this process is for all Australians if reconciliation is to be more than polite superficiality. Because of their historical experience, NATSIAC felt the need to remind black Australians they could 'stand up as equals…we have all been made in the image of God'. It seems extraordinary that this statement had to be made at the end of the twentieth century in an appeal for financial support that was aimed primarily at non-Indigenous Anglicans. The NATSIAC appeal concluded: 'There is a long way to go, for God's spirit is moving us into action'.[29]

There was indeed a long way to go, but at least Aboriginal and Torres Strait Islander Anglicans had a fragile structure that potentially reached out to the whole of Australia, one that could yet relate to the established Anglican Church. In June 2001, NATSIAC was allotted five representatives on General Synod; Vivienne Sahanna came from Perth, Rose Elu from Brisbane, Rev. Di Langham from Newcastle, Deacon Charles Loban from Thursday Island, and Bishop Arthur Malcolm from Cairns.[30]

The continuing denial of the Stolen Generations and the failure of the Howard Government to implement all the recommendations of the *Bringing Them Home* report were again emphasised, as was 'the weak response from the Church'. The official representatives wanted to focus again on mandatory sentencing and reconciliation. To these, were added the request 'for secure and adequate resources' for NATSIAC, which should be the 'visible voice' of Indigenous Australians within the national church and within the dioceses. NATSIAC members did not want to depend on the charity of the rest of the church to function. The whisper was at least starting to become a shout.[31] The national synod had supported NATSIAC on the Stolen Generations and mandatory sentencing issues when, dramatically, history reached forward into the present.

A white priest, the Rev. Greg Ezzy, reported that a massacre site containing the bodies of about forty Aboriginal men, women, and children had been discovered in 2000 in the East Ballina region of northern New South Wales. A memorial service was to be conducted on 11 August and a memorial stone and plaque blessed in a project that involved the Bundjalung nation, the Anglican Church, the shire council and some community members.[32] The Anglican journal, *Market Place*, captioned this: 'Bones of Reconciliation'.

* * * *

Some living flesh had started to appear on the dry bones of the Christian communities that had come to know a white Christ through high church Anglicanism as they experienced the holocaust of colonisation.

As I have observed elsewhere, in some dioceses Indigenous Australians are more important spiritually to the existence of the dioceses than the dioceses are to the spiritual wellbeing of the Indigenous Australians. The successful incorporation of the first Australians into the Anglican Church nationally is just as essential. Otherwise the Anglican Church will remain an artifact of colonialism, replete with rigid structures and seemingly irrelevant values, failing to confront the challenge of dispossession that has created it. If such is the case, Aboriginal Christians will increasingly have alternatives through which they can explore and express their spirituality.

Although Christianity has become quite an important part of contemporary Aboriginal culture, there is no guarantee that this situation will continue. It is in the nature of Christianity to see its eventual triumph although there are various interpretations of what this means. To non-Christians this is foolishness or at least muddleheaded mysticism. The historian can point to modern Turkey, the heartland of Paul's evangelism, or north Africa, to show the eclipse of Christianity by a competing religious faith embedded in imperialist expansionism. In the western world, except in the United States, Christianity seems in full flight to the fringes of a society whose faith is secular humanism or consumerism. At present, I suspect that the Aboriginal Christians I have met would consider the possibility of the demise of Christianity as just another example of western rationalism and an effete denial of the spiritual dimension. They would see it as a statement of unfaith.

The Anglican Church, through the ABM, took the story of a triumphant white Christ to a conquered, impoverished black people, some of whom took up the cross of Christ's sacrifice and suffering and identified with it. To them the cross also held the promise of ultimate triumph over their past and present suffering. In effect the missionaries and ABM had been part of this whole process but were no longer central to it. They had become the fringe dwellers of the Aboriginal people's past. The contemporary church could support their present pilgrimage wherever it might lead, or be irrelevant to it.

Christianity had not been taken to Aboriginal people by the likes of Paul or Peter or John or any of the major actors in the Christian story, but by very ordinary people doing the best they could to spread the faith that had made their own lives significant. They had been sent or supported by a missionary body of ordinary Christian people, servants of their church, whose dedication was, they believed, their salvation. A few personalities flare forth from this history of high church Anglicans at mission — but not many. Most of the ordinary Christians who helped create the Aboriginal communities are now forgotten, as well as their mission experience with its dedication, achievements, and human limitations. What is extraordinary is that the white missionaries seem more appreciated in the communities where they worked than they are by the white church that sent them. Many Aboriginal people remember with gratitude such people as John and Bunty Warby, Ernest Gribble, Mary Gribble, John Best, Cyril Brown, 'Chappie' Chapman, Joy and Philip Freier, David Thompson, Eileen Heath, and a host of others who worked in the communities and became part of their lives. They know in a different way their own people such as Patrick Brisbane, James and Angelina Noble, Stephen Giblet, Jimmy Doctor, Nancy Dick, Alma Wason, Muriel Stanley, Valentine Clumpoint, Norman and Alan Polgen, Kevin Baird, Wayne Connolly, Lesley and Mercy Baird, Lloyd Fourmile, Michael Connolly, Jim Leftwich, and Arthur Malcolm. These people and many like them are living the faith the white man brought. Yet it is their faith. For them, increasingly a black man looks down from a black cross.

Appendix

The Forrest River Massacres

Dr Reim enclosed this report in a letter to me dated 7 September 2003. His report was made after a visit to the Forrest River Mission in 1968. It reconstructs the events as told to him by Aborigines at the mission 42 years after the massacre occurred, and 40 years after Gribble had been dismissed from the mission. There is no mention here of Hay's dealings with Lumbia's wife and other details are not mentioned elsewhere and some are confused or questionable, as one would expect after such a long interval. Reim remains convinced a large scale massacre occurred.

> Account in 1968 by native Ron Morgan and others, compiled by anthropologist Dr H Reim, of Karl Marx University, Leipzig, and read from his notes to journalist Tony Thomas, December 1968.

> A native Lumbia from Forrest River Mission and his two wives were on walkabout to Karanjie for initiation ceremonies. They passed Nulla-Nulla station and the man lay under a tree by a lagoon sleeping while his wives gathered water lilies' roots.[1] Around the lagoon was a mob of cattle, which were disturbed and started spreading. On the station the whites realised this and the foreman Hay set out on horse and beat the women out of the lagoon and broke the weapons the man had dropped on the bank. But the man had still a short woomera and a 'juble-spear', (tipped with iron from a shovel — other accounts say 'shovel-nosed', probably wrongly). He woke from the noise and ran away, and a bit off from the lagoon he laid ambush and when Hay raced after him on horse, he threw the spear and killed him. Hay fell down and the horse ran back to the homestead with blood on the saddle. The natives disappeared. The whites found the corpse of Hay, and got word to Wyndham Police and Turkey Creek and the stations around, and they organised a revenge party and set out for the Forrest River Mission. At Galagari they took natives on a chain and the trackers did the dirty work, shot down the natives at

close quarters, first the men and at another spot the women, and did the same at other places. The trackers took axes and tomahawks and chopped up the corpses and poured kerosene over them and burnt them, and put the bones in a sack and sank it in a water hole. Whole sub-tribes were annihilated.

Hereafter the account is verbatim:

The revenge party set out overland to Bundala, that is now McNamara station, and on the lower course of the Durack River, they met a camp of the natives, two men and three women, and shot them all. (Most of the dead natives were not bush people but lived on the mission.) From there they go to Wimbali country that belongs to the Alumbalu subtribe and captured all the Alumbalu people and chained them up. They got about ten men and women but no children because they were at the mission. The party kept another young man separately on a chain and forced him to guide them to Mararan, here they captured Galangari people and chained them up too. Then they go back to Wimbali and make camp. Next day they go to hill country near the Ernest River or Forrest River, and here they grabbed a mob of hilltop Walar, but a man and woman escaped and ran to the Berkeley River northward.

Next morning the party drove all their prisoners to Gudgudmidi water hole, in the hilly country on the right bank of the Forrest River near Ernest River. To stage the mass execution of the captured men, there was a depression in the rocky surface, the natives had to sit down, chained to a tree on each side, in a circle. They sat round a rocky basin facing the middle, chained by the neck. When this was ready some black trackers and white men went around and shot one after another in the forehead with a revolver, after the execution they took the victims away from the chain and tied them in bundles.

They dragged them with mules 100 yards, and here the trackers took axes and tomahawks and chopped the corpses to pieces, poured [kerosene] over and burnt them, after this they put the bones in a sack, and sunk it in Gudgudmidi water hole with rocks.

After this execution, they drove the women in a chain gang about three miles upstream to Balara water hole. Here some way from the water on sandy ground they shot them in the same way. But before they shot them they forced them to gather firewood for the burning of their corpses. The burnt bones were dried (tried) to take away, but a tracker from Derby native welfare office found the bones. There were 17 women, six from Yunduran, five from Kalamari and the rest from Malangani.

After this the party went to the mission, but told the missionaries nothing about what was going on. They picked up two young married men, Wumar and Alidour (Aldoa tt) to guide them to the Berkely River and went to Jarar, north-west of the mission.

Here they found a native hunting group of three men and four women, poisoning fish by stunning them with bark and seeds in the water, and another man was cooking a kangaroo. Trackers seeing smoke encircled the natives and chained them up to a tree. The police party camped and ate the roo, the natives were tied up for a fortnight. Next morning the bulk of the party set out on foot to Berkely River, two whites and two trackers stayed with the prisoners and horses, and shot the prisoners the same as at Gudgudmidi and Balara. Three days after, the party came to Moreigano country, on the upper course of the Berkely River, and here they captured Lumbiar, the man who killed Hay. They chained many natives there and drove them to the previous camp, where seven prisoners had been murdered. The new prisoners asked where the others were, for they could read their tracks, but the police lied and said they had released them, chased them away.

With all the Berkely River prisoners they came close to the mission, near the present airstrip and camped... Now my main informant Ron Morgan went out early to bring mission horses to the horse yard, he saw the prisoners. The police asked for Father Krobl (Gribble tt), thanks to Gribble the massacres were stopped. The police asked Morgan what he was doing, didn't hurt him, and were quite kind and gave him some plug tobacco. Morgan caught the horses and then told Gribble what he had seen. Gribble was having breakfast. Gribble ordered Ron to saddle four horses, and just after breakfast Gribble, a lay half-cast preacher Jim Snowball,[2] his wife Angelina, Robert Roberts, Morgan and James Wanmaru rode out and saw the police camp and prisoners, who were climbing a hill south of the mission on the north bank of the Forrest River. The two guides had been released and returned. Gribble's party pursued the police party and stopped them, and induced them to return to the airstrip camp. Gribble disarmed the white people and trackers and released the natives, and sent the police party back to Wyndham and brought the whole case to court. The white men involved in the atrocities were sentenced and spent a couple of years in gaol (not true, acquitted. tt).

Gribble's stockboys then were Morgan, Wanmaru and Roberts (still alive), Wuibram, Goror and Barara. He had been going to Wyndham to get cattle to port, and they camped at Wumbali Creek, and now Father Gribble had a dream: he was dreaming he found a human tooth in a camp fire and he wrote the dream down on paper. They drove [sic].

From Wyndham they returned on horseback, but Gribble returned by launch which his son Brother Jack Gribble had brought to Wyndham. At that time news came to the mission about the massacre, it was told to Gribble from the man from the upper course of the Berkely and Ulumbalu, from the native who escaped. He sent a letter to the NWD Derby, and the officer came with a blackfellow from Wamala (desert) overland to Wyndham...They reconstructed the story from the tracks, finally found the sack of bones in the waterhole, and then Gribble's dream came true; according to Ron Morgan he put his hand in the ashes of a deserted fire and found a tooth...[sic] .[3]

Reim says he heard of all this when asking natives about their relatives [sic] set-up and their burial practices and beliefs in ghosts of the dead.

He said Elin[4] [Elkin] in an article of 1932–3 mentioned Forrest River atrocities.

Of all the natives there, each seemed to have lost a relative in the massacres; he estimated the toll at 80–100.

Tony Thomas

Notes

1. The Triumph of the Mynah Bird

1. I have used my own knowledge of Yarrabah and its people built up over approximately 20 years, as well as J Thomson, *Reaching Back: Queensland Aboriginal People Recall Early Days at Yarrabah Mission*, Aboriginal Studies Press, Canberra, 1989, Map 1, and passim, and *Consecration of Bishops at Townsville, 13 October 1985, and Welcome to Bishops at Yarrabah, 14 October 1985*, videotape, Nungalinya College, Darwin, 1985.
2. It is also referred to in English as the Eternal Dreaming, my preferred term, or the Dreaming.
3. Nungalinya College, *Annual Report of the Principal, 9 August 1984*, Darwin, 1984, p. 5.
4. Bishop J Lewis, North Queensland, to Rev. G Braund, Anglican Consultative Council Office, 21 April 1988, North Queensland Diocesan Correspondence. Loos, personal conversation with Canon Boggo Pilot, 1980.
5. A Brent, *Cultural Episcopacy and Ecumenism: Representative Ministry in Church History from the Age of Ignatius of Antioch to the Reformation, with special reference to contemporary ecumenism*, EJ Brill, Leiden, 1992, pp. 174–180.
6. *The Northern Churchman*, October 1984; *Church Scene*, 6 September 1985, 'General Synod 1985: The Primate's Charge'.
7. Lewis to Denton, General Secretary, General Synod Office, 4 October 1984, Bishop of North Queensland Correspondence, Diocesan Registry, Townsville.
8. *Church Scene*, 17 May 1985.
9. Brent, *Cultural Episcopacy and Ecumenism*, p. 176.
10. *The Northern Churchman*, November 1985.
11. Lewis to Diocesan Council of North Queensland, 22 October 1984, Bishop of North Queensland Correspondence.
12. Bishop of North Queensland, 'Bishop for the Aboriginal and Torres Strait Islander People', 27 August 1984, 1985 North Queensland Synod Papers, Diocesan Registry, Townsville.
13. See A Markus, *Governing Savages*, Allen and Unwin, Sydney, 1990, ch. 5 for a balanced account.
14. J Harris, *One Blood: 200 Years of Aboriginal Encounter with Christianity: A Story of Hope*, Albatross Books, Sydney, 1990, pp. 12–15.

15. A Haebich, *For Their Own Good: Aborigines and Government in the Southwest of Western Australia, 1900–1940*, University of Western Australia Press, Nedlands, WA, 1988, p. 74.

16. R Broome, *Aboriginal Australians: Black Responses to White Dominance, 1788–1980*, George Allen & Unwin, Sydney, 1982, ch. 7, gives a balanced account. CD Rowley, *A Matter of Justice*, Australian National University Press, Canberra, 1978, pp. 167–74.

17. Harris, *One Blood*, pp. 9–10, 562–3, 585, 590–2, 722, 794.

18. Discussion with residents of Yarrabah, 13 April 1992. Dr John Taylor, an anthropologist at James Cook University who had had extensive contact with all North Queensland Aboriginal communities also found no resentment of the early missionaries. Harris, *One Blood*, p. 591.

19. NA Loos, Aboriginal-European Relations in North Queensland, 1861–1897, PhD thesis, History Department, James Cook University, 1976, ch. 10.

20. The understanding of first generation converts at Edward River Mission is well brought out in J Taylor, 'Goods and Gods: A Follow Up Study of 'Steel Axes for Stone Age Australians'' in T Swain and DB Rose (eds) *Aboriginal Australians and Christian Missions: Ethnographic and Historical Studies*, Australian Association for the Study of Religions, Bedford Park, South Australia, 1988, passim.

21. Djiniyini Gondarra, *Series of Reflections of Aboriginal Theology: Let My People Go*, Northern Synod of the Uniting Church in Australia, Darwin, 1986, pp. 13–35.

22. G Rosendale, 'Aboriginal Myths and Customs: Matrix for Gospel Preaching'. This paper was distributed by a group of Palm Island Aborigines of the Aboriginal and Islander Catholic Council at *Signs of Peace Seminar*, 17 June 1990.

23. Djiniyini Gondarra, *Father You Gave Us the Dreaming*, Northern Synod of the Uniting Church in Australia, Darwin, 1988, passim.

24. Harris, *One Blood*, p. 659.

25. *The Northern Churchman*, November 1985, p. 4; June 1986, p. 3. Bishop Lewis has since assured me that there were no tears in his eyes.

2. Agents of the Aboriginal Holocaust

1. Bowen Historical Society (ed.), *The Story of James Morrill*, Bowen Independent, 1964, pp. 1–19.

2. N Loos, *Invasion and Resistance: Aboriginal-European Relations on the North Queensland Frontier, 1861–1897*, Australian National University Press, Canberra, 1982, pp. 24–7, ch. 2, 'The Pastoral Frontier', ch. 3, 'Conflict on the Mining Frontier 1869–1897' and ch. 4, 'Resistance from the Rainforest'.

3. *The Story of James Morrill*, pp. 15–26.

4. QSA, Governor's correspondence, outward dispatch, 77 of 1865, Bowen to Sec. of State, Cardwell, 4 December 1865.

5. J Bonwick, *The Wild White Man and the Blacks of Victoria*, Ferguson and Moore, Melbourne, 1863, 2nd edition. Bonwick had a brief comment on Morrill inserted just before publication; *PDT*, 1 November 1865.

6. QSA, Governor's correspondence, outward dispatch, 74 of 1861, 16 December 1861; *PDT*, 10 June 1865.

7. *The Story of James Morrill*, p. 26.

8. 'Report of Commissioner of Police Upon Tour of Inspection', 1868 *V&P*, pp. 51, 52; Loos, *Invasion and Resistance*, p. 40. The nineteenth century north Queensland material is derived from this source.

9. *ibid*, see GC Bolton, *A Thousand Miles Away: a History of North Queensland to 1920*, ANU Press, Canberra, 1963, pp. 38–42.

10. 'Liddle' is probably a misprint for 'Little'. See Loos, *Invasion and Resistance*, p. 37, fn.27.

11. *PDT*, 21 July 1866; 1875 *V&P*, p. 624; *PDT*, 24 August 1872.

12. *PDT*, 16 June 1866.

13. *MM*, 7 September 1867; C Eden, *My Wife and I in Queensland: An Eight Years' Experience in the Above Colony with Some Account of Polynesian Labour*, Longmans, London, 1872, pp. 108, 211–12.

14. Eden, *My Wife and I in Queensland*, pp. 308–9. RH Anning, Sun on the Right (unpublished typed manuscript, written 1960s), p. 12. A draft in the History Department library, James Cook University.

15. *MM*, 7 September 1867.

16. Interviews with Dick Hoolihan at Townsville on 8 April and 14 April 1972. Interview with Harry Gertz at Valley of Lagoons Station on 14 October 1972. Interview with Alf Palmer at Palm Island on 19 December 1972. When interviews were made, Hoolihan was approximately 65 years old, Gertz 84 years old, and Palmer 82 years old.

17. H. Reynolds, *An Indelible Stain? The Question of Genocide in Australia's History*, Viking, Penguin Books, Ringwood, Victoria, 2001, pp. 49–66.

18. *ibid*, p. 99.

19. *ibid*, pp. 120–30.

20. *ibid*, p. 134.

21. O Burt, Permanent Head of Colonial Secretary's Department, to Premier John Forrest, July 1895, cited in Reynolds, *An Indelible Stain*, p. 136.

22. *CC*, 21 February 1878.

23. A Markus, *Australian Race Relations 1788–1993*, Allen and Unwin, Sydney, 1994, p. 18.

24. M Dewar, *The 'Black War' in Arnhem Land: Missionaries and the Yolngu 1908–1940*, North Australian Research Unit, Australian National University, Darwin, 1992, pp. 38–76; CD Rowley, *The Destruction of Aboriginal Society*, Penguin, Harmondsworth, 1978, pp. 289–97.

25. NA Loos, *Invasion and Resistance*, ch. 6, 'The Decent Disposal of the Native Inhabitants'.

26. NA Loos, 'A Chapter of Contact: Aboriginal-European Relations in North Queensland, 1606–1992' in H Reynolds (ed.), *Race Relations in North Queensland*, Department of History & Politics, James Cook University, Townsville, 1993, pp. 4–39.

27. F Brennan, *Land Rights Queensland Style. The Struggle for Aboriginal Self Management*, University of Queensland Press, Brisbane, 1992, pp. 57–116.

28. NA Loos, 'The Frontier Revisited', *Meanjin*, vol. 36, no. 4, December 1977, pp. 508–15; Loos, *Invasion and Resistance*, 160–2.

29. M Franklin, *Black and White Australians: An Inter Racial History*, 1788–1975, Heinemann, South Yarra, Victoria, 1976, pp. 123–4.

30. See PH Russell, *Recognizing Aboriginal Title: The Mabo Case and Indigenous Resistance to English-Settler Colonialism*, University of Toronto Press, Toronto, 2005, *passim*, for an analysis of how *terra nullius* came to be imposed in Australia, uniquely among English-settled states, and how it was rejected by the High Court *Mabo* decision.

31. A Haebich, *Broken Circles: Fragmenting Indigenous Families 1800–2000*, Fremantle Arts Centre Press, Fremantle, 2000, p. 240; Broome, *Aboriginal Australians*, p. 100.

32. R Callick, 'Power and the Dreaming', *Time*, 19 November 1990, pp. 36–7.

33. Human Rights and Equal Opportunity Commission, *Bringing Them Home: The Report of the National Inquiry into the Separation of Aboriginal and Torres Strait Children from their Families*, Commonwealth of Australia, 1997, passim.

34. Harris, *One Blood*, pp. 562–3; 568–603.

35. Thomson, *Reaching Back*, pp. 13–14, 16–28; Haebich, *Broken Circles*, p. 240.

36. Thomson, *Reaching Back*, pp. 13–14.

37. R Kidd, *Black Lives, Government Lies*, University of New South Wales Press, Sydney, 2000, passim. This is a 63 page book that crystallises the findings of her doctorate and her detailed analysis: Rosalind Kidd, *The Way We Civilise: Aboriginal Affairs the untold story*, University of Queensland Press, St Lucia, 1997, ch. 3, 4, 5; see also pp. 160–1, 192–227.

38. Haebich, *Broken Circles*, pp. 188–9, 220–2, 519.

39. *ibid*, pp. 240–44, 266, 271–87, 475–80.

40. Harris, *One Blood*, pp. 633–7.

41. Kidd, *The Way We Civilize*, pp. 73–8, 233.

42. *ibid*, pp. 92–97, 113, 170, 188–9.

43. *ibid*, pp. 128–9.

44. *ABM Review*, 1 February 1937.

45. Kidd, *The Way We Civilize*, p. 218.

46. Kidd, *Black Lives Government Lies*, pp. 32, 33.

47. Kidd, *The Way We Civilize*, pp. 66, 74.

48. Harris, *One Blood*, p. 585.

49. *ibid*, p. 509.

50. Kidd, *The Way We Civilize*, pp. 84–5.

51. *ibid*, pp. 63–4.

52. Philip Freier, Living with the Munpitch: The History of Mitchell River Mission, 1905–1967, PhD, James Cook University, 1999, pp. 299–302.

53. L Smith, 'How many people had lived in Australia before it was annexed by the English in 1788?', in G Briscoe and L Smith (eds), *The Aboriginal Population Revisited*, Aboriginal History Monograph 10, Canberra, 2002, pp. 11–12; Markus, *Australian Race Relations*, p. xi; W Jonas, M Langton, and AIATSIS staff, *A Short Guide to Indigenous Australia: The Little Red, Yellow and Black and Green and Blue and White Book*, Australian Institute for Aboriginal and Torres Strait Islander Studies, Canberra, 1993, p. 27; D Horton (editor), *The Encyclopaedia of Aboriginal Australia: Aboriginal and Torres Strait Islander History*

Society and Culture, Aboriginal Studies Press, 1994, vol. 2, p. 889 (author Dr KHW Gaminiratne). Some early estimates were as low as 200,000 but this figure was soon revised upwards.

54. Markus, *Australian Race Relations*, p. xi; Loos, Aboriginal-European Relations in North Queensland, 1861–1897, pp. 459–77.

3. In the Beginning

1. G White, *Round About the Torres Straits: A Record of Australian Church Missions*, Society for Promoting Christian Knowledge, Sydney, 1917, p. 8. White was the first bishop of the missionary diocese of Carpentaria (1900–1915).

2. Australian Board of Missions [hereafter ABM], *ABM 1984*, Sydney, 1984, passim; ABM, *Budget '85*, Sydney, 1986; *Partners*, February–April 1990, 'ABM Budget 1989'. The amounts budgeted for Aboriginal and Islander Ministries were: 1984, $258,300 (31.8%); 1986, $362,340 (31.1%); 1989, $330,000 (27.5%). In 2001, $280,140 (24.2%) was budgeted for Aboriginal and Islander Ministries in six dioceses.

3. K Cole, *From Mission to Church: The CMS Mission to the Aborigines of Arnhem Land 1908–1985*, K Cole Publications, Bendigo, 1985, pp. 9–10; 'A Snapshot of our missionary giving, and where the money went in 1986', *Church Scene*, 13 May 1988. Roper River, Oenpelli, Numbulwar, Angurugu and Umbakumba were established by the CMS.

4. Loos, *Invasion and Resistance*, passim.

5. L Oates, 'The Impact of Christianity on a Primitive Culture', *Journal of Christian Education*, 1963, vol. VI, pp. 72–81.

6. S Neill, *A History of Christian Missions*, Penguin Books, Harmondsworth, 1984, pp. 15, 325; AE David, *Australia: Handbooks of English Church Expansion*, AR Mowbray, London, 1908, pp. 34–6.

7. *Sydney Morning Herald*, 2 November 1850; RM Ross, 'Evolution of the Melanesian Bishopric', *The New Zealand Journal of History*, vol. 16, no. 2, October 1982, pp. 132–3.

8. D Hilliard, *God's Gentlemen: A History of the Melanesian Mission, 1849–1942*, UQP, St Lucia, Brisbane, 1978, p. 14.

9. *ibid*, p. 13. Quotations from the Bible throughout are from the *Revised Standard Version*, Collins Fontana Books, London, rev. 1952.

10. *Sydney Morning Herald*, 2 November 1850.

11. Cole, *From Mission to Church*, pp. 10–14; D Wetherell, *Reluctant Mission: The Anglican Church in Papua New Guinea 1891–1942*, UQP, St Lucia, Queensland, 1977, p. 49; S Judd and K Cable, *Sydney Anglicans: A History of the Diocese*, Anglican Information Office, Sydney, 1987, p. 219.

12. Cole, *From Mission to Church*, pp. 10, 12; Harris, *One Blood*, pp. 33, 56–71, 133.

13. Determination No.III (20 October 1872), Resolution for the Constitution of the Church in the Dioceses of Australia and Tasmania. ABM Board Minutes, 4–5 February 1942, 'Chairman's Report', p. 1.

14. ABM Executive Council Minutes, 19 April 1879; Loos, Aboriginal–European Relations in North Queensland, 1861–1897, pp. 625–42.

15. ABM Executive Council Minutes, 17 October 1876–9 November 1884; ABM Sydney Diocesan Corresponding Committee Minutes, 15 August 1885.
16. Determination No.I, General Synod, 1886; ABM Board Minutes, 4–5 February 1942, 'Needham Report', p. 2.
17. ABM Executive Council Minutes, 20 June 1891; 29 July 1891.
18. ER Gribble, *Forty Years with the Aborigines*, Angus and Robertson, Sydney, 1930, p. 58.
19. ABM Gribble Papers, a six page letter from JB Gribble, presumably to Executive Council, date obliterated, concerning his preparations for establishing Bellenden Ker [Yarrabah] Mission, commencing: 'On reaching Townsville a meeting of the Diocesan Council'. The Gribble Papers are a part of the ABM Papers held at the Mitchell Library.
20. ABM Gribble Papers, Journal of Rev. JB Gribble: Early Days of Yarrabah 1891–92, 16 May 1892.
21. ABM Gribble Papers, Journal of Rev. JB Gribble, 2 June 1892; 3 June 1892.
22. ABM Executive Council Minutes, 6 June 1893.
23. Gribble, *Forty Years with the Aborigines*, pp. 58, 60.
24. ABM Executive Council Minutes, 14 December 1892; 3 February 1893; 7 April 1893. EC Rowland, *The Tropics for Christ: Being a History of the Diocese of North Queensland*, Diocese of North Queensland, Townsville, 1960, p. 93.
25. Cited in David, *Australia*, pp. 202, 203.
26. See Judd and Cable, *Sydney Anglicans*, chapter 13, for the significance of diocesanism.
27. Australia had been created as a diocese in 1836 with its cathedral at Sydney; Tasmania in 1842; Sydney, Melbourne, Newcastle (including what is now southern Queensland), and Adelaide (including Western Australia) in 1847; Brisbane in 1859; Goulburn in 1864; Grafton and Armidale in 1867; Bathurst in 1870; Ballarat in 1875; and North Queensland in 1878. New Zealand had been created a diocese in 1841 and was, until 1857, under the jurisdiction of Sydney. The Northern Territory was excised from Carpentaria in 1968.
28. Judd and Cable, *Sydney Anglicans*, pp. 208, 214.
29. Hilliard, *God's Gentlemen*, pp. 1–26; Wetherell, *Reluctant Mission*, pp. 46–55; Judd and Cable, pp. 218–19.
30. Wetherell, *Reluctant Mission*, pp. 44–5.
31. ABM Board Minutes, 1 October 1896; ABM, *The Jubilee Festival*, p. 34.
32. *ibid*, 1 October 1896.
33. *ibid*, 4–5 February 1942, 'Needham Report', p. 2.
34. Judd and Cable, *Sydney Anglicans*, pp. 4–5, 13; Cole, *From Mission to Church*, p. 13.
35. J Bayton, *Cross Over Carpentaria: Being a History of the Church of England in Northern Australia from 1865–1965*, Smith and Paterson, Brisbane, 1965, pp. 29–40; AdeQ Robin, *Matthew Blagden Hale: The Life of an Australian Pioneer Bishop*, Hawthorn Press, Melbourne, 1976, pp. 18, 45–56. For the earliest missions in New South Wales and Tasmania, see J Woolmington, 'The First Missions to Aborigines in Eastern Australia' and NJB Plomley, 'The Aborigines of Tasmania and Christianity: An Essay', in Swain and Rose, *Aboriginal Australians*

and Christian Missions, pp. 78–99. See also Harris, *One Blood*, pp. 21–76, 205–20, 340–57.

36. JS Needham, *White and Black in Australia*, National Missionary Council, London, 1935, pp. 95–101; Harris, *One Blood*, pp. 411–30.

37. David, *Australia*, pp. 192–3.

38. Judd and Cable, *Sydney Anglicans*, p. 13.

39. ABM Archives, Executive Council Minutes, 17 April 1879.

40. *ibid*. For Sir Alexander Stuart (1824–1886), see G Serle and R Ward (eds), *Australian Dictionary of Biography*, vol. 6: 1851–1890, R–Z, Melbourne University Press, Melbourne, 1976.

41. ABM Executive Council Minutes, 22 October 1881.

42. *Ibid.*

43. *ibid*; NA Loos, 'Concern and Contempt: Church and Missionary Attitudes towards Aborigines in North Queensland in the Nineteenth Century', in Swain and Rose (eds), *Aboriginal Australians and Christian Missions*, pp. 100–20.

44. ABM Board Minutes, 12–13 November 1952, 'Chairman's Report'.

45. Loos, 'A Chapter of Contact: Aboriginal–European Relations in North Queensland 1606–1992', pp. 20–39.

46. ABM Board Minutes, 4–5 February 1942, 'Needham Report', p. 3.

47. *ibid*, p. 3.

48. ABM Executive Council Minutes, 21 March 1890.

49. ABM Board Minutes, 4–5 February 1942, 'Needham Report'; David, *Australia*, pp. 166–8.

50. Bayton, *Cross Over Carpentaria*, pp. 83–5.

51. The five missions were Yarrabah (North Queensland), Mitchell River, Edward River, and Lockhart River Missions (Carpentaria), and Forrest River Mission (North West Australia).

52. ABM Executive Council Minutes, 13 October 1899–20 April 1900; ABM, *The Jubilee Festival*, pp. 60–2.

53. ABM Executive Council Minutes, 14 December 1900.

4. The Golden Age of Missions 1900–1950

1. Ignatius, 'Epistle to the Syrnaeans', in H Bettenson (ed.), *Documents of the Christian Church*, 2nd edn, Oxford University Press, Oxford, 1979, p. 64.

2. Bayton, *Cross Over Carpentaria*, p. 38.

3. Journal of ER Gribble, 14 November 1893, Gribble Papers, ABM Archives.

4. ER Gribble to Dixon, 18 October 1900, Gribble Papers.

5. Journal of ER Gribble, 3 August 1908, Gribble Papers; *Diocese of North Queensland Yearbook*, Diocesan Registry, Townsville, 1908, p. 78.

6. *Missionary Notes*, 18 June 1900, p. 42.

7. See *Brisbane Courier*, 7 September 1901, 'Aboriginal Mission Work: Mapoon Mission Station', p. 26; and 'Substance of an Address Delivered by the Rev. N Hey on Foreign Mission Night ... on May 14th 1912', p. 443, Presbyterian Board of Mission Papers, Mitchell Library, MSS 1893 carton no. 4.

8. D Craig, *The Social Impact of the State on an Aboriginal Reserve in Queensland, Australia*, PhD dissertation, University of California, Berkeley, 1980, (University Microfilms International facsimile), pp. 54–5.

9. *Missionary Notes*, 22 June 1896, p. 54.

10. Roth to Pol. Com., 'A Report on the Bellenden Ker Mission Station' [typed copy], encl. Roth to Pol. Com., 6 August 1898, QSA COL/142 [typed copy].

11. *1898 V. & P.*, IV, p. 501.

12. Craig, *The Social Impact of the State on an Aboriginal Reserve in Queensland*, p. 54.

13. 'Report of the Northern Protector of Aborigines for 1899', *1900 V. & P.*, V, p. 591.

14. *The Carpentarian*, 1903, 'Diocese of Carpentaria', QSA Lands Res no.03–117.

15. See Loos, Aboriginal–European Relations in North Queensland, 1861–1897, ch. 10.

16. Interview with Rev. John Best, Perth, 18, 22 August 1988.

17. *Missionary Notes*, 18 June 1900, p. 1.

18. Craig, *The Social Impact of the State on an Aboriginal Reserve in Queensland*, p. 62.

19. ABM Board Minutes, 3–4 February 1942, 'Chairman's Report', p. 6.

20. ABM Executive Council Minutes, 16 February 1903.

21. Bayton, *Cross Over Carpentaria*, pp. 85–93; ABM Board Minutes, 4–5 February 1942, 'Chairman's Report', p. 6.

22. Su-Jane Hunt, 'The Gribble Affair: A Study in Colonial Politics', in JB Gribble, *Dark Deeds in a Sunny Land or Blacks and Whites in North-West Australia*, republished 1987, University of Western Australia Press, with Institute of Applied Aboriginal Studies, Western Australian College of Advanced Education, Perth, 1987, pp. 62–73.

23. ABM Board Minutes, 3–4 February 1942, 'Chairman's Report', p. 5; NJ Green, European Education at Oombulgurri an Aboriginal Settlement in Western Australia, an abridged version of MEd thesis, University of Western Australia, 1986, pp. 61–2.

24. Superintendents' Diaries, 1917 to 1953, Battye Library; Green, European Education at Oombulgurri, passim.

25. Diocesan Council of the North West Minutes, 'A Survey of the Oombulgurri Community: July 1985', a report by Rev. Keith Cole, quoting from John Best, 'A Closed Chapter of Church History', *Anglican Messenger*, September 1968.

26. Neville Green, *The Forrest River Massacres*, Fremantle Arts Centre Press, Fremantle, pp. 74–5, 97, 121–2, 129; Christine Halse, *A Terribly Wild Man*, Allen & Unwin, Sydney, 2002, pp. 108–11, 114–5.

27. ABM Board Minutes, 18 June 1919, 'Memorandum from the Aboriginal Sub-Committee of the A.B.M.', p. 2.

28. *ibid.*, p. 2.

29. *ibid.*, p. 4.

30. ABM Board Minutes, 18 June 1919.

31. *ibid.*, 5 October 1921.

32. *ibid.*, 6 December 1920.

33. *ibid.*, 2–3 April 1924, 'Organisation Committee Report'; Bayton, *Cross Over Carpentaria*, pp. 153–4.

34. JJE Done, *Wings Across the Sea*, Boolarong Publications, Brisbane, 1987, pp. 66–74. See also Loos, *Invasion and Resistence*, chapter 5.

35. A Chase, 'Cultural Continuity: Land and Resources among East Cape York Aborigines', in NC Stevens and A Bailey (eds), *Contemporary Cape York Peninsula*, The Royal Society of Queensland, Brisbane, 1980, pp. 84–8.

36. D Thompson, *Bora is Like Church: Aboriginal Initiation Ceremonies and the Christian Church at Lockhart River, Queensland*, ABM, Sydney, 1985, p. 10.

37. ABM Board Minutes, 11–13 April 1961, 'Carpentaria Mission Study', passim. See also ABM Board Minutes, 15–16 March 1933, 'Budget', p. 3; and, for this period, especially Board Minutes, 11–14 July 1939, Agenda Item No.14, 'The Bishop of Carpentaria writes', passim.

38. JW Chapman, 'The Founding of Edward River Mission', *A.B.M. Review*, June 1962, pp. 80–1; *Queensland Government Gazette*, 14 January 1922, p. 129.

39. *A.B.M. Review*, 12 June 1928, pp. 46–55, 'Our Annual Report'.

40. ABM Board Minutes, 11–12 July 1939, 'Agenda Item No.14: The Bishop of Carpentaria writes'.

41. Bayton, *Cross Over Carpentaria*, pp. 151, 152; interviews with Frank Coleman, John Colman, Mickey Walker of Edward River, 11–12 April 1988; *A.B.M. Review*, 1 June 1933, pp. 17–19, 32–41; 'Chairman's Report'; and 1 August 1939, pp. 113–49, 'Chairman's Report'.

42. Queensland Department of Community Services and Ethnic Affairs, 'Annual Report for the Year Ended 30th June 1988', Queensland Government, 1988, pp. 4–7.

43. Discussions with Bishop Arthur Malcolm, now retired, Bishop James Leftwich, his successor, and the Reverend Wayne Connolly of Yarrabah, at Townsville, 12–13 July 2003.

5. An Expanding Perspective 1900–1950

1. See NA Loos, 'The Frontier Revisited', *Meanjin*, 4, 1977, pp. 509–15.

2. A Haebich, *For Their Own Good: Aborigines and Government in the Southwest of Western Australia, 1900–1940*, University of Western Australia Press, Nedlands, 1988, passim.

3. *ibid*, pp. 196–7.

4. *ibid*, p. 220.

5. *A.B.M. Review*, 7 March 1921, pp. 6–7; 7 August 1921, pp. 86–7; 7 September 1922, p. 108; 12 January 1925, pp. 150–1; 12 May 1927, pp. 38–9.

6. *A.B.M. Review*, 7 August 1921, p. 86.

7. *ibid*, 12 May 1927, p. 39.

8. *ibid*, p. 38.

9. *ibid*.

10. *A.B.M. Review*, 1 November 1935, p. 144. See also Haebich, *For Their Own Good*, passim.

11. E Heath to Needham, 26 August 1938; 20 February 1939; 27 March 1939; 25 September 1939; 5 June 1941; ABM Chairman's Correspondence, Personal File.

12. Heath, St Mary's Church of England Hostel, Alice Springs, to Robertson, 14 May 1951; 4 November 1952; ABM Chairman's Correspondence, Personal File; ABM Board Minutes, 25–26 July 1945, 'Report of the Moore River Native Settlement'.

13. ABM Board Minutes, 24–25 November 1948, 'The Forrest River Mission'.

14. *A.B.M. Review*, 12 April 1925, pp. 2–3; 15 September 1930, p. 100.

15. *ibid*, 15 May 1931, p. 29.

16. *ibid*, 1 August 1949, p. 120; 1 January 1938, p. 15.

17. *ibid*, 1 July 1948, p. 106.

18. *ibid*, 15 November 1931, p. 139.

19. *ibid*, 1 November 1941, pp. 206–7.

20. ABM Board Minutes, 25–6 July 1945; *A.B.M. Review*, 1 July 1949, p. 106; Rowland, *The Tropics for Christ*, pp. 100, 103. See also Halse, *A Terribly Wild Man*, pp. 186–7.

21. *A.B.M. Review*, 15 May 1931, p. 29.

22. ER Gribble to Chairman, ABM, 30 June 1945, ABM Chairman's Correspondence on Aborigines (Palm Island).

23. Feetham to Needham, 26 July 1933, ABM Chairman's Correspondence on Aborigines (Palm Island); Halse, *A Terribly Wild Man*, p. 4.

24. 'Report of Palm Island', encl. Feetham to Cranswick, 27 November 1945, ABM Chairman's Correspondence on Aborigines (Palm Island).

25. ER Gribble to Bishop (Feetham), 10 March 1947, ABM Chairman's Correspondence on Aborigines (Palm Island).

26. Feetham to Needham, 26 July 1933, ABM Chairman's Correspondence on Aborigines (Palm Island). See also Rowland, *The Tropics for Christ*, p. 102.

27. ABM Board Minutes, 4–5 November 1936, 'Agenda Item No.11'.

28. Feetham to Needham, 26 July 1933; Feetham to Archbishop of Brisbane, 14 December 1945, copy encl. Feetham to Chairman of ABM, 16 December 1945, ABM Chairman's Correspondence on Aborigines (Palm Island).

29. Feetham to Cranswick, 16 December 1945, ABM Chairman's Correspondence on Aborigines (Palm Island).

30. ABM Board Minutes, 8–9 November 1939, 'Report on Yarrabah and Palm Island'.

31. *A.B.M. Review*, 1 October 1948, p. 161. There were four girls and five boys away at this time.

32. ABM Board Minutes, 30 April–1 May 1925, 'Missions and Missionaries Committee Report'.

33. *ibid*, 19–20 August 1925, 'Chairman's Report' and 'Missions and Missionaries Committee Report'; *A.B.M. Review*, 15 July 1929, pp. 87–9.

34. *A.B.M. Review*, 1 March 1933, pp. 177–8; 1 April 1934, p. 212; ABM Board Minutes, 19–20 November 1930, 'Missions and Missionaries Committee Report'.

35. ABM Board Minutes, 14–15 March 1945, 'Standing Committee Report'.

36. *A.B.M. Review*, 1 December 1947, p. 187.

37. *ibid*, 1 March 1949, p. 36; 1 April 1949, pp. 53–4; ABM Board Minutes, 13–14 November 1946, 'Missions and Missionaries Committee Report'.

38. ABM Board Minutes, 'Missions and Missionaries Report', 22–3 August 1928; 26–27 March 1930; 'Chairman's Report', 29–31 October 1968.
39. *A.B.M. Review*, 1 June 1933, p. 36.
40. *ibid*, 1 June 1935, p. 49.
41. *ibid*, 1 August 1939, p. 140.
42. AE Clark to [Robertson], 19 December 1952, ABM Chairman's Correspondence re Aborigines [Lake Tyers].
43. *A.B.M. Review*, 1 September 1951, p. 129.
44. ABM Board Minutes, 20–21 November 1929, 'Report of Tasmanian Committee'; 19–20 November 1930, 'Missions and Missionaries Report: Report on Half-Castes in SW Australia and Tasmania'; 29–30 July, 'Organisation Committee Report'.
45. Haebich, *For Their Own Good*, pp. 353–4.
46. ABM. Board Minutes, 18–19 March 1931; 29–30 July 1931; 4–5 November 1936, 'Agenda Item No.11'; 16–17 March 1938, 'Agenda Item No.10', 20–21 November 1940, 'Chairman's report'.
47. ABM Board Minutes, 4–5 February 1942, 'Chairman's Report'; 29–31 July 1942, 'Chairman's Report'. Interview with Rev. J Best, Perth, 18–22 August 1988; Interview with Rev. J Warby, Rockhampton, 11 October 1988.
48. ABM Board Minutes, 19–20 November 1930, Agenda Item No.9(a) (I): 'Aborigines and Half-castes in South-West Australia' and 'Cape Barren Island'.
49. ABM Executive Council Minutes, 19 August 1910.
50. *ibid*, 5 September 1910.
51. ABM Board Minutes, 23–24 November 1927; 21–23 March 1928, 'Chairman's Report'; 18–19 November 1942, 'Missions and Missionaries Report'; 24–25 February 1943, 'Missions and Missionaries Report'; 5–6 July 1944, 'A National Policy for Aborigines'. See also *A.B.M. Review*, 1 October 1933, p. 108, 'A Despised Race'.
52. ABM Board Minutes, 24–25 February 1943, 'Chairman's Report'.
53. *ibid*, 20–21 November 1940, 'Report on the Aborigines of Australia and the Work Being Done for Them by Government and Missionary Bodies', pp. 4–5.
54. *ibid*, 16–17 March 1938, 'National Missionary Council Aboriginal Advisory Committee'.
55. *ibid*, 13–14 March 1935, 'Notes on Budget Proposed for 1935'.
56. *ibid*, 20–21 November 1940, 'Report on the Aborigines of Australia', p. 5.
57. ABM Chairman's Correspondence, Hann to Robinson, 28 March 1950, Alice Hann Personal File.
58. Loos, personal observations, commencing in the 1960s.
59. ABM Board Minutes, 11–14 July 1939, Minister, Department of Health and Home Affairs, to Needham, 29 June 1939 [copy]; ABM Board Minutes, 13–14 March 1935, 'Missions and Missionaries Report'.
60. W Moore, Minister for Health and Home Affairs, to Secretary, Diocese of North Queensland, 17 September 1951, ABM Chairman's Correspondence on Aborigines (Yarrabah).
61. *Church Chronicle*, 1 June 1951, p. 167.

62. Cranswick to Gregory, 27 November 1946, ABM Chairman's Correspondence, Personal File PC Gregory; ABM Board Minutes, 24–25 November 1948, 'The Forrest River Mission'.

63. Craig, *The Social Impact of the State on an Aboriginal Reserve in Queensland*, pp. 72–5; ABM Board Minutes, 6–7 October 1937, 'Chairman's Report', pp. 1, 2.

64. ABM Board Minutes, 15–16 November 1950, p. 4.

65. *ibid*, p. 3.

66. *ibid*, 24–25 November 1948, p. 5.

67. *ibid*.

68. 'Native Affairs Report', *QPP*, 1950–51, 2, p. 1047; Green, European Education at Oombulgurri, p. 178.

69. ABM Board Minutes, 29–30 June 1932, pp. 378ff.

70. J Jones, Chairman, *Annual Report for the Nine Months Ended December 31ˢᵗ, 1918*, ABM, Sydney, 1919, p. 6.

71. *ibid*, pp. 6–10.

72. *ibid*, p. 8.

73. 'Report of the Australian Board of Missions to the General Synod, 1944', *Summary of Proceedings of the General Synod of the Dioceses in Australia and Tasmania Session 1945: Official Report*, Sydney, The Church of England in Australia and Tasmania, p. 97.

74. EC Rowland, *Faithful Unto Death: The Story of the New Guinea Martyrs*, ABM, Sydney, 1964.

75. 'ABM Report to General Synod, 1944', pp. 97–8, 107–8.

76. *ibid*, p. 104; 'Missions and Missionaries Committee Report', ABM Board Minutes, 18–19 November 1942, 28–29 July 1943, and 17–18 November 1943; *A.B.M. Review* 1 April 1946, p. 35.

77. 'A.B.M. Report to General Synod 1944', p. 104; ABM Board Minutes, 30–31 July 1941, 'Chairman's Report'.

78. ABM Board Minutes, 18–19 November 1942, 'Notes on the Budget' and 'Missions and Missionaries Reports'; *A.B.M. Review*, 1 July 1942, pp. 102–3, 'News from Carpentaria'.

79. Interview with Rev. John Best, Perth, 18, 22 August 1988; *A.B.M. Review*, 1 August 1942, pp. 116–18.

80. *A.B.M. Review*, 1 June 1942, p. 91.

81. *ibid*, 1 August 1942, p. 118; 1 October 1942, p. 152.

82. *ibid*, 1 May 1943, p. 68.

83. *ibid*, 1 December 1949, p. 180.

84. *ibid*, 1 March 1943, p. 44.

85. *ibid*, 1 May 1943, p. 66.

86. ABM Board Minutes, 24–25 November 1958.

87. *ibid*, 'Chairman's Report'.

88. *ibid*.

89. Mission Agency Conference, Brisbane, 8–13 December 1986. I attended as an observer.

90. 'Report of the Australian Board of Missions to General Synod', *Summary of Proceedings of the General Synod of the Dioceses in Australia and Tasmania, Session 1950*, Sydney, Church of England in Australia and Tasmania, 1951, p. 96; *A.B.M., Past-Present-Future*, A.B.M., Sydney, 1977.

6. Of Massacres, Missionaries, Myths and History Wars

1. Green, *The Forrest River Massacres*, pp. 129–49, 159, 166, 177; Journals re Forrest River, 16 April 1922–20 August 1926 [typed copy] Mitchell Library, Item 10/13, pp. 16–26.
2. *ibid*, pp. 14–15, 160, 162. See also Halse, *A Terribly Wild Man*, pp. 132–35.
3. Halse, *A Terribly Wild Man*, p. 134.
4. *ibid*, p. 140.
5. Royal Commission proceedings, p. 6, quoted in Halse, *A Terribly Wild Man*, p. 148.
6. Green, *The Forrest River Massacres*, pp. 206–7.
7. *ibid*, pp. 218, 219, cited.
8. *ibid*, pp. 207–8, 220, 228–9.
9. e.g. Harris, *One Blood*, pp. 512–17. See Rod Moran, *Massacre Myth*, Access Press, Bassandean, 1999, pp. 226–40.
10. The High Court's 1992 Mabo decision (Mabo No. 2) overturned the legal principle of *terra nullius* upon which Australia was founded; that is, that Australia was a colony of settlement, not a colony of conquest. Its land belonged to no-one that British law recognised as civilised enough to have ownership and sovereignty. Consequently, the English Crown took possession of New South Wales and subsequently the other Australian colonies. *See* Noel Loos and Koiki Mabo, *Edward Koiki Mabo: His Life and Struggle for Land Rights*, UQP, St Lucia, 1996.
11. Green, *The Forrest River Massacres*, passim; Halse, *A Terrible Wild Man*, chapters 5, 6, 7, 8.
12. N Green, 'Ahab wailing in the wilderness', *Quadrant*, June 2003, no.397, pp. 30–34.
13. Rod Moran, *Sex Maiming and Murder: Seven Case Studies into the Reliability of Reverend ERB Gribble, Superintendent Forrest River Mission 1913–1928, as a Witness to the Truth*, Access Press, Bassandean, 2002, passim.
14. Halse, *A Terribly Wild Man*, pp. 164–5.
15. Kate Auty, 'Patrick Bernard O'Leary and the Forrest River massacres, Western Australia: examining "Wodgil" and the significance of 8 June 1926', *Aboriginal History*, vol. 28, 2004, pp. 122–55.
16. Green, 'Ahab wailing in the wilderness', pp. 30–34. See also Halse, *A Terribly Wild Man*, pp. 81–92 for her account of Gribble's affair with Janie and his subsequent dismissal from Yarrabah.
17. Cited Green, *The Forrest River Massacres*, pp. 143–4. See also Hay's death certificate 4/26 Wyndham, dated 1/6/1926, cited Auty, 'Patrick Bernard O'Leary'.
18. Moran, *Massacre Myth*, pp. 18, 125, 140, 148–9, 157, 181.
19. ER Gribble, *The Problem of the Australian Aboriginal*, Angus & Robertson, Sydney, 1932, p. 77; N Green, *The Oombulgurri Story: A Pictorial History of*

the People of Oombulgurri 1884–1988, Focus Education Services, Perth, 1988, pp. 80–2.

20. ABM Board Minutes, 26–27 July 1950, 'Chairman's Report'.

21. *ibid*, 24–25 July 1929, 'Mission and Missionaries Committee Report – Action'.

22. Keith Windschuttle, 'The myths of frontier massacres in Australian history, Part I The invention of massacre stories', *Quadrant*, vol. XLIV, no. 10, October 2000. I read this recently on Windschuttle's Internet site at http://www.sydney-line.com/Massacres, pp. 6–7. See also at the same site: 'The Myths of frontier massacres in Australian history, Part II The fabrication of the Aboriginal death toll', *Quadrant*, vol. XLIV, no. 11 November 2000, and 'The myths of frontier massacres in Australian history, Part III Massacre stories and the policy of separation', *Quadrant*, vol. XLIV, no. 12, December 2000. There is a vast amount of literature now most conveniently available on the Internet, including other articles by Windschuttle, his supporters and his critics.

23. H Reynolds and N Loos, 'Aboriginal Resistance in Queensland', *Journal of Politics and History*, vol. 22, no. 3, 1976, pp. 214–26.

24. Windschuttle, 'Part II The fabrication of the Aboriginal death toll', p. 10. See also pp. 4–7.

25. Windschuttle, *The Fabrication of Aboriginal History, Vol.1, Van Diemen's Land 1803–1847*, Macleay Press, Sydney, 2002; R Manne (ed), *Whitewash: On Keith Windschuttle's Fabrication of Aboriginal History*, Black Inc., Melbourne, 2003; S Macintyre, *The History Wars*, Melbourne University Press, Melbourne, 2003; J Dawson, *Washout: On the Academic Response to the Fabrication of Aboriginal History*, Macleay Press, Sydney, 2004; B Attwood and SG Foster (eds), *Frontier Conflict: The Australian Experience*, National Museum of Australia, Canberra, 2003; B Attwood, *Telling the Truth about Aboriginal History*, Allen and Unwin, Crow's Nest, NSW, 2005. In this book, pp. 2–3 Attwood details the controversy, the associated 'travelling circus', and the articles, debates, and radio and television coverage.

26. Attwood, *Telling the Truth about Aboriginal History*, pp. 65–84, 119, 152.

27. Attwood, *Telling the Truth about Aboriginal History*, pp. 80, 81, 119

28. Russell, *Recognizing Aboriginal Title*, p. xi.

29. 'The myths of frontier massacres in Australian history, Part III Massacre stories and the policy of separation'. See also Attwood, *The Truth about Aboriginal History*, pp. 122–3.

7. The End of an Era

1. 'The Aims of Native Welfare Policy in Australia by the Hon. Paul Hasluck, MP, Minister for Territories', ABM Board Minutes, 17–19 November 1953; AT Yarwood and MJ Knowling, *Race Relations in Australia: A History*, Methuen, Australia, North Ryde, NSW, 1982, p. 265.

2. Yarwood and Knowling, *Race Relations in Australia*, pp. 254, 264–6; Markus, *Governing Savages*, pp. 130–57.

3. 'The Aims of Native Welfare Policy in Australia by the Hon. P Hasluck, MP, Minister for Territories', ABM Board Minutes, 17–19 November 1953; Elkin to FW Coaldrake, 3 October 1967, ABM Chairman's Correspondence, Series 23, Box 6, Folder 32.

4. Cranswick to Sister Eileen Heath, 5 December 1945, ABM Chairman's Correspondence, Personal File: Sister Eileen Heath.

5. 'Report on Forrest River Mission by Professor Elkin', ABM Board Minutes, 13–14 November 1946; 'Report on Forrest River Mission July to December 1947', ABM Chairman's Correspondence, Personal File: RB Cranswick; Robertson, Chairman, ABM, to Archdeacon RE Freeth, ABM, Perth, 18 June 1954, ABM Chairman's Correspondence, Forrest River Mission.

6. 'Report for Year July '52 to June '53', ABM Chairman's Correspondence, Series 6.

7. 'Report on Forrest River Mission by Professor Elkin', ABM Board Minutes 13–14 November 1946.

8. M Hogan, *The Sectarian Strand: Religion in Australian History*, Penguin Books, Ringwood, Vic., 1987, pp. 220–1.

9. N Loos and R Keast, 'The Radical Promise: The Aboriginal Christian Co-operative Movement', *Australian Historical Studies*, vol. 25, no. 99, October 1992, pp. 286–301.

10. L Kelly (ed.), 'Salute to Alf Clint', *Goorialla*, Summer 1980/81, 2. This is unpaginated. *Aboriginal Welfare Bulletin*, vol.1, no.1, [1957?], p. 3, ABM Chairman's Correspondence re Aborigines, Series 14.

11. Robertson to Clint, 17 September 1952, ABM Chairman's Correspondence relating to Aborigines, Series 14; A Clint, 'Report to the Standing Committee on Co-operatives', October 1961, ABM Chairman's Correspondence re Aborigines, Series 16.

12. Loos and Keast, 'The Radical Promise'.

13. 'Native Affairs Report', *QPP*, 1953–4, vol. 2, p. 1009 and *QPP*, 1955, p. 1113.

14. 'Native Affairs Report', *QPP*, 1957–8, vol. 2, p. 1165, *QPP*, 1958–9, vol. 2, p. 1088, and *QPP*, 1953–4, vol. 2, pp. 959, 1010.

15. 'Native Affairs Report', *QPP*, 1956, pp. 1112–16. I have also used figures supplied by John Warby, 22 February 1989, personal communication.

16. 'John Warby's Report, June 1958', ABM Chairman's Correspondence re Aborigines, Series 19.

17. 'Native Affairs Report', *QPP*, 1956–7, vol. 2, p. 1280.

18. 'Native Affairs Report', *QPP*, 1957–8, vol. 2, p. 1165.

19. K Tennant, *Speak Ye So Gently*, Angus and Robertson, London, 1959, p. 107.

20. The 1985 Tranby/NSWIT Link course (eds), *The Meeting Tree*, Co-operative for Aborigines, 1986, pp. 8–11.

21. J Warby, 'The Formation of the First Aboriginal Co-operative', in 'Salute to Alf Clint', *Goorialla*, Summer, 1980/81, 2.

22. Rev. WA Brown, 'Report on Interview with Dr Noble, Minister for Health and Home Affairs (Qld)', ABM Chairman's Correspondence re Aborigines, Series 9; Tennant, *Speak Ye So Gently*, p. 146. Personal communication, Warby to Loos, 1 May 1989.

23. 'Lockhart River Co-operative Society, 1 May 1960'; Williams to Coaldrake, 18 September 1960; Williams to Coaldrake, 5 January 1961; Coaldrake to SJ Matthews, Bishop of Carpentaria, 15 February 1961, ABM Chairman's Correspondence re Aborigines, Series 10.

24. Hudson to Coaldrake, 18 March 1959, ABM Chairman's Correspondence re Aborigines, Series 14; Hooper-Colsey, Superintendent, Mitchell River, to Coaldrake, 15 July 1960, ABM Chairman's Correspondence re Aborigines, Series 5; J Hudson, Bishop of Carpentaria, to Clint, 4 March 1961, ABM Chairman's Correspondence, Series 14.

25. Telephone interviews, John Warby, Keppel Sands, 20 November 1990, and Fred Thompson, Townsville, 17 November 1990.

26. C Lack, *Three Decades of Queensland Political History 1929–1960*, SG Reid, Government Printer, Brisbane [n.d. 1961?], pp. 486–92.

27. Warby to Bishop of Carpentaria, 7 October 1959, ABM Chairman's Correspondence, Series 14. See also 'Report on Interview with Dr Noble, Minister for Health and Home Affairs for the Queensland Government , by Rev. WA Brown', ABM Chairman's Correspondence, Series 9. The date of this interview is given as 27 November but no year is indicated; it was probably 1958. See also 'Report Cape York Peninsula Torres Strait Islands', ABM Chairman's Correspondence, Series 11, 1958[?].

28. Warby to Bishop of Carpentaria, 7 October 1959.

29. SJ Matthews, Bishop of Carpentaria, to Coaldrake, 28 February 1961, ABM Chairman's Correspondence, Series 14; Kelly, 'Salute to Alf Clint'; Matthews to Clint, 4 March 1961, Chairman's Correspondence, Series 14.

30. Matthews to Coaldrake, 2 October 1960, and Coaldrake to Matthews, 13 October 1960, ABM Chairman's Correspondence, Series 10.

31. SJ Matthews, Bishop of Carpentaria, to Coaldrake, 2 October 1960, ABM Chairman's Correspondence re Aborigines, Series 15; Matthews to Clint, 4 March 1961, ABM Chairman's Correspondence re Aborigines, Series 14; Minutes, Lockhart River Aboriginal Co-operative Society Ltd, 29 March 1963; Deputy Commissioner of Taxation to Diocesan Registrar, 16 August 1966, Tax Receipt, 12 July 1967, for $1990; Diocese of Carpentaria Papers, Oxley Library. The letters concerning tax are filed in the back cover of 1960 Minute Book.

32. Clint to Coaldrake, 20 November 1965, ABM Chairman's Correspondence, Series 14.

33. 'Report to Standing Committee re Co-operatives', October 1961, ABM Chairman's Correspondence, Series 16; *The Co-operative for Aborigines Newsletter*, vol. 1, no. 2, June 1967; Interview with Jacob Abednego by Noni Sharp, cassette 092, SPII/Cn/1/81.

34. 'Co-operative for Aborigines Limited, News Sheet', January 1974, ABM Chairman's Correspondence, Series 14.

35. ABM Board Minutes, 24–26 October 1967, 'Chairman's Report: A New ABM Policy for Aborigines', p. 2.

36. Cranswick to Eileen Heath, 5 December 1945, ABM Chairman's Correspondence, Personal File: Eileen Heath; ABM Board Minutes 28–29 July 1948, 'Chairman's Report'.

37. '*Instructions*: issued to the Rev. Keith Coaldrake on the occasion of his assumption of the office of Priest-Superintendent of the Forrest River Mission', 19 February 1948, ABM Chairman's Correspondence, Series 6, Box 2, Folder 10.

38. ABM Board Minutes, 26–28 July 1955, 'Forrest River Mission: Report by Canon MA Warren'; K Coaldrake to Chairman, ABM, 2 December 1954, ABM Chairman's correspondence, Series 6, Box 2, Folder 10.

39. ABM Board Minutes, 29–31 October 1968, 'Forrest River Mission Closed'; Green, *The Oombulgurri Story*, pp. 114–5.

40. Robertson to Sister Delaney, 21 March 1951, ABM Chairman's Correspondence, Personal File: D. Delaney.

41. ABM Board Minutes, 3–5 May 1966, 'Chairman's Report', p. 10.

42. *ibid*, 27–29 September 1960, 'Chairman's Report'.

43. *ibid*, 11–13 April 1961, 'Chairman's Report'.

44. *ibid*, 11–13 April 1961, 'Carpentaria Mission Studies'.

45. *ibid*, 26–28 October 1965, 'Report from Division of Mission of the Australian Council of Churches 1964–65'.

46. See also David Trigger, *Whitefella Comin: Aboriginal responses to colonialism in northern Australia*, Cambridge University Press, Cambridge, 1992, passim.

47. 'Report on Forrest River July to December 1947', ABM Chairman's Correspondence, Personal File: RB Cranswick. Aborigines at Yarrabah made this comment in discussion with me on visits to Yarrabah in the early 1970s. In 1989, two of my Aboriginal students interviewed older relatives about the dormitory system and found that the three women they interviewed presented the complete spectrum from strong approval to bitter disapproval.

48. 'Report for Year July '52 to June '53', ABM Chairman's Correspondence, Forrest River Mission.

49. ABM Board Minutes 13–14 November 1946, 'Report on Forrest River by Professor Elkin'.

50. *ibid*.

51. *ibid*.

52. ABM Board Minutes, 26–28 July 1955, 'Aborigines: Forrest River Mission'.

53. *ibid*, 13–14 March 1935, 'History Compiled from Official Documents in the Possession of the Board Concerning the Relationship of the Bishop and Diocese of North Queensland, the Australian Board of Missions and the Yarrabah Mission'; ABM Board Minutes, 14–15 April 1937, 'Chairman's Report: Yarrabah'.

54. Craig, *The Social Impact of the State on an Aboriginal Reserve in Queensland*, pp. 75–7.

55. Discussion with Bishop Arthur Malcolm at Yarrabah during 1988 and 1989 and interview at Townsville, 10 November 1989. Sister Muriel Stanley was a trained nursing sister, but 'Sister' was also the title given to female Church Army Officers. Male graduates were referred to as 'Captain'.

56. *QPP*, 1956–7, Vol. 2, p. 1250.

57. 'Native Affairs Report', *QPP*, 1958–9, vol. 2, pp. 1060–1 and *QPP*, 1959–60, vol. 2, pp. 1160–1; *QPP*, 1959–60, p. 1189.

58. Warby to Bishop of Carpentaria, 7 October 1959, ABM Chairman's Correspondence re Aborigines, Series 14.

59. Diocese of North Queensland, *Yearbook*, Diocesan Registry, Townsville, 1959, p. 61; ABM Board Minutes, 27–29 October 1959, 'The Future of Aboriginal Reserves'.

60. ABM Board Minutes, 27–29 October 1959, 'Special Visit to the Diocese of Carpentaria by the Board's Representatives'.

61. Matthews to Coaldrake, 28 August 1961, ABM Chairman's Correspondence, Personal File: A Lupton. The letter referred enthusiastically to Lupton. Telephone discussion with Bishop A Hall-Matthews, 18 March 1991.

62. ABM Board Minutes, 1–3 May 1962, 'Missions Commission'; 23–25 October 1962, 'Memorandum on the Removal of Lockhart River People: Chairman's Response to the Board'.

63. Hudson to Director of Native Affairs, 30 June 1961; Memorandum of Interview of Minister of Health and Home Affairs with Right Rev. SJ Matthews, 30 June 1961, QSA Health and Home Affairs 6694 N.A. of 1961; Coaldrake to Matthews, 16 December 1965, Diocese of Carpentaria Papers, Oxley Library; ABM Board Minutes 27–29 April 1965, 'Chairman's Report'; 23–25 October 1962, 'Memorandum on the Removal of the Lockhart River People'; 3–5 May 1966, 'Chairman's Report'; 25–27 October 1966, 'Chairman's Report: Future of Cape York Mission'; 4–6 April 1967, 'Chairman's Report: Cape York Transfer'.

64. ABM Board Minutes, 23–25 October 1962, 'Memorandum on the Removal of Lockhart River People'; 25–27 October 1966, 'Standing Committee: Transfer of Cape York Missions to Government'.

65. *ibid*, 11–13 April 1961, 'Report on Full Situation at Edward River Mission', and 'Report on Mitchell River Mission to The Lord Bishop of Carpentaria'.

66. *ibid*, 3–5 May 1966, 'Chairman's Report: Aborigines'.

67. *ibid*, 25–27 October 1966, 'Chairman's Report: Future of Cape York Missions' and 'Standing Committee: Transfer of Cape York Missions to Government'.

68. *ibid*, 23–25 October 1962, 'Chairman's Report to the Board: Memorandum on the Removal of Lockhart River People'.

69. 'Native Affairs Report', *QPP*, 1960–61, pp. 1167, 1190; 1961–2, pp. 1353–5; 1962, pp. 1370, 1377–8; Craig, *The Social Impact of the State on an Aboriginal Reserve in Queensland*, pp. 79–80.

70. JC Taylor, *Of Acts and Axes: An Ethnography of Socio-Cultural Change in an Aboriginal Community*, Cape York Peninsula, PhD thesis, Department of Behavioural Sciences, James Cook University, 1984, pp. 338–40.

71. Craig, *The Social Impact of the State on an Aboriginal Reserve in Queensland*, pp. 74–5. Craig cites a number of reports.

72. *Courier Mail*, 25 August 1959.

73. Taylor, *Of Acts and Axes*, p. 607.

74. 'Chairman's Memorandum on Parochial Aboriginal Work', 12 June 1961.

75. ABM, *Acceptance: The Next Step Forward*, Sydney, October 1967, passim.

76. ABM, *Acceptance: The Next Step Forward*, Sydney, October 1967, passim.

77. Ellemor to Coaldrake, 1 November 1967, ABM Chairman's Correspondence, Series 23. Ellemor was late in replying.

78. ABM Board Minutes, 14–16 April 1980, 'Chairman's Report'. This review and analysis, no doubt derived from the Minutes, confirms my reading of the Minutes.

79. *ibid*, 30 April–2 May 1968, 'Chairman's Report'; 29–31 October 1968, 'Standing Committee Report'.

80. *ibid*, 30 April–2 May 1968, 'Chairman's Report'.

81. *ibid*, 26–28 October 1971, 'Chairman's Report: Report of the Representative for Aboriginal Affairs'.

82. *ibid*, 7–9 April 1970, 'Chairman's Report: Programme for Aboriginal Work'.

83. *ibid*, 24–26 September 1972, 'Chairman's Report: Report of the Representative for Aboriginal Affairs'.

84. *ibid*.

85. *ibid*, 24–26 October 1972, 'Chairman's Report: Report of the Representative for Aboriginal Affairs'; [New South Wales] Provincial Synod 1974, 'Report of the Committee on the Church's Ministry to Aborigines', ABM Chairman's Correspondence re Aborigines, Series 22 Box 61, Folder 31.

86. 'A Survey by the Australian Board of Missions of the State of Development of Aboriginal and Islander Ministries in the Anglican Church of Australia, January 1991', enclosed Right Rev. Ken Mason, Chairman of ABM, to Loos, 10 April 1991.

87. ABM Board Minutes, 26–27 October 1971, 'Chairman's Report'.

88. Mason to Loos, 10 April 1991; ABM Board Minutes, 3–5 April 1978, 'Chairman's Report'; 22–24 April 1985, 'Chairman's Report'.

89. ABM Board Minutes, 3–5 April 1978, 'Chairman's Report'; 29–30 October 1980, 'Personnel Report and the Commission Report'.

8. A Black Church

1. *Missionary Notes*, 20 May 1901, p. 35.

2. Journal of Rev. ER Gribble, 1 August 1896; 30 January 1897; 8, 18, 22 February 1897; 10, 15, 18 April 1897, Gribble Papers.

3. *ibid*, 14 September 1896.

4. *Missionary Notes*, 15 April 1897, p. 27; and 15 October 1897.

5. Journal of Rev. ER Gribble, 24 November 1892; 7 August 1896; 20, 24 May 1899; Gribble Papers; *Missionary Notes*, 24 June 1899, p. 43.

6. Loos, Aboriginal–European Relations in North Queensland, 1861–1897, pp. 569–71.

7. Journal of Rev. ER Gribble, 1899: Yarrabah, page 'Memorandum for 1898' and various entries in his journal to this time, e.g. 14 September, 19 December 1896; 10 September 1897.

8. G Higgins, *James Noble of Yarrabah*, Mission Publications of Australia, Lawson, New South Wales, 1981, pp. 18, 19, 32–4; *ABM Review*, 1 February 1942, pp. 21–2, 27, 'The Late Rev. James Noble'.

9. *A.B.M. Review*, June 1962, 'The Founding of Edward River Mission' by JW Chapman.

10. ABM Board Minutes, 30 April–1 May 1925, 'Missions and Missionaries Report'.

11. *ibid*, 25–26 November 1925, 'Report of ABM Committee in Victoria' and 'ABM Tasmania'; *A.B.M. Review* 1 August 1934, p. 88; 1 February 1942, pp. 21–2, 27, 'The Late Rev. James Noble'.

12. *ibid*, 1 February 1942, p. 22. He was approximately fifty-six years old.

13. *ibid*, 1 August 1934, p. 88.

14. *ibid*, 1 October 1946, pp. 134–5; 1 October 1947, p. 155.

15. Rowland, *The Tropics for Christ*, p. 100.

16. *A.B.M. Review*, 1 July 1949, p. 106; ABM Board Minutes, 25–27 October 1982, 'Chairman's Report'.

17. *Church Scene*, 23 March 1978, p. 17: 'The Passing Scene'.

18. AR Tippett, *Introduction to Missiology*, William Carey Library, Pasadena, California, 1987, pp. 175–8; DL Whiteman, *Melanesians and Missionaries: An Ethno-Historical Study of Social and Religious Change in the Southwest Pacific*, William Carey Library, Pasadena, California, 1983, pp. 364–93.

19. Djiniyini Gondarra, *Series of Reflections of Aboriginal Theology*, p. 12. David Thompson helped me to clarify my description of the Aboriginal Church. Thompson to Loos, 17 November 1992 [pers. comm.].

20. The Diocese of Carpentaria Conditions of Surrender Canon 1996 and The Diocese of Carpentaria Surrender Canon 1995, Diocese of North Queensland.

21. *Sydney Morning Herald*, 2 December 1974: A Gill, 'Father Patrick—a historic calling'.

22. Cole, *From Mission to Church*, pp. 85, 203–10.

23. Bishop C Wood, 'Diocesan Report for Northern Territory' to Queensland and Northern Territory Regional Advisory Committee 16–18 February 1987, Diocese of Northern Territory Registry.

24. Interview with Bishop C Wood, Darwin, 2 July 1991. Discussions with Rev. Robert Bos and Rev. David Thompson at various times. See also Thompson to Loos, 17 November 1992 [personal communication].

25. Wontulp-Bi-Buya, *Information Booklet*, Rockhampton, 1992, p. 8.

26. ABM Board Minutes, 24–26 October 1972, 'Chairman's Report', p. 9.

27. Thompson, *Bora is like Church*, 'Foreword'.

28. *ibid.*

29. ABM Board Minutes, 24–26 October 1972, 'Chairman's Report', p. 14.

30. *ibid.* See Matthew 14, 25–6.

31. *ibid*, p. 16.

32. J Taylor, 'Goods and Gods: A Follow-up Study of "Steel Axes for Stone Age Australians"', in Swain and Rose (eds), *Aboriginal Australians and Christian Missions*, p. 447.

33. *ibid*, pp. 439–40.

34. *ibid*, p. 450.

35. *ibid.*

36. ABM Board Minutes, 24–26 October 1972, 'Chairman's Report', p. 14.

37. Thompson, *Bora is like Church*, pp. 8, 9; Conversation with Bishop Hall-Matthews, Cairns, 17 June 1992.

38. *ibid*, p. 10.

39. Djiniyini Gondarra, *Series of Reflections of Aboriginal Theology: Let My People Go*.

40. *ibid*, p. 12.

41. *ibid*, pp. 17–18.

42. *ibid*, p. iv.

43. *ibid*, pp. 10, 11.

44. *ibid*, p. 26.

45. *ibid*, p. 1–12.
46. Djiniyini Gondarra, *Father You Gave Us the Dreaming*, Northern Synod of Uniting Church, Darwin, 1988.
47. ABM Board Minutes, 24–26 October 1972, 'Chairman's Report', pp. 14–6.
48. Thompson to Loos, 16 April 1991 [personal correspondence].
49. 'Report of the Provincial Secretary [AG Fellows] on His Visit to the Diocese of Carpentaria, June 15th–July 16th, 1983', ABM Queensland, Executive Committee Minutes, Brisbane; Rev. P Freier, Report on Preliminary Consultation with Lockhart River Church Community [17–24 April 1985] [copy provided by Rev. P Freier]; ABM Board Minutes, 22–24 October 1979, Chairman's Report, quoting from the report of the Head Brother to the Synod of the Church of Melanesia. See also B Macdonald-Milne, *Spearhead: The Story of the Melanesian Brotherhood*, Melanesian Mission, Walford, England, [n.d.].
50. Bishop Hudson of Carpentaria to Chairman, ABM, 5 July 1951, ABM Chairman's correspondence, Personal file: AE Biggs. See also Coaldrake, chairman of ABM, to Rev. E Baldwin, 28 October 1958, ABM Chairman's Correspondence, Personal file: E & J Baldwin; Rev. P Freier, Report on Preliminary Consultation with Lockhart River Church Community, [17–24 April 1985].
51. *Church Scene*, 27 September 1991, p. 9: 'Carpentaria, a missionary diocese in transition'; 'A Report by the Bishop of Carpentaria to the Provincial Committee of the Australian Board of Missions, Brisbane, 16–17 February 1978', Minutes of the Executive Committee of ABM, Brisbane.
52. Thompson, *Bora is Like Church*, front and back covers; *Church Scene*, 31 May 1985, p. 6: 'Lockhart River men ordained'.
53. *Nungalinya News*, March 1988.
54. Far Northern Zone Aboriginal and Torres Strait Islander Commission, in Conjunction with the Cape York Land Council, Aboriginal Land Issues Workshop, Cairns, 27–28 August 1992.
55. Personal communication from a Torres Strait Islander priest, 21 June 1992, to an acquaintance who has asked me to regard the writer's identity as confidential.

9. A New Beginning

1. Issues of *Yaburru: The Yarrabah Christian Youth Centre Newsletter, National Boomerang: The National Anglican Aboriginal Newsletter, Sunrise Times*, a Wontulp newsletter, carry testimonies of Aborigines whose lives were changed by a conversion experience which they sought in their despair. See *Sunrise Times*, March 1985, p. 1: 'He beat the grog'; *Yaburru*, April 1984, 'Testimony by Lloyd Fourmile Jnr'; *National Boomerang*, April 1986, pp. 10, 11, testimonies by Bettie Walsh of Palm Island, and Wayne Connolly of Yarrabah; December 1986, pp. 10, 11, testimonies of Kate Higgins and Leslie Baird of Yarrabah. Over the years a number of Yarrabah, Palm Island, Kowanyama, Edward River and Woorabindah people have told me of similar experiences or of those of friends or relatives.
2. D Thompson, 'Nungalinya participates in renewal', *Partners*, vol. 3, no. 2, 1987, p. 6.
3. *National Boomerang*, August 1986, pp. 1, 7; *Yaburru*, July 1984, passim. This issue 'King Jesus Came', is devoted to the early series of visions and reproduces in colour Carl Nicholas's painting.

4. *National Boomerang*, August 1986, p. 7.

5. *ibid.*

6. *ibid*, p. 2, an interview with John Noble, son of James.

7. *ibid.*

8. *ibid*, Interview with Rev. Lloyd Fourmile, Yarrabah, 22 October 1988; *Yaburru*, July 1984, 'Poor Fella — My Culture?'

9. *Yaburru*, July 1984, 'Poor Fella — My Culture?'

10. *ibid.*

11. Wayne Connolly addressing the North Queensland Synod, 3 July 2004.

12. *Yaburru*, July 1984, 'Poor Fella — My Culture?'

13. *National Boomerang*, August 1986, p. 6, reproducing a *Northern Churchman* article.

14. 1982 North Queensland Synod. A motion to support an Aboriginal Treaty was modified to become a motion in support of Aboriginal Land Rights. L Hume, 'Christianity Full Circle: Aboriginal Christianity on Yarrabah Reserve', in Swain and Rose (eds), *Aboriginal Australians and Christian Missions*, pp. 250–62.

15. *National Boomerang*, November 1985, p. 7.

16. 'The Aboriginal Bishopric Rule of Life', 18 January 1990. This was assented to by Bishop Arthur Malcolm and the Reverends Neil Fourmile, Kevin Baird, Lloyd Fourmile and Wayne Stafford.

17. Conversations with D Thompson, P Freier and others at Cairns and Yarrabah, 17 June 1992; *Sunday Mail*, 23 April 1989; *Townsville Bulletin*, 23 March 1987.

18. *Northern Churchman*, June/July 1988, p. 4.

19. Report by the Bishop of North Queensland, 13 October 1976, to Provincial ABM Committee, Annual Meeting, 25 October 1976, Minutes of Executive Committee of ABM, Queensland, Brisbane.

20. J Harris, *One Blood*, p. 659.

21. *Church Scene*, 10 July 1992, pp. 1, 18.

22. *Church Scene*, 31 July 1992, pp. 5, 6. See also *Partners*, May 1992, p. 1 and *Church Scene*, 10 July 1992, pp. 1, 18.

23. *Church Scene*, 31 July 1992, pp. 5, 6; *Missionary Review*, August 1984, p. 3; Gondarra, *Series of Reflections of Aboriginal Theology*, pp. 11–12.

24. Harris, *One Blood*, pp. 553ff.

25. Harris, *One Blood*, p. 671.

26. Hodge, ABM, to Loos, 7 May 2003 [email].

27. 'The National Aboriginal and Torres Strait Islander Council', an appeal for financial support, [n.d.], enclosed C Hodge, ABM, to Loos, 22 November 2000.

28. Press Release: 'The National Aboriginal and Torres Strait Islander Anglican Council', [n.d., probably 2000], enclosed Hodge to Loos, 22 November 2000.

29. Appeal for financial support: 'National Aboriginal and Torres Strait Islander Council', [n.d.], enclosed Hodge to Loos, 22 November 2000.

30. *Market Place*, May 2001, p. 4.

31. *Market Place*, August 2001, pp. 12–13.

32. *Market Place*, August 2001, p. 13: 'Bones of Reconciliation'.

Appendix

1. In the text, there is an exclamation mark, instead of an apostrophe.
2. Probably the Aboriginal deacon James Noble, ordained in 1925 (HR, August 03).
3. The verbatim report by Dr Reim presumably ends here.
4. That is, Elkin (Reim, August 2003).

Index

Page locators printed in *italics* refer to illustration and captions when the person or subject referred to is not mentioned elsewhere on the page.

DATE DUE

#47-0108 Peel Off Pressure Sensitive